Valle-Inclán
and the Theatre

Valle-Inclán and the Theatre

Innovation in *La cabeza del dragón,*
El Embrujado, and
La Marquesa Rosalinda

Xavier Vila

Lewisburg
Bucknell University Press
London and Toronto: Associated University Presses

© 1994 by Associated University Presses, Inc.

All rights reserved. Authorization to photocopy items for internal or personal use, or the internal or personal use of specific clients, is granted by the copyright owner, provided that a base fee of $10.00, plus eight cents per page, per copy is paid directly to the Copyright Clearance Center, 222 Rosewood Drive, Danvers, Massachusetts 01923. [0-8387-5267-5/94 $10.00 + 8¢ pp, pc.]

Associated University Presses
440 Forsgate Drive
Cranbury, NJ 08512

Associated University Presses
25 Sicilian Avenue
London WC1A 2QH

Associated University Presses
P.O. Box 338, Port Credit
Mississauga, Ontario
Canada L5G 4L8

The paper used in this publication meets the requirements of the American National Standard for Permanence of Paper for Printed Library Materials Z39.48–1948.

ISBN 0-8387-5267-5
LC 93-70385

PRINTED IN THE UNITED STATES OF AMERICA

als meus pares

Benjamí Vila Campderròs
María Estrada Herrero

Contents

Acknowledgments	ix
Introduction	3
1. The Aesthetic Overview	9
The Mystic Norm: The Grecian Mode, 9	
The Literary Context, 16	
The Play of Contrasts, 26	
Reflection, 28	
2. The Structural Consequences	32
The Symmetrical Frame, 32	
Language, 38	
Object, 41	
Character, 43	
Self-Presence, 48	
3. The Dynamics	55
Mise en Scène: Authorial Interplay, 55	
Mocking: Mechanical Entrenchment, 65	
Subversive Mirroring, 74	
De-Hierarchization, 81	
4. Dissemination	92
Provenance, 92	
Proposition and Development, 99	
Perspectival Stance, 121	
Select Bibliography	131
Index	149

Acknowledgments

I would like to thank Luis Fernández Cifuentes and José Muñoz Millanes for their comments on an earlier version of this book. Any commendable passages in the following pages derive from the lessons learned in two classes I had the immense good fortune to take some years ago. In these classes, Alban Forcione did more than show me how to begin to write literary criticism. I thank him for showing me how a critic is to read. Finally, as a fellow student, Jorge Checa taught me a great deal of what I know about literature.

Valle-Inclán
and the Theatre

Introduction

With the *esperpentos*, Valle-Inclán effectively consolidated his position at the very forefront not only of the Spanish, but of the international, theatrical avant-garde. The revolutionary impact of the *esperpentos* has tended to obscure the importance of earlier plays. In particular, three plays published in a brief nine-month period in 1913–14 have attracted relatively little scholarly attention. Nonetheless, many of the characteristics of Valle-Inclán's later theatre are present in *El Embrujado: Tragedia de tierras de Salnés* (published 23 May 1913), *La Marquesa Rosalinda: Farsa sentimental y grotesca* (10 July 1913), and *La cabeza del dragón: Farsa* (12 January 1914). In addition, these characteristics are closely linked with the norms detailed in *La Lámpara maravillosa: Ejercicios espirituales*.

El Embrujado, *La Marquesa Rosalinda*, and *La cabeza del dragón* are no exception to Valle-Inclán's method of writing as a process of rewriting. *La cabeza del dragón*, already staged in 1910,[1] ultimately becomes *Farsa infantil de la cabeza del dragón* in 1926 as part of a work entitled *Tablado de marionetas para educación de príncipes*. Similarly, in 1927, Valle-Inclán incorporates *El Embrujado* into *Retablo de la avaricia, la lujuria y la muerte*. Characters, situations, even entire passages are evoked, quoted, or misquoted in a later context.[2] Works are distinct less in kind and underlying aesthetic conception than in degree of development—the thread of a common past stitches together the various segments of an entire oeuvre.[3]

---

1. Jean-Marie Lavaud, "Realidad y esperpento en *La cabeza del dragón*," in H. Wentzlaff-Eggebert, *Ramón del Valle-Inclán (1866–1936)* (Tübingen: Max Niemeyer, 1988), 115.
2. Examples of Valle-Inclán's textual reciprocity are myriad. *El Marqués de Bradomín: Coloquios románticos* (1907), for instance, derives from *Sonata de otoño* (1902). *El yermo de las almas: Episodios de la vida íntima* (1908) is based on *Cenizas* (1899), itself derived from the short story *Octavia Santino* (1895).

Bounded on the one hand by the first two *Comedias bárbaras* (*Aguila de blasón* [1907]; *Romance de lobos* [1908]) and on the other hand by *La lámpara maravillosa* (1916), the three plays studied herein lie at the very center of an intertextual movement. The broad-ranging aesthetic, mystic, and ethical precepts of *La lámpara maravillosa* (*Lámpara*), in particular, are patently indebted to preceding theatrical works. *Lámpara* dates from at least 1910, according to the information provided by "a lecture Valle gave in Buenos Aires ["una conferencia que Valle dio en Buenos Aires"],[4] and further expands on the concerns already expressed in works such as the *Comedias bárbaras* (*Comedias*). To be more specific, don Juan Manuel, the principal character of *Romance de lobos*, engages in a quest of spiritual dimensions. His pilgrimage to doña María's manor, his desire to transcend the moral degeneration of his sons, his acute recognition of finitude, both of individual and of class, give voice to issues crucial to *Lámpara*—the confrontation with lust, avarice, and death. Moreover, the *Comedias* evince the disinterested, nontemporal perspective required, as *Lámpara* makes clear, to transcend the confines of the particular. Unlike earlier plays where characters conflict with their environment, in the *Comedias* each character fuses with his milieu.[5] Whereas *Cenizas*, for example, progresses in a linear fashion with a conflict leading to a climax and a resolution, the *Comedias* posit an eternal present—the characters/ambiance on display in an ostentation of stage world plasticity. Time is conceived less as a vectorial progression than as a play of shadows, contrasts, diurnal and nocturnal

---

3. In his classic essay, "Significación del esperpento o Valle-Inclán, hijo pródigo del 98," P. Salinas hints at the links between Valle-Inclán's works and periods (reprinted in *Literatura española siglo XX* [Madrid: Alianza, 1972], 86–114). Roberta L. Salper studies Valle-Inclán's repeated characters, recognizing, as did Salinas, that "many of Valle-Inclán's apparently disconnected and diversified texts, in reality, formed part of a larger unity" ["muchos de los textos aparentemente inconexos y diversificados de Valle-Inclán en realidad formaban parte de un conjunto mayor"] (*Valle-Inclán y su mundo: ideología y forma narrativa* [Rodopi: Amsterdam, 1988], 26).\

4. V. Garlitz, "El centro del círculo: *La lámpara maravillosa* de Valle-Inclán," diss., University of Chicago, 1978, 3. See also R. Lima, *Valle-Inclán: The Theatre of His Life* (Columbia: University of Missouri Press, 1988), 262. J. de Entrambasaguas indicates that, given the importance of Molinos in *Lámpara*, the work is begun "after 1906, when don Ramón would have been able to obtain Miguel de Molinos's *Guía espiritual* (Rome, 1675), reprinted in Barcelona in that year by Rafael Urbano, a book which was not available in other editions" ["después de 1906, en que pudo caer en manos de don Ramón la *Guía espiritual* de Miguel de Molinos [Roma, 1675], reimpresa en Barcelona en aquella fecha por Rafael Urbano y de la cual no había otra edición asequible"] ("Leyendo a Valle-Inclán," *Cuadernos de literatura contemporánea* 18 [1946]: 565).

5. The following discussion in the body of the text derives from J. Lyon, *The Theatre of Valle-Inclán* (Cambridge: Cambridge University Press, 1983), 38–57.

shifts. Galician boundaries are broadened and temporal/historical markers expanded. Perspectives clash as the texts evoke the Trojan wars amidst the conflation of Galician peasants with biblical figures. Don Juan Manuel appears as much the doomed titan of a crumbling aristocracy as the locus for the cosmic struggle of satanic and redemptive forces. Specificity as such blurs. The *Comedias* tend toward the depiction and visualization of universal constants.

Like the *Comedias*, the plays written from 1910–14 indicate theatrical discourse's privileged position in the formulation of Valle-Inclán's aesthetic and mystic vision—indeed, the entire period is devoted exclusively to theatre. Dramatic resources exemplify and/or annunciate *Lámpara* principles.

The *Comedias* bequeath yet another legacy. Valle-Inclán begins his career as an *enfant terrible* distrusted and misunderstood by members of the literary *status quo*. The *Sonatas* testify to an espousal of norms, both aesthetic and ethic, in complete variance with accepted practices. The *Comedias* add grist to this nonconformist trend, with a vengeance.

In the theatrical context of the period, Jacinto Benavente situates innovative plays in various types of middle-, upper-, or peasant-class interiors. Joaquín Dicenta presents proletarian characters and conflicts that broaden the scope of Spanish theatre. Amidst such innovators, Valle-Inclán stands in a class of his own. His plays quite simply shatter the Spanish theatrical horizon of expectations. As written texts, the *Comedias* are denied the status of theatre works and are classified as dialogued novels.[6] As stage texts, directors (and public) are at a loss. Skiffs at sea, prancing horses, a couple's sexual frolic synchronized with the sounds emanating from a cauldron boiling away the remains of a disinterred hag comprise but a few of the difficulties companies (and potential audiences) find insurmountable. The *Comedias* mark a point of no return. Reigning conventions are left behind. The Galician writer is on his own.

From 1910–14, Valle-Inclán forges a replacement for standard theatrical canons.[7] A dramatic code in the making seeks new forms. Uncertainty is the byword. In the travails of a "moral crisis" ["crisis moral"], Valle-Inclán even begins to doubt his literary vocation.[8]

6. See, in this text, chapter four, footnote 41.
7. In response to an interviewer's question on a possible Spanish theatrical crisis, Valle-Inclán counters by asking if theatres actually exist in Spain (Frederico Navas, *Las esfinges de Talía* [Escorial: Real Monasterio de El Escorial, 1928], 50). The response, dated from 1928, admittedly reflects the writer's bitterness at the failure of his own theatre to gain public acceptance. At the same time, the general tenor of Valle-Inclán's assessment of prevalent theatre practices is evident.

Neologisms proliferate, attesting to the level of creative tension—only in the period of the *esperpento* does standard language prove to be so inadequate.[9] Personal expression grapples with an ever-present unknown.

Valle-Inclán's struggle against theatrical convention forms part of a more general (and visceral) repudiation of the prevailing cultural climate. The Galician envisages a broad aesthetic renewal and considers himself engaged in an "educational enterprise" ["labor educadora"].[10] Specifically, theatre becomes the Galician writer's chosen instrument[11] for the renovation of a moribund Spanish discourse—a language completely asphyxiated by outmoded rhetorical strictures and useless for those writers who feel "the imperative of the hour" ["el imperio de la hora"].[12] Valle-Inclán determines to "untwist the Spanish tongue,"[13] burst the bonds of rhetoric, and base his theatre on such Spanish essentials as vocalic harshness, accentuation, rapid rhythm, and elocutionary vigor. *La Marquesa Rosalinda*, *El Embrujado*, and *La cabeza del dragón* are examples of Valle-Inclán's ongoing battle to set theatre on an autochthonous and contemporary foundation.[14]

  8. M. Fernández Almagro, *Vida y literatura de Valle-Inclán* (Madrid: Editora Nacional, 1943), 174.
  9. Ciriaco Ruiz Fernández, *El léxico del teatro de Valle-Inclán* (Salamanca: Ediciones Universidad de Salamanca, 1981), 277. Ruiz Fernández compares the number of neologisms used in 1910–13 and 1920–23 (the gestation period of the *esperpento*).
  10. C. Rivas Cherif, "El viaje de Valle-Inclán," *España* 11 May 1916: 10 (reprinted in J. A. Hormigón, *Valle-Inclán: Cronología y documentos* [Madrid: Imprenta del Ministerio de Cultura, 1978], 77–81). Rivas Cherif cites a long roster of innovative artists, particularly in the plastic arts, whom he feels owe their inspiration, in great measure, to the suggestive power of Valle-Inclán's word. See also J. Moya del Pino, "Valle-Inclán y los artistas," *La Pluma* 32 (1923): 63–65.
  11. Theatre enjoys a privileged status not only with respect to the formulation of Valle-Inclán's aesthetic principles (in *Lámpara*) but throughout his career. The Galician's entire oeuvre appears conceived "*sub specie theatri*" (Pérez de Ayala, *La Pluma* 32 [1923]: 24). Valle-Inclán himself confesses: "I write all my works in dialogue because they emerge from my soul in this fashion; and because my sense of world order imposes it upon me" ["Yo escribo todas mis obras en diálogo porque así salen de mi alma; y porque mi sentido de la vida así me lo ordena"] (F. Navas, *Las esfinges de Talía*, 52).
  12. *Lámpara*, 86. See the Bibliography, section 1, for the editions of Valle-Inclán's works utilized in this text.
  13. Taken from Carol S. Maier, "Untwisting the Castillian Tongue: Some Suggestions from Valle-Inclán's *La lámpara maravillosa*," *Hispanic Journal* 6.2 (1985): 59.
  14. Valle-Inclán never fails to stress the singularity of theatre's ties to a "people": "Theatre is the least universal of existing things. Every country has its own. The more unique the surroundings whose development allows a country this artistic expression, the more difficult it also is to be brought to other latitudes. Therefore, it is naive to try to transplant misty Northern theatre to the South. In the former, fog holds sway, here the sun is outlined [as] with punch holes over Castile. Moreover, theatre needs above

Valle-Inclán's endeavor to construct drama on (an avowedly *sui generis* conception of) what is distinctly "Spanish" unveils a unique personal aesthetic.[15] Already in the *Sonatas*, the Marqués de Bradomín affirms that "having learned how to smile is Humanity's greatest conquest [achievement]" ["haber aprendido á sonreír, es la mayor conquista de la Humanidad"] (*Sonata de invierno*, 237). And indeed, the Marqués smiles, listening as a tearful ex-soldier, inspired by the chronicles of Cortés, expresses his desire to return "these Indies" ["estas Indias"] to the "Empire" ["Imperio"]—a smile accompanied by "a mocking touch" ["una punta de burla"] (*Sonata de estío*, 226). The aristocrat mockingly looks down at the cause of his mirth, and Valle-Inclán makes this lesson the cornerstone of his art. The writer stands above, distinct from, a world he contemplates for amusement. The vision of a Spain living the present in the past comes to be written and viewed from the position that a sage, also of Iberian heritage, denominated "*sub specie aeternitatis*"[16]—under the light "of the other shore" ["de la otra ribera"] (*Los cuernos de don Friolera*, 22). The *esperpento* is most famous for characters who speak of the living from the perspective of the dead.

The unique aesthetic vantage point of Valle-Inclán's later theatre results from the development of previous experiments, particularly

---

all an audience, even more so than the actual author. And the specific condition of this audience is to be united by a common sentiment, something that is peculiar to a single milieu. This necessary cohesion is perfected and purified until it becomes a religious base (re-ligari), an intimate and supreme community, towards which the sheaf of aesthetic emotions should converge" ["El teatro es lo menos universal que existe. Cada país tiene el suyo. Cuanto más típico es un medio cuyo desarrollo le permite esa expresión de arte, mayor impedimiento también para ser llevada a otra latitud. Así resulta cándido querer trasplantar el teatro brumoso del Norte al Mediodía. Allá impera la niebla, aquí el sol se recorta con sacabocados sobre Castilla. Además, el teatro antes que nada exige un público, incluso antes que el propio autor. Y la condición específica de este público es estar ligado por un sentimiento común, lo cual es privativo de un solo ambiente. Esta imprescindible cohesión se perfecciona y encarece hasta convertirse en fondo réligioso (re-ligari), íntima y suprema comunidad hacia donde debe converger el haz de incitaciones estéticas"] (Valle-Inclán, in J. Lyon, *The Theatre of Valle-Inclán*, 205).

15. Valle-Inclán constantly refers to a guiding system or theory governing the specific artistic manifestation. Regardless of his medium, the artist requires a personal credo. In judging paintings: "Few, very few [artists] in this exhibition appear to have an aesthetic concept prior to and superior to the desire to paint" ["Pocos, muy pocos, son los que en esta Exposición parecen tener un concepto estético anterior y superior al propósito de pintar"] (Valle-Inclán, in J. M. Lavaud, "Une collaboration de Valle-Inclán au journal *Nuevo Mundo* et l"Exposition de 1912," *Bulletin Hispanique* 71 [1969]: 307).

16. Baruch Spinoza, in *The Collected Works of Spinoza*, ed. and tr. Edwin Curley (Princeton: Princeton University Press, 1985), 636.

those dealing with theatricality, the manipulation of literary codes, and perspectival alternacy. The following pages are a contribution to the study of these experiments, their sources and their implications. The opening chapters are largely devoted to *La Marquesa Rosalinda*, a veritable pinnacle in the Galician's repertoire. The amorous misadventures of Marquesa Rosalinda and of Arlequín, the head of an Italianate troupe of barnstormers, reveal the implications of pagan/Castilian, commedia dell'arte/Calderonian differences. Special attention is given to an issue that will be discussed in subsequent chapters: the crucial importance of the nontemporal view in Arlequín's pagan aesthetics and the manner in which this view is attained. The analyses of the third chapter are concerned with the authorial viewpoint that will become fundamental to the *esperpento*—the "in the air" ["en el aire"] position where the characters are regarded, as well as conceived, from above.[17] At the same time, the characters rebel against their inferior, manipulated status. The ensuing author/character shifts in perspective are studied in the context of *La cabeza del dragón*, a text constituted by an ever-present interplay that breaks with hierarchical conceptions of order. The role of *El Embrujado* in Valle-Inclán's search for a new theatre is examined in the fourth and final chapter. This apparently conventional play cannot mask a fundamental affinity with the aesthetic-spiritual disquisitions of *La Lámpara maravillosa*—disquisitions that are shown to be inseparable from the affirmation and evolution of Valle-Inclán's dramatic voice.

17. See, in this text, chapter 3, footnote 7.

1
The Aesthetic Overview

The Mystic Norm: The Grecian Mode

As author of *La lámpara maravillosa* (*Lámpara*), Valle-Inclán urges the artist to labor under a spiritual aegis. As dramaturge, Valle-Inclán does indeed give voice to issues of a mystic nature. This chapter is a study of the relationship extant between *Lámpara* and undoubtedly the most important of the plays written in the 1913–14 period, *La Marquesa Rosalinda: Farsa sentimental y grotesca*. The stylized garden of *La Marquesa Rosalinda* is, in many respects, an example of the paradisiacal setting so prevalent in the writings of the *Modernistas*. The elegant Grecian evocations, though, more than a triumph of stylistic virtuosity, are a means to a sensuous/mystic apprehension of the world. Arlequín, the leader of the commedia dell'arte troupe in *La Marquesa Rosalinda*, is largely responsible for highlighting the mystic import of the pagan world and for contextualizing the Grecian view within a Spanish literary framework. The Pagan/Spanish opposition is, to a great extent, seen in terms of a commedia versus a noncommedia presence. For the commedia character, this presence, as Arlequín often reveals, bears the ethic and aesthetic responsibility of transcending temporal confines.

In *Lámpara*, Valle-Inclán quite clearly indicates the artist's "eternal responsibility" ["responsabilidad eterna"] (*Lámpara*, 51): "The work of beauty, creation of poets and prophets, comes close to the creation of God" ["La obra de belleza, creación de poetas y profetas, se acerca á la creación de Dios"] (*Lámpara*, 91). The poet, like the prophet, embarks on a mission—a pilgrimage in search of "the mystery of Eternal Beauty" ["el misterio de la Eterna Belleza"] (*Lámpara*, 15). Artistic creation becomes a "discipline to transmigrate into the essence of things and by its paths seek God" ["disciplina para transmigrar en la esencia de las cosas y por sus caminos buscar á Dios"] (*Lámpara*, 112).

From the beginning, *La Marquesa Rosalinda* (*MR*) bears witness to an aesthetic-mystic link. When the ever-wandering commedia dell'arte troupe descends on the estate of a Marquis, the aristocrat immediately recognizes that the troupe "[g]oes in search of a star / as the Three Wise Men of the Orient" ["Va detrás de una estrella, / Como los Reyes Magos del Oriente"] (*MR*, 28). The mystic implications of the artistic world are underscored time and again throughout the play. The enamored Marquesa Rosalinda, for example, finds that her lover Arlequín confronts her with one excuse after another in order to forestall her fleeing the garden with the troupe. Arlequín finally admits, "I think about your [Rosalinda's] bones, / about the cart jolting along those paths, / about the constant running from one village to another, / [we are] pilgrims who never arrive in Judea" ["Pienso en tus pobres huesos, / En los tumbos del carro por los caminos esos, / En el rodar constante de una aldea á otra aldea, / Peregrinos que nunca llegamos á Judea"] (*MR*, 141). Art remains the province of those few who, like Arlequín, can withstand the travails of pilgrimage.[1]

---

1. Valle-Inclán describes artistic endeavor in ascetic terms. Expression begins with the acceptance of solitude and the imposition of discipline: "I was able to punish myself in the manner of a holy monk tempted by the Devil" ["supe castigarme como pudiera hacerlo un santo monje tentado del Demonio"] (*Lámpara*, 23). The need to purge "vanity" ["vanidad"] and exalt "pride" ["orgullo"] (see *Lámpara*, 23) recalls the oft-quoted statement made by the Marquis of Bradomín, "Disparage everyone else and not love oneself" ["Despreciar a los demás y no amarse a sí mismo"] (*Sonata de estío*, 197). The artist must cultivate a supreme pride—a pride born of a categorical conviction in his own artistic enterprise. Pío Baroja testifies, somewhat bewildered, that Valle-Inclán is capable of going "through pain or sickness in order to produce an art work" ["hasta el dolor y la enfermedad para producir una obra de arte"] (*El escritor según él y según los críticos. Obras completas VII* [Madrid: Biblioteca Nueva, 1949], 407). In matters of conviction, conformity, be it literary or social, is irrelevant: "I believe that an artist, above all, should have norms to impose on an audience, and impose them, and if there is no audience, create it. That is a [source of] great pride" ["Yo creo que un artista, ante todo, debe tener normas que imponer al público, e imponerlas, y si no hay público, crearlo. Ese es un gran orgullo"] (D. Dougherty, *Un Valle-Inclán olvidado: entrevistas y conferencias* [Madrid: Fundamentos, 1983], 72). This aesthetic credo, taken in the context of the Spanish cultural climate of the period, explains in part why the Modernist artist/bourgeois and the Romantic Davidsbündler/Philistine clashes are so evident in Valle-Inclán's works. His characters are, by necessity it seems, at one with the beggar, the oppressed and those elements proscribed from society—the artistic product cannot but evince the context to which creation has been relegated. The artist struggles against the incomprehension of an entire society. Despite the struggle, *MR* is a continuous affirmation of the worth of artistic creation, *Luces de bohemia* a passionate declaration of faith. Society overwhelms, the artist (Max Estrella) dies, but the *esperpento* is revealed—the perspective of the artist cannot and will not be crushed.

The extent to which Arlequín and the troupe are identified as working within the parameters of a mystical activity is directly linked to their evocation of a Grecian world.

> *Amaranta* — Here Greek loves do not dance
>   in the garden, under the laurels.
> *Rosalinda* — Here the nymphs do not play
>   their riding games on the centaurs.
> *Amaranta* — Here furtive kisses do not fly
>   behind the branches of Trianon.
> *Rosalinda* — With the branches of the copses
>   here the Inquisition lights bonfires.
> *Arlequín* — My ladies, how am I to believe you
>   when in your lips you have Grecian bees
>   and Eros hides his arrows
>   between the nards at your grates!
>   You are the muses of the rondels
>   and in the bowknots around your waists
>   you carry roses from Grecian, Latin, and Versaillesque laurels.
>   Versailles, that loves Grecian breezes!
>   By the lady of Montespán,
>   in her groves, Lutetia hears
>   Pan's rustic flute resound! [. . . .]
>   Bifrontal Hermes rules in the parks
>   Venus and Adonis feign combats
>   and Anacreon's aged wine
>   stains the abbots' frocks.
>   The arid fountains have crystals
>   when Diana hunts in the thicket,
>   swarms of cantharides are heard
>   when she passes nude and blonde.
>
> [*Amaranta* — Aquí no danzan amores griegos
>   En los jardines, bajo los lauros.
> *Rosalinda* — Aquí las ninfas no hacen sus juegos
>   De cabalgadas en los centauros.
> *Amaranta* — Aquí no vuelan, tras los ramajes,
>   Furtivos besos del Trianón.
> *Rosalinda* — Con los ramajes de los boscajes
>   Aquí hace hogueras la Inquisición.
> *Arlequín* — ¡Señoras mías, cómo creeros
>   Si en vuestros labios tenéis abejas
>   Griegas, y esconde sus flechas, Heros,
>   Entre los nardos de vuestras rejas!
>   Si sois las musas de los rondeles
>   Y en las lazadas de vuestros talles,
>   Portáis las rosas de los laureles
>   Griegos, Latinos y de Versalles.
>   ¡Versalles, que ama brisas de Grecia!
>   ¡Por la señora de Montespán,
>   En sus florestas oye Lutecia

> Sonar la agreste flauta de Pan! [. . . .]
> Reina en los parques Hermes bifronte,
> Venus y Adonis fingen combates
> Y el viejo vino de Anacreonte
> Mancha la chupa de los abates.
> Tienen cristales las fuentes áridas
> Cuando Diana caza en la fronda,
> Se oye el enjambre de las cantáridas
> Cuando ella pasa, desnuda y blonda].
>
> (MR, 64–66)

Mythology comes into being in the largely hostile Spanish environment with the arrival of the commedia troupe. Arlequín never ceases to proclaim the Grecian presence. Indeed, he implores the Spaniards, as does Valle-Inclán in *Lámpara*, to open "the five roses of the senses" ["Las cinco rosas de los sentidos"] and to heed "the flute with which Pan makes merry" ["la flauta con que hace fiesta / Pan"] (*MR*, 190) with evident proselytizing intent.[2]

The fascination with the Grecian mode in *MR*[3] can be attributed, at least in some measure, to its very novelty. Valle-Inclán is among the first of the Peninsular writers to feel the impact of Darío,[4] a poet in whose work, as in the entire Modernist *Weltanschauung*, the Grecian element figures prominently.[5] *MR* pays eloquent tribute to the Nicaraguan's influence, and indicates at the same time the degree of confluence between the two writers.[6] Valle-Inclán does not simply appropriate the literary trappings of his mentor, he identifies with

---

2. Valle-Inclán emphatically signals the Grecian element as a cornerstone of his aesthetics. "In my disposition, I have as a precept to be neither historical nor of the present time, rather, to hear the Grecian flute" ["Yo para mi ordenación tengo como precepto, no ser histórico ni actual, pero saber oír la flauta griega"] (*Lámpara*, 86–87). *MR* overlaps in this fundamental issue with *Lámpara*. The created work (*MR*) proclaims the principles governing creation (given in *Lámpara*). Arlequín, like Max Estrella in *Luces de bohemia*, serves as the spokesman of an aesthetic, or, to be more precise, as a spokesman striving to define an aesthetic.

3. *La cabeza del dragón* [*CdD*] also evokes, to a much lesser degree, the Grecian world. The "Elf" ["Duende"], a character who cannot be assigned to a precise temporal period, "still has the scars of the horns with which the poets one day saw him in the Grecian forests" ["aún tiene las cicatrices de los cuernos con que le vieron un día los poetas en los bosques de Grecia"] (*CdD*, 19).

4. See Juan Ramón Jiménez, *El Modernismo* (México: Aguilar, 1962), 157. See also G. Díaz Plaja, *Las estéticas de Valle-Inclán* (Madrid: Gredos, 1965), 265–66.

5. See, for example, George D. Schade, "La mitología clásica en la poesía hispanoamericana," in Luis Monguió, ed., *La cultura y la literatura Iberoamericanas* (México: Audrea, 1957), 123–29.

6. "[W]hat Valle-Inclán found in his friend Darío was a profound affinity with regard to a conception of art, as an absolute value, and moreover, a system of thinking

their underlying significance. "What is Greek" ["*Lo griego*"] means "a kind of paradise" ["una especie de paraíso"], less a historical recollection than a projection of "visions" ["visiones"].[7] The Modernists (Darío is not alone) are engaged in a quest that seeks to root man in a world from which he has become deracinated.[8] The construction (or reconstruction) of paradise(s) presents the all too fleeting vision of man in a world before the acknowledgment of his separation from the world—a vision of man that forever points back to the nebulous moment antedating the beginning of time (the presence of death) and the realization of guilt. At the very dawn of human existence, man neither occupies a position of dominance, nor does he stand separated from creation, he is simply one among the created. An "analogical vision" ["visión analógica"] provides the perspective with which to view the world, and Valle-Inclán, alone among the Peninsular writers, makes this vision, this "true and secret originality of Modernism" ["verdadera y secreta originalidad del modernismo"],[9] his own. He voices the "ecstasy of the sum" ["éxtasis de la suma"] (*Lámpara*, 33) and projects a world governed by "rhythm and its repetitions and conjunctions [. . . where] all exceptions, even mankind, find their double and their correspondence" ["el ritmo y sus repeticiones y conjunciones [donde . . .] todas las excepciones, inclusive la de ser hombre, encuentran su doble y su correspondencia"].[10]

> And in that moment, in turning to the sea, I again became ecstatic, my eyes full of innocence, and my heart magnetized toward all things. The most spurious were in me with love's unity, brought near on similar paths, that opened in a circle like the rays of a lamp. All my paths were of love and all of them were joined in the light of the soul that was becoming ecstatic. The bramble's thorn and the snake's venom told me a secret of harmony as did the girl, the rose, and the star. I enjoyed the beauty of the world

---

oriented towards the mysterious very similar to the one which the Galician writer elaborated in *La lámpara maravillosa*" ["lo que hallaba Valle-Inclán en su amigo Darío era una profunda afinidad en cuanto a una concepción del arte, como valor absoluto, y por lo demás un sistema de pensamiento orientado hacia el misterio muy parecido al que expuso el escritor gallego en *La lámpara maravillosa*"] (A. W. Phillips, *Temas del modernismo hispánico y otros estudios* [Madrid: Gredos, 1974], 201).

7. Pedro Salinas, *La poesía de Ruben Darío* (Buenos Aires: Losada, 1948), 78–79.

8. The perpetual wanderings of the commedia cart in *MR* are a manifestation of this rootlessness. A displaced status is also evident, albeit on a different level, in the role played by the artist in a mechanized/industrialized society that considers artistic activity itself to be of minor importance. See, in this chapter, footnote 1.

9. Octavio Paz, *Los hijos del limo* [Barcelona: Seix Barral, 1974], 137. The observation that Valle-Inclán is the only Spanish writer to grasp the secret of Modernism is found on the same page.

10. O. Paz, *Los hijos del limo,* 100.

permeated by a genetic feeling, I felt born from the earth as the flowers in green fields. Speaking in me was the twin voice of all slime, hymen of all forms, sacred memory that governs the knowledge of the senses.

[Y en aquel momento, como mirase hacia el mar, volví á extasiarme, llenos los ojos de inocencia, y el corazón imantado hacia todas las cosas. Las más espúreas estaban en mí con unidad de amor, allegadas por veredas iguales, que se abrían en círculo como los rayos de una lámpara. Eran de amor todos mis caminos, y todos se juntaban en la luz del alma que se hacía extática. La espina de la zarza y la ponzoña de la sierpe me decían un secreto de armonía, igual que la niña, la rosa y la estrella. Yo gozaba la belleza del mundo penetrado de un sentimiento genesíaco, me sentía nacido de la tierra como las flores del campillo verde. Hablaba en mí la voz melliza de todos los limos, himen de todas las formas, memoria sagrada que pauta el conocer de los sentidos] (*Lámpara*, 234–35).[11]

In *MR*, the pagan tidings Arlequín brings to the garden also relay this (spiritual) experience of unity with the world. The ability to hear the Grecian flute, as Marquesa Rosalinda discovers, constitutes the first step in the path leading to mystical awareness.

> *Rosalinda* — It was in Greece where one day, hearing the cicades
> surrounded by golden sprigs and under green vines sing,
> a blind man sang with a sovereign rhythm
> the divine romance of Helen and the Trojan.
> Let my soul soar as a butterfly
> [would soar] coming out of the humid depths of a pit [grave]!
> My soul, that was dying of old age, Amaranta,
> and is now rising in two light wings

> [*Rosalinda* — Fué en Grecia donde un día, oyendo á las cigarras
> Entre espigas de oro y bajo verdes parras,
> Cantar, cantaba un ciego con ritmo soberano,
> El divino romance de Elena y del troyano.
> ¡Deja que mi alma vuele como una mariposa
> Que saliese del húmedo socavón de una fosa!
> Mi alma, que de vieja se moría, Amaranta,
> Y que en dos leves alas ahora se levanta]. (MR, 105)

The Marquesa's soul begins to recover in the context of a poet whose verse portrays a world before "the symbolic apple contaminated with science and experience the immaculate knowledge of the senses" ["la simbólica manzana, contaminó de ciencia y de experiencia el inmaculado conocer de los sentidos"] (*Lámpara*, 182–83). An unmediated, sensuous apprehension of the world precedes the

---

11. See, among others, Paul De Man, "The Double Aspect of Symbolism," *Yale French Studies* 74 (1988): 7–8, for the Neoplatonic and occult sources underlying "the fundamental unity of all being" (7).

moment experience introduces a temporal framework. In Homer's world, the world before the onset of time, knowledge rests on "intuitions" ["intuiciones"] taken from the "celestial entrails of the Sun" ["celeste entraña del Sol"] (*Lámpara*, 97). Man shares the divine perspective since the Earth is not yet separated from the Heavens. A "solar lust" ["lujuria solar"] binds the now sundered realms of "gods and animals" ["dioses y bestias"] (*Lámpara*, 189) in Homer's epic. Erotic yearning underlies the Grecian experience of cosmic unity."[12] Love unveils the apparent particularity of Creation and reveals its *de facto* oneness—this constitutes the significance of the Grecian model. The paradisiacal view is attainable, even in a fallen world, by means of a sensual comprehension. Marquesa Rosalinda acknowledges that if "the star of love / illuminates our path, a divine taste / of honey will we find in the rye loaf / broken by the innkeeper serving our supper" ["la estrella de amor / Nos alumbra la senda, un divino sabor / De miel, encontraremos en la hogaza centena / Que parta el mesonero al servirnos la cena"] (*MR*, 106–7). And indeed, quotidian things undergo a transformation as Marquesa Rosalinda, under Arlequín's tutelage, embarks on the discovery of "the arcane secret of things / that seem vulgar and that are marvellous" ["el arcano secreto de las cosas / Que parecen vulgares y son maravillosas"] (*MR*, 104). The seemingly disparate elements of Creation are viewed in their essential unity as a new order of things is revealed to the Marquesa. Arlequín "carries it [Marquesa Rosalinda's heart] through the meadows to catch butterflies / and he explains the divine mystery of the roses / and the birds to it. / He sings it the song of the pines" ["Lo lleva por los prados á cazar mariposas, / Y le explica el divino misterio de las rosas / Y las aves. Le canta la canción de los pinos"] (*MR*, 103). "To love is to understand" ["Amar es comprender"] explains the writer, "on its [love's] paths we again see the world under the sacred dew of the first dawn" ["por sus caminos tornamos á ver el mundo bajo el rocío sagrado de la primera aurora"] (*Lámpara*, 110).[13]

12. Valle-Inclán's contemporaries share this "mixture of eroticism and mysticism" ["mezcla de erotismo y misticismo"] (Ricardo Gullón, "Ideologías del modernismo," *Insula* 291 [1971]: 11) to varying degrees. See Cathy L. Jrade, *Rubén Darío and the Romantic Search for Unity: The Modernist Recourse to Esoteric Tradition* (Austin: University of Texas Press, 1983), above all chapters 1, "Modernism and the Romantic/Esoteric Tradition" and 5, "Paradise Found: Sexual Love in Esoteric Tradition." Valle-Inclán makes the erotic/mystic symbiosis fundamental to his art. Access to "the mystery of eternal beauty" ["el misterio de la eterna belleza"] implies: "First transit, painful love; Second transit, joyful love: Third transit, love with renouncement and stillness" ["Primer tránsito, amor doloroso: Segundo tránsito, amor gozoso: Tercer tránsito, amor con renunciamiento y quietud"] (*Lámpara*, 112).

13. The mystic implications of erotic fulfillment are freely evinced in *MR*. When

The Literary Context

Arlequín's presence remains crucial to the progressive revelation and dissemination of the pagan pretemporal view. The view itself, though, is descried, albeit remotely, even before the commedia troupe interacts with the inhabitants of the garden. Certain characters, such as Marquesa Rosalinda's young daughter, Estrella, are in a privileged position with respect to the pagan perspective:

> *Doña Estrella* — And the swan sighs in the wave
> that the afternoon covers with gold.
> And the grove has a murmur
> in order to say to me: May God be with you!
> And the silver fountain cries,
> as I do, in the autumnal anguish!
> And the cricket of the serenade
> plays a funeral march!
> *The Duenna* — The fountain, swans, the cricket! . . .
> Too many complications
> for my science [understanding].
> *Doña Estrella* — And how simple
> it is for the heart!
> *The Duenna* — A cathedral music master
> could clear up the matter for you
> with a musical explanation
> along the lines of point and counterpoint.
> *Doña Estrella* — All mysterious voices,
> once explained, are no longer heard.
>
> [*Doña Estrella* — Y el cisne suspira en la onda
> Que cubre de oro la tarde.

---

wooing, the Page tells his beloved Estrella: "Since you are the Spring / let a bird sing! / Perched in your heart, / with its two wings extended, / Let it tell you the song / of all born things" ["¡Ya que sois la Primavera, / Dejad á un pájaro cantar! / Posado en vuestro corazón, / Con las dos alas extendidas, / Dejad que os diga la canción / De todas las cosas nacidas"] (*MR*, 42). The image of the "two wings extended" ["dos alas extendidas"] resembles the "gnostic wings" ["alas gnósticas"] cited in *Lámpara* (190) and the "two light wings" ["dos leves alas"] (*MR*, 105) Marquesa Rosalinda uses to express the regenerative effect of love—for a reason. The transcendence of self begins with the comprehension of this "song / of all born things" stressed by the Paje. "A power of erotic evocations sleeps in all things. Some appear to awake hardly after approaching, others take time to show themselves, others are not yet revealed, others will never be revealed. But, if one day we could ever know them totally, we would see them link in a mathematical sequence and take shape in one unique impulse of love" ["En todas las cosas duerme un poder de evocaciones eróticas. Algunas parecen despertarse apenas nos aproximamos, otras tardan en revelarse, otras aun no se revelaron, otras no se revelarán jamás. Pero si un día pudiésemos conocerlas íntegramente, las veríamas enlazarse en sucesión matemática y concretarse en un solo impulso de amor"] (*Lámpara*, 47–48).

        Y tiene un murmullo la fronda
        Para decirme: ¡Dios os guarde!
        ¡Y llora la fuente de plata,
        Como yo, en la angustia otoñal!
        ¡Y el grillo de la serenata
        Toca una marcha funeral!
La Dueña — ¡La fuente, los cisnes, el grillo! . . .
        Demasiada complicación
        Para mi ciencia.
Doña Estrella — ¡Y tan sencillo
        Como es para el corazón!
La Dueña — Un solfista de catedral
        Podría daros del asunto
        Una explicación musical
        Dentro del punto y contrapunto.
Doña Estrella — Todas las voces misteriosas,
        Explicadas, dejan de oírse.]   (*MR*, 37–38)

Childlike innocence playfully, yet significantly, bridges the gap that separates the external object from the enunciating subject.[14] Yet,

14. The identification with the exterior world results from a fundamental disinterestedness: "Only the ecstatic look can make you [the soul] the center of love and knowledge. But as long as you look at things with the greed of self-advantage, you are blind" ["Sólo la mirada extática puede hacerte centro de amor y de conocimiento. Pero en tanto mires las cosas con codicia de buena pro, estás ciega"] (*Lámpara*, 190). St. Francis of Assisi serves as the model for the disavowal of personal gain: "a voice is heard that speaks with the ant, and with the water, and with the weeds and the wormwood of the mountains. It is the soul of the humble [saint] from Assisi" ["se oye una voz que habla con la hormiga, y con el agua, y con las yerbas y los ajenjos del monte. Es el alma del Pobrecito de Asís"] (*Lámpara*, 117). Many of Valle-Inclán's characters (of which Adega, the child protagonist of *Flor de Santidad* constitutes perhaps the principal example) present the Franciscan perspective. Indeed, the child, as a result of his simplicity, stands in a privileged position vis-a-vis the Franciscan view. Valle-Inclán admits that an "infantile secret [. . . .constitutes] the moment of an initiation where all things explained to me their mystic and beautiful eternity" ["secreto infantil [. . . .] el momento de una iniciación donde todas las cosas me dijeron su eternidad mística y bella"] (*Lámpara*, 195). In *MR*, the child (Doña Estrella) becomes the Franciscan foil to a character (the Duenna) who bases her understanding on self-interest.
    Doña Estrella — The nightingale, in the foliage,
        is saying goodbye to me, somewhat sad
        wishing me a good trip.
    The Duenna — Since you gave it birdseed!
    Doña Estrella — The peacocks sigh
        in the penumbra of the garden,
        and the roses on the rosebushes
        also send me a nod
        shedding their petals with dismay
        which is their way of crying.
    The Duenna — They probably think to themselves
        that no one is going to water them."

Doña Estrella's simple intuitive grasp of the world is decried by the Duenna.[15] Spanish traditionalists adopt a similair attitude and do not simply belittle but actively rebuff Arlequín's (pagan) insistence on the importance of such "mysterious voices." The pagan message is proclaimed in a Christian land and Grecian mores clash with Iberian habits: "Versailles that loves Grecian breezes" ["Versalles que ama brisa de Grecia"] (65) contrasts with the Spanish garden where "the Inquisition lights bonfires" ["hace hogueras la Inquisición"] (65). Marquesa Rosalinda differentiates and needs to choose between the evocative pagan and the imprisoning Spanish views of love.[16] The

> [*Doña Estrella* — El ruiseñor, entre el follaje,
> Me dice adiós, un poco triste,
> Deseándome buen viaje.
> *La Dueña* — ¡Como solías darle alpiste!
> *Doña Estrella* — Suspiran los pavos reales
> En la penumbra del jardín
> Y las rosas en los rosales
> También me hacen un mohín
> Deshojándose con desmayo,
> Que es su manera de llorar.
> *La Dueña* — Tal vez piensan para su sayo
> en que nadie las va á regar.]   (*MR*, 36–37)

15. The "mysterious voices" are not only beyond the ken of the Duenna but outside the realm of explanation itself. Reason does not understand the revelations of intuition: "But the wise men of the schools were never able to penetrate the mystic forest" ["Pero los sabios de las escuelas en ningún tiempo alcanzaron á penetrar en la selva mística"] (*Lámpara*, 16). Valle-Inclán's plays echo this deprecatory view of the intellect in a lighthearted fashion. *La cabeza del dragón* [*CdD*] opens with a discussion about the Prime Minster, proclaimed a wise man, who has a "head full of smoke" ["cabeza llena de humo"] (*CdD*, 15); the head of the dragon is presumed to be authentic, since it weighs as much as doctoral thesis (*CdD*, 129). In *MR*, the Marqués philosophizes (*MR*, 32), and this meditative tendency is the butt of the characters' mockery (*MR*, 177). In *Divinas palabras* (*DP*), more somber aspects of the issue are revealed in the role played by "knowledge" ["saber"] (DP, 257) and the opposition between the sacristan, Pedro Gaila, and the outlaw, Séptimo Miau. Nonrational, mystic, even demonic means of comprehension fascinate Valle-Inclán. Arlequín reportedly posesses the powers of a "sorcerer" ["hechicero"] (*MR*, 165). Dark and unknown forces are concretized and made visible in *Divinas palabras* and *Comedias bárbaras*—the characters Trasgo Cabrío and Fuso Negro, respectively. An occult power lies at the very heart of the writer's art—in the word itself. Witness the incantatory spell of the Latin phrases at the end of *Divinas palabras* or of the confession throughout *Sacrilegio*.

16. *Rosalinda* — The smell of orange blossoms fills the air
  the stars are juggling,
  and the harmonious wave of the fountains
  trembles with the nightingales' song.
  What a beautiful spot for swoons
  of love [. . . .] A sigh has at least three echoes here!

conflict between the Spanish and pagan/Italian/French worlds is fundamental to the structuring parameters of *MR*, and indeed, to many of the pieces written before 1916.[17] The specifically aesthetic implications of the conflict, though, are particularly emphasized in *MR*. The commedia troupe, with its pagan roots, presents an art that runs counter to Spanish expectations.

Arlequín brings a decidedly foreign tradition to the garden. "*Arlequín* — I am from Bergamo, I lived in Venice, / but for some time now, I have been wandering at will. / Paris has given me what it most prizes: / debts, teachers, and a wife!" ["*Arlequín* — Soy de Bergamo,

> *Amaranta* — A laugh, a sigh, a kiss, and a lament
> on the grate also have three echoes.
> *Rosalinda* — The grate is no more than a cage!
> Eros's eyes had their court
> of love in the arbor, near the water,
> waiting for the baths of goddesses and nymphs.
> The green vine leaves and the green apple
> are from Attic and Roman fields.
> The grate is moorish without pagan grace,
> I prefer the merry window over the grate
>
> [*Rosalinda* — Penetra la brisa olor de azahares,
> Las estrellas hacen juegos malabares
> Y la onda armoniosa de los surtidores
> Tiembla con el canto de los ruiseñores.
> ¡Qué lindo paraje para los desmayos
> De amor [. . . .] ¡Lo menos tres ecos tiene aquí un suspiro!
> *Amaranta* — Tres ecos los tiene también en la reja
> La risa, el suspiro, el beso y la queja.
> *Rosalinda* — ¡La reja no pasa de ser una jaula!
> Los ojos de Heros tuvieron el aula
> De amor, en la fronda, cerca de las linfas,
> Acechando el baño de diosas y ninfas.
> Los pámpanos verdes y la verde poma
> Son de los ejidos de Atica y de Roma.
> La reja es moruna, sin gracia pagana,
> Prefiero á la reja, la alegre ventana"] (*MR*, 46–47).

This choice resembles Estrella's observation in that it is made before the commedia troupe establishes itself as an effective presence in the garden. The characters adopt a position with respect to pagan/Christian differences prior to their realization of its (mystic) significance—a significance made evident, in the case of Marquesa Rosalinda, by Arlequín.

17. The Spanish/non-Spanish dichotomy in itself indicates Valle-Inclán's interest in depicting and defining the nature of things Spanish, a tendency evident even in such early works as the first two *Comedias bárbaras* (1907 and 1908). In *Voces de gesta* (1911), El Rey Pagano contrasts with El Rey Carlino. In *Cuento de abril* (1910), Provençal lyric sensuousness stands in opposition to ironclad Castilian harshness. In *El*

viví en Venecia, / Pero años hace vuelo á placer. / París me ha dado lo que más precia: / ¡Deudas, maestros, y una mujer!"] (*MR*, 63). In addition to detailing biographical information about the character Arlequín, the passage provides a genetic explication of his role. Commedia dell'arte, of course, originated in Italy and then moved to France. The "teachers" Arlequín finds in Paris do indeed change the troupe's attributes, and these changes are evident in *MR*.[18] Arlequín comes to Spain with this background, this "old coffer, all covered with tinsel / that I call the Ossuary of History" ["cofre viejo, todo de oropeles, / Al que llamo el Osario de la Historia"] (*MR*, 31), in order to fulfill a dream: "For my dream, I ask good luck" ["Para mi ensueño pido fortuna"] (*MR*, 64). Marquesa Rosalinda immediately points out the obstacles confronting this dream: "Think [be aware] that this is a very Christian land" ["Pensad que es tierra muy cristiana"] (*MR*, 64). Arlequín remains imperturbable and intends not simply to counter the Spanish resistance to his pagan ideals, but to bridge the differences and unite the two positions: "Divine mouth [Marquesa Rosalinda], do not make faces at the divine pagan monsters. / You will see the same brooding hen cover your dancers and my sylvans" ["A los divinos monstruos paganos, / Boca divina, no hagas la mueca. / Tus bailarines y mis silvanos / Verás que cubre la misma clueca"] (*MR*, 66).

The implications of Arlequín's dream are not immediately recognized by the Marquis, who orders Arlequín to erect his stage in the garden (*MR*, 31) and to entertain. Aristocratic "sorrows" ["penas"] will be dispelled by Arlequín's "jingle bells" ["cascabeles"] (*MR*, 29).[19] Theatrical and nontheatrical positions are clearly defined.

Yermo de las almas (1908), Octavia Goldoni vacilates between her natural inclination (love for Pedro) and social obligation (the return to a husband whom she does not love)—a dilemma presented essentially as a further extension of the fundamental difference between her Italian grandfather and her inflexible Spanish grandmother. Marquesa Rosalinda, caught between her desire to flee with Arlequín and the socially imposed need to remain with her husband, is in a position similar to that of Octavia Goldoni. The psychological exposition of the suffering caused by (Spanish) cultural and social realities present in *El yermo de las almas*, however, remains largely absent in *MR*. As in Valle-Inclán's later plays, the emphasis on character development comes to be replaced in *MR* by a focus on aesthetic concerns in the context of (Spanish) cultural/social values and issues.

18. The character Polichinela, for example, has two humps (*MR*, 88), as distinct from the single Italian hump. "Pulchinela was amongst our first buffoons to pass the Alps [. . . .] But in France they made him change his appearance, gave him two humps, one in front, the other behind" (Michele Scherillo, "The Genealogy of Pulcinella," *The Mask* 3 [1910–11]: 27). See also Giacomo Oreglia, *The Commedia dell'Arte* (London: Methuen, 1968), 97.

19. The complete phrase reads: "By shaking your crazy bells, / you will drive off courtly sorrows" ["Al sacudir tus locos cascabeles / Ahuyentarás las cortesanas penas"]

Commedia art stands relegated to the stage, and the Marquis remains free of its bounds—he can choose either to suscribe to the theatrical pact (become a spectator) or to ignore it completely. The Marquis then believes himself to be safely distanced from commedia space, largely as a result of its isolation.

Commedia art, though, hardly tolerates circumscription. The attempt to limit Arlequín's play to the stage meets with little success. Commedia is a "devouring theatricality"[20] that endows the nominally nontheatrical Spanish garden with theatrical presence. The troupe converts what appears to be a preparation for the play (on the stage) into the play itself. The Marquis and the inhabitants of the garden find themselves enmeshed in a commedia frame with every succeeding moment.

The extension of the pagan influence beyond its (Marquis demarcated) stage confines elicits a response that, as might be expected, finds expression in aesthetic terms. On Arlequín's stage, the "entertainment / of an Italian Farce" ["diversión / De una Farsa Italiana"] compares with (confronts) "[t]he plays of yesteryear, written by / don Pedro Calderón" ["Las comedias de antaño, que escribía / Don Pedro Calderón"] (MR, 92), and the "theatricalization" of the pagan/Spanish difference comes slowly but steadily to the foreground in MR. The Marquis, for example, at first espouses the Versaillesque manner of ignoring conjugal infidelity. Spanish surroundings will (apparently) be inconsequential to the manner in which the Marquis regards his wife's affair with Arlequín. Marquesa Rosalinda knows that "The Marquis D'Olbray will not commit absurdities / in the fashion of a lamentable Spanish nobleman" ["El Marqués D'Olbray no hará disparates / Al modo de un pobre hidalgo español"] (MR, 51).[21] Any similarity between the Marquis and honor-bound Spanish husbands is eschewed. When the Page gives evidence to the contrary, The Duenna dismisses the evidence as a nice story (MR, 96), and Marquesa Rosalinda (who uncovers this information from other sources) laughs so much that she starts coughing (MR, 97). The change may be laugh-

---

(MR, 29). Later versions of the play change the phrase to emphasize a theatrical presence: "Your stage of farce and bedlam / will drive off courtly sorrows" ["Tu tablado de farsas y babeles / ahuyentará las cortesanas penas"] (*Obras completas de Don Ramón del Valle-Inclán* [Madrid: Plenitud, 1954], 220).

20. The term is from Roland Barthes, "Baudelaire's Theater," *Critical Essays* (Evanston: Northwestern University Press, 1972), 26.

21. Later versions stress that the behavior of Spanish husbands is based on theatrical roles: "the Marquis smiles at the absurdities / and at the husbands of Spanish theatre" ["el Marqués sonríe de los disparates / y de los maridos del Teatro Español"] (*Obras completas de Don Ramón del Valle-Inclán*, 230).

able (and indeed its farcical nature certainly comes to the fore), but the Marquis does change: "with a jump he has changed, with his tassel of stoical / doctorate in Versailles, into a heroic Castillian" ["de un brinco ha pasado con su borla de estoico / doctorado en Versalles, á castellano heroico"] (*MR*, 101). The once disparaged Spanish example, immortalized in countless theatrical works, becomes the model on which the Marquis bases his actions. The cuckold will take revenge: "For the lady [Marquesa Rosalinda] the convent opens its doors / and for the actor [Arlequín] the galleys [are waiting]" ["Para la dama abierto está el convento / Y para el comediante las galeras"] (*MR*, 96)—an outcome that indeed merits the Duenna's literary epithet "story" ["cuento"] (*MR*, 96).

The Marquis's effort to counter Arlequín's desire results in the evocation of a literary/dramatic atmosphere—instancing a pattern inscribed in the very structure of *MR*. Gestures are redolent of preceding aesthetic movements. Characters become, as it were, figures in bas-relief, blurred with their background despite (feeble) protestations and efforts to the contrary. When Marquesa Rosalinda, for example, confesses her desire to elope with Arlequín and join the commedia troupe, Amaranta pleads against the action, basing her arguments on potential literary repercussions. "A Marquise kidnapped in a farceur's cart! / You will appear in stories as an example for lovers! / Blind men and barnstormers will sing your looseness / in ribald ballads and in chaconne couplets" ["¡Raptada una Marquesa en carro de farsantes! / ¡Saldrás en las historias para ejemplo de amantes! / Ciegos y bululues cantarán tu rabona / En romances de jácara y en coplas de chacona"] (*MR*, 105). The elopement does not take place, but Amaranta's desire to stand clear of a literary backdrop, itself the expression of a fear—the fear of literary engulfment—meets with little success. Literary (and dramatic) presence become ever more accentuated.

MR evinces the progressively central role of the citation in Valle-Inclán's drama. Evolving from a primarily passive, ambiance-creating status in earlier texts, the citation actually comes to determine the perspective from which the characters are to be viewed.[22] The Grecian

22. *Luces de bohemia* [*Luces*], of course, culminates this process. Scene 11 of *Luces*, with the mother whose child has been shot by the guards, illustrates the crucial importance of literature. Max Estrella acknowledges the quite evident tragic nature of the incident: "This tragic voice has shaken me up!" ["¡Me ha estremecido esa voz trágica!"] (*Luces*, 126). At the same time, *sainete* echoes envelope the expression of this tragedy: "*The Mother of the Child* — Oh, how cold, mouth of nards!" ["*La Madre Del Niño* — ¡Qué tan fría, boca de nardo!"] (*Luces*, 128). As a result, the whole situation exudes, as Don Latino points out, "a lot of theatre" ["mucho de teatro"] (*Luces*, 128). The literary quotation changes the dominant perspective from which to view the scene.

elements, for example, can hardly be regarded as isolated instances, dashes of color added to highlight the events and actions of the characters on the stage. The (mythological) quotation begins to shed its adjectival role. Arlequín, of course, as noted in the previous section, continuously underscores the crucial importance of the Grecian world, and other characters follow his example. "*Silvia* — [. . .] the Marquesa sighed / throwing laments to the wind / who blowing up her skirt, was becoming happy" ["*Silvia* — [. . .] la Marquesa suspiraba / Dando quejas al viento, / Que inflándole la falda, se alegraba] (*MR*, 166). The mythological allusion simply alternates on an equal footing with the other various elements constituting the characters' world. "[Silvia is speaking] There is no [better] devil than Love. The winged child / shot his golden arrow in the blue" ["No hay más diablo que Amor. El niño alado / Lanzó su flecha de oro en el azul"] (*MR*, 167).

From the vantage point of the stage directions, the author also indulges in Arlequín's desire to confuse the distinction between the garden of the play and the Grecian world. "Alas!. . . [The Page and Doña Estrella] They become lost in the thicket / fatal to Leda and to Diana!" ["¡Ay! . . . ¡Se pierden en el boscaje / Fatal á Leda y á Diana!"] (*MR*, 172). Characters are instructed to imitate mythological figures: "As an old Silenus [. . .] Polichinela runs through the gardens" ["Como un Sileno viejo [. . .] Corre por los jardines Polchinela"] (*MR*, 90). In fact, Eros is actually instructed to appear onstage in a problematic stage direction, given that Eros does not appear listed as one of the Dramatis Personae: "Eros shoots an arrow from his bow / behind the Grecian laurels of the garden" ["Heros lanza una flecha de su arco, / Tras los griegos laureles del jardín"] (*MR*, 147).[23]

Foregrounding the Grecian quotation becomes a manner of emphasizing its intrinsic (mystic) significance. The act of foregrounding a

---

23. Silvia's testimony corroborates the presence of Eros onstage. The author would have liked (stage directions take the form of perlocutionary phrases, see R. Ohman, "Speech Acts and Style," in S. Chatman, ed. *Literary Style: A Symposium* [London: Oxford University Press, 1971], 241–54) the following sequence of events to be carried out in the proceeding fashion: "Eros shoots an arrow from his bow / behind the Grecian laurels of the garden / and it goes flying through the light blue sky / to pierce Arlequín's chest. / The actor insinuates a smile, / brings his hand to his pierced chest / and from his chest he feels a breeze fly. / Spirit is air in the Grecian language" ["Heros lanza una flecha de su arco, / Tras los griegos laureles del jardín, / Y va volando por el cielo zarco / A clavarse en el pecho de Arlequín. / El comediante ensaya una sonrisa, / La mano al pecho traspasado llega, / Y del pecho volar siente una brisa. / ¡El espíritu es aire en lengua griega!"] (*MR*, 147). Silvia reports the manner in which the events actually take place: "There is no [better] devil than Love. The winged child / shot his golden arrow in the blue / and with it piercing his chest / the actor [Arlequín] arrives at the Palace" ["No hay más diablo que Amor. El niño alado / Lanzó su flecha de oro en el azul, / Y con ella clavada en el costado, / Llega al Sitio Real, Don Farandul"] (*MR*, 167).

preceding aesthetic manifestation, however, as a method of writing stems,[24] in part, from Valle-Inclán's conviction that art is a means to communion with the Infinite—the Source, the ultimate Fountainhead of all possible meanings that works can suggest and language display. All things are subsumed under the One, and nothing can be created as such, no new elements can be added. The artist works with (and within) a fixed group of elements that he can combine as imaginatively as his "Daemonium" (*Lámpara*, 27) requires, but which he cannot create:

> The poet combines them [words], connects them and with known elements he also invents a line of monsters. His own. In this fashion, he succeeds in awakening slumbering emotions, but create them, never. What is not in us, [either] as a larva or consciously, will never be given to us by someone else's words [. . . .] We can only understand what has its larva in our conscience and what goes with us from when we are born to when we die. Sometimes the music of a word manages to awaken these larvae, and another stirs them, and another gives them wings, but we never learn anything. Everything is always found in us, and the only thing that we achieve is to decrease the ignorance of ourselves.
>
> [El poeta las combina ["las palabras"], las ensambla, y con elementos conocidos inventa también un linaje de monstruos. El suyo. Logra así despertar emociones dormidas, pero crearlas, nunca. Lo que no está en nosotros larvado ó consciente, jamás nos lo darán palabras ajenas [. . . .] Sólo podemos comprender aquello que tiene sus larvas en nuestra conciencia, y que va con nosotros desde que nacemos hasta que morimos. A veces la música de una palabra logra despertar estas larvas, y otra las hace remover, y otra les da

---

24. Although the progressive importance of the quotation in the structure of Valle-Inclán's dramatic text is particularly noticeable in the Grecian context, citations from other sources are also utilized. In the brief "Prelude" ["Preludio"] that precedes the first act, the poet clearly relies on the moon for aid in descrying the events in the garden. "In order to spy behind the bush / the moon offers me her horns / and I must tell you the secret / of the Marquesa Rosalinda" ["Para espiar detrás del seto, / La luna sus cuernos me brinda, / Y he de contaros el secreto / De la Marquesa Rosalinda"] (*MR*, 13). The author further accentuates the continued importance of the moon in the very progression of *MR*: "And the moon spins the silver flax of the little play" ["Y la luna devana el lino / Argentino de la Comedieta"] (*MR*, 56). Within this imbrication of the moon and the development of the piece resides the plethora of literary allusions evoked by the moon, allusions noted by *MR* itself. A "silhouette" ["silueta"] is "[s]wathed in the chimerical halo / given by the metaphorical moon" ["Envuelta en el halo quimérico / Que da la luna metafórica"] (*MR*, 17). In consequence, this "silhouette" "[d]rags an esoteric prestige / as an allegorical figure" ["Arrastra un prestigio esotérico / Como una figura alegórica"] (*MR*, 17). The metaphors and Romantic imagery associated with the moon play an active role in the burlesque/stylized atmosphere of *MR*—see P. Ilie, "The Grotesque in Valle-Inclán," *Ramón del Valle-Inclán* ed., A. Zahareas [New York: Las Américas, 1968], 502–7.

alas, pero jamás aprendemos nada. Todo se halla desde siempre en nosotros, y lo único que conseguimos es ignorarnos menos]. (*Lámpara*, 60; 62–63)

Originality, then, lies in the ability of the artist to evoke latent and as yet unrecognized elements of the One. The oft-quoted, and as often misrepresented, phrase "So that the poet, the more obscure, the more divine!" ["¡Así el poeta, cuanto más obscuro más divino!"] (*Lámpara*, 63) indicates the extent to which Valle-Inclán regards suggestion as central to the artistic process. "Always choose your words making a little mistake" ["Elige tus palabras siempre equivocándote un poco"] (*Lámpara*, 68]). The interstice of juxtaposition generates meaning. The artist remembers "and shakes the chain of centuries" ["y sacude la cadena de siglos"] (*Lámpara*, 87), to combine the similar with the almost similar. "There where the rest of mankind only finds differentiations, poets find luminous bonds of an occult harmony" ["Allí donde los demás hombres sólo hallan diferenciaciones, los poetas descubren enlaces luminosos de una armonía oculta"] (*Lámpara*, 48–49). The revelation of hitherto unrecognized harmonies lies at the very center of the artistic/mystic endeavor. Allusion has a temporal dimension—the present is united with the past and carries into the future. The (poet's) discovery of "luminous bonds" provides a means with which to transcend temporal divisions. The desire to create leads Valle-Inclán perforce to the already created (the preceding aesthetic manifestation) in order to beget the creation:

> The aesthetic conscience of the past is always in the future [. . .] when looking for the beauty of the primitive poems of bygone times we are like weavers of a seamless and golden cloth! Our souls, restless with modernity, pour in old rhythms the treasure of their new emotions.
>
> [La conciencia estética del pasado está siempre en lo futuro [. . .] al buscar la belleza en los rudos poemas de otro tiempo somos como tejedores de una tela inconsútil y dorada! Nuestras almas inquietas de modernidad vierten en los ritmos viejos el tesoro de sus emociones nuevas]. (*Lámpara*, 89–90)

As artist, the writer creates beauty and "all action of beauty is a center of love that engenders the infinite circles of the sphere" ["toda accion de belleza es un centro de amor que engendra los infinitos círculos de la esfera"] (*Lámpara*, 89–90). The art work (the text that highlights its connection with previous texts), like the eye of a storm, centers the generation of an ever-expanding ("infinite") web of allusion. Valle-Inclán calls for the text to manifest "in the vertigo of movement, the secret aspiration to stillness" ["en el vértigo del movimiento la secreta aspiración á la quietud"] (*Lámpara*, 174), for it is in this fashion that the nontemporal view is unveiled.

The Play of Contrasts

The image of the "brooding hen" ["clueca"] (see page 20 of this text) unites the pagan (Arlequín's "sylvans") with the nonpagan (Spanish "bailarines"). The feasibility of such a union, however, is, at best, difficult to envisage. Marquesa Rosalinda, for example, maintains that "I will go blind before!" ["¡Cegaré antes!"] (*MR*, 67). Given the dichotomy of the two positions, the mere presence of pagan actors in a Spanish setting is problematic, engendering, of course, a temporal vector. The progression of *MR* depends on overcoming the very dichotomy on which it is based—a progression measured by the extent to which the pagan entourage succeeds (or fails) in the drive toward union with Spanish identity. The dramatic repercussions of this drive for union are evinced at all levels of the text. Shifts of perspective are constant. One moment the action fulfills the requisites demanded from a Christian perspective, while in the next moment, pagan imperatives are followed.

> *Rosalinda* — Have you brought, Aldonza, the two candles
>   to the Discalced Nuns?
> *The Duenna* — Yes, ma'am.
> *Rosalinda* — Did the Mother Superior give you
>   a prayer for toothaches?
> *The Duenna* — Yes, ma'am. And Mother Prudenciana
>   a crock of prune jam
>   and another crock of apple jam [. . . .]
> *Rosalinda* — Enough! Enough! Lord, what gibberish!
>   Deliver this note. In the garden,
>   Aldonza, you will find,
>   Mr. Arlequín.
>
> [*Rosalinda* — ¿Habéis llevado, Aldonza, las dos velas
>   A las Madres Descalzas?
> *La Dueña* — Si señora.
> *Rosalinda* — ¿Os entregó la Madre Superiora
>   Una oración para el dolor de muelas?
> *La Dueña* — Si, señora. Y la Madre Prudenciana
>   Una orza con jalea de ciruelas,
>   Y otra orza con jalea de manzana [. . . .]
> *Rosalinda* — ¡Basta! ¡Basta! ¡Jesús, qué jerigonza!
>   Llevad este billete. En el jardín
>   Encontraréis, Aldonza,
>   Al señor Arlequín].
>
> (*MR*, 98–99)

The observance of Christian ritual is cast to the winds. From an instrument in the service of pious obligations, the Duenna becomes a means by which Marquesa Rosalinda can pursue sensual satisfaction.

Often, a pervasive uncertainty tints the perspective from which to view an action. Spanish (Pagan) characteristics are endowed with Pagan (Spanish) attributes. The shifting ground of the struggle for unison stands revealed, and neither view triumphs over the other. In conversation with Marquesa Rosalinda, Arlequín comments that Estrella, the Marquesa's young daughter, "[s]he seems a doll carried by her Duenna, / a present of the Magi to a little queen. / The beau who kisses her will have doubts / whether to take her in his arms or whether to kneel" ["Parece una muñeca que llevase su Dueña, / Regalo de los Magos á una reina pequeña. / Al galán que la bese, le ocurrirá dudar / Si ha de tomarla en brazos ó se ha de arrodillar"] (*MR*, 145). The gesture of adoration envelopes both the "present" of the Three Wise Men and the "kiss" of the "beau." The "beau," however, makes the kiss either an expression of adoration (kneeling) or the expression of desire preceding consumption (taking her into his arms). The bridge from the sensual to the spiritual spans the shortest of distances. The two alternatives are largely made equivalent. Desire and pagan/Christian adoration lie in the most amicable of harmonies.

The alternating play of perspectives implied by Arlequín's dream has implications beyond its structural (and structuring) role in *MR*. Art overcomes temporal limitations in the search for Unity. The confines of the present are surpassed by the desire to "unite contrary forms, contrary movements" ["enlazar las formas contrarias, los movimientos contrarios"] (*Lámpara*, 140). The artist can endow his work with transcendental meaning by the conscious use of two contrasting features—even if it be but "[t]he beginning and the end of the smile" ["El nacer y el declinar de la sonrisa"] (*Lámpara*, 141) on da Vinci's *Gioconda*. The mystic significance of "[t]he flaming motif in the ogival arch" ["El motivo flamígero en el arco ojival"] (*Lámpara*, 142), for example, derives precisely from the fact that "[w]hat is weightless is united to a substance with weight in a divine harmony of contrasts" ["Lo ingrávido se enlaza con la substancia grávida en una divina armonía de contrarios"] (*Lámpara*, 143). The omnipresence of the two moments in *MR*—the latter in some manner contradicting, undermining, or even overpowering the former—plays a fundamental suggestive role in revealing the mystic goals of artistic expression.[25] "The heart is a garret, Marquesa, / and neglected in it,

---

25. The oppositional interplay derives, in part, from the direct relationship Valle-Inclán deems extant between theatre and the specificity of a language. The Spanish language is one of "subjugators" ["sojuzgadores"] (*Lámpara*, 78), with harsh, violent contrasts that need to be incorporated into the very structure of (Spanish) theatre. The natural and popular forces of language, then, give rise to an art form (theatre) that, in

one finds everything" ["Es un desván el corazón, Marquesa / Y arrinconada en él, se halla de todo"] (*MR*, 195) proclaims Arlequín. The "garret" opens to display a patchwork of contrasts. Arlequín's love affair with Marquesa Rosalinda, for example, has a spiritual effect on the Marquesa (see *MR*, 102–7), yet he freely admits to exploiting her for pecuniary reasons (see *MR*, 70 –71). Arlequín's "lust" ["lujuria"] and "avarice" ["avaricia"], to cite from the title of Valle-Inclán's last collection of plays, seem on the surface to have little to do with the mystic position; nonetheless the three are intertwined in *MR*.[26] Arlequín's explanation is as simple as it is direct: "The moral of life is the following: A harmony of opposites!" ["La moral de la vida es esa: / ¡Una armonía de contrarios!"] (*MR*, 135). This ethical dictum, drawn from the contradictions apparent in the activity of the garden's inhabitants, proves to be inseparable from aesthetic formulation. Indeed, in *Lámpara*, the ethic and the aesthetic are one and the same: "All aesthetic doctrine is a lesson to love what is good" ["Toda la doctrina estética es una enseñanza para amar el bien"] (*Lámpara*, 114). In *MR*, the barnstormers' vicissitudes in preparation for the play on the stage that the Marquis orders them to erect in the garden (*MR*, 31) become the actual enactment of the play. The acceptance of life as a harmony of opposites gathers significance as an aesthetic norm when life is theatre-in-the-making.

Reflection

The strength of the spell cast by the Graeco-Roman legacy on the contemporaries of Valle-Inclán can be measured not only by the prevalence of mythological citations in their works but also by the

---

turn, reveals the mystic significance of the forces inherent to the language (the contrasts). See, in this text, the first section of chapter four.

26. In *Retablo de la avaricia, lujuria y muerte* (1927), "lust" ["lujuria"] and "avarice" ["avaricia"] are presented in the context of the distancing (and distanced) perspective of death. The topics are prevalent in Valle-Inclán's works. Their mystic significance derives from the fact that lust and greed enclose man in the confines of the self and hence limit him to the realm of the particular (see, in this chapter, footnote 14). In *MR*, the contrast between self-centered and disinterested views appears, as the subtitle of *MR* itself suggests, in a "sentimental and grotesque" light. In *Divinas palabras* (*DP*), one of the many works where this contrast appears repeatedly, pictorial vividness comes to be emphasized. The couple and child—"a martyr virgin between two aged retable figures" ["una virgen mártir entre dos viejas figuras de retablo"] (*DP*, 174)— stand in sharp contrast to the drunken, avarice-, and lust-charged atmosphere of the tavern (see Robert Marrast, "Quelques clés pour *Divines paroles*" *Cahiers Renaud-Barrault* 43: [1963]: 18–35).

use of such themes as the Horatian *carpe diem*. The reintroduction of the *carpe diem* "is the work of Rubén Darío [. . .] and has two aspects: the melancholy reflection on the passing of time and the need [urgency] to make the most of life" ["es obra de Rubén Darío [. . .] y tiene dos aspectos: la reflexión melancólica del paso del tiempo y la urgencia de aprovechar la vida"].[27] Both aspects are presented in *MR* and, as might be expected in Valle-Inclán, are endowed with aesthetic implications. Arlequín's commedia follows pagan dictates and, as such, situates "the world's images outside of Time" ["las imágenes del mundo fuera del Tiempo"] (*Lámpara*, 136). The artistic process serves as a refuge from the irreversible progression of time.

The contrast between commedia and noncommedia characters heightens the particular (nontemporal) status of the art work. Marquesa Rosalinda, as a character in *MR*, "grows old" ["envejece"] and attempts, as the Duenna reveals in conversation with the adolescent Estrella, to forestall this aging:

> *The Duenna* — You should be more reasonable
> and understand, my lady
> that it is no longer feasible for your mother
> to have you in her company.
> You grew without giving it a thought
> so very quickly,
> Doña Estrella, that it is a public announcement
> to courtly maliciousness.
> Your mother has this complaint
> because she suddenly grows old
> near you, and she is not old
> nor will she [ever be old], most likely
>
> [*La Dueña* — Debíais ser más razonable
> Y comprender, señora mía,
> Que á vuestra madre no le es dable
> Teneros en su compañía.
> Crecisteis tan sin reflexión,
> Tan de la noche á la mañana,
> Doña Estrella, que es un pregón
> A la malicia cortesana.
> Vuestra madre tiene esa queja,
> Porque envejece de repente
> Cerca de vos, y ella no es vieja
> Ni lo será, seguramente]. (*MR*, 39)

Colombina, on the other hand, is both a character in a specific play and a role that has been played for centuries. Arlequín indicates the

---

27. Guillermo Díaz Plaja, *Modernismo frente a noventa y ocho* (Madrid: Espasa-Calpe, 1951), 258.

distinction in a comment to Colombina, referring to her attributes as role rather than as character: "*Arlequín* — Between the myrtles and the peacocks, / Colombina, your immortal laughs will find a platform" ["*Arlequín* — Entre los mirtos y los pavos reales / Van á tener estrado, / Colombina, tus risas inmortales"] (*MR*, 31). Colombina stands in the confines of *MR* and simultaneously pertains to an (essentially) immortal or nontemporal context to which Marquesa Rosalinda finds herself barred access. "How old are you" ["¿Cuántos años cumpliste?"] asks the Marquesa, to which Arlequín responds: "Whatever people say. / Do not seek, Marquesa, the age of an actor" ["Los que dice la gente. / La edad de un comediante, Marquesa, no persigas"] (*MR*, 140). Marquesa Rosalinda would like to hear, in the Duenna's words, that she is neither "old / nor will she [ever be old]" ["vieja / Ni lo será"]; she stands, however, firmly within a temporal framework.[28]

Dread accompanies the recognition of being within the bounds of temporal progression. Even Estrella, quite unexpectedly given her youth, fears death: "Your blessing in case I die, Father!" ["¡Tu bendición por si me muero, / Padre!"] (*MR*, 35). Death and the possibility of death are omnipresent in *MR* and, indeed, quite simply fascinate the characters: "*Rosalinda* — [. . .] this tremor, that turns / all of love's trysts into a wedding night, / only charms, scares, and stalks us / when jealous Othello with his scimitar intrudes" ["*Rosalinda* — [...] ese temblor, que convierte todas / Las citas de amor en noche de bodas, / Sólo nos encanta y espanta y asedia / Si Otelo celoso con su alfanje media"] (*MR*, 50).[29] Death, as the Marquesa points out, constitutes the Damoclean sword that adds a special "tremor" to every action—and this "tremor" comes to be constantly elicited in *MR*. An action is not complete without the added realization that in complet-

28. This Marquesa Rosalinda/Colombina or character/role difference has a direct bearing on why Marquesa Rosalinda's elopement with Arlequín never comes to pass—the differences between commedia and noncommedia are (apparently) impossible to bridge. Commedia, Italy, and the innovatory perspective stand on one side; Calderón, Spain, and the Inquisition on the other. The final corroboration of this fundamental schism is revealed near the end of the play with Marquesa Rosalinda's disavowal of the pagan ideals that inform commedia art: "*Rosalinda* — [to Arlequín] Your pagan language / makes me sad" ["*Rosalinda* — ¡Vuestros discursos de paganía / Me causan pena!"] (*MR*, 192).

29. The Eros/Thanatos confluence as well as the simple and sheer delectation in the presence of death are characteristic of Valle-Inclán's work. See, for example, *Sonata de estío* (57–66) or *Ligazón*, which date from 1903 and 1926 respectively. The explications given in *Lámpara* reveal the underlying significance of this confluence. Love (either in the pagan or Franciscan sense) and death (the ultimate liberation from the self) provide a disinterested vantage point—a detachment from the encircling rings of self-centered action required of the mystic perspective (see, in this chapter, footnote 26).

ing the action, death is thwarted. In this sense, *MR* betrays its links to the improvisatory nature of commedia art.³⁰ The ability to conjure the dramatic from a nondramatic presence that never entirely disappears characterizes an essential feature of theatrical improvisation. The special thrill of improvisation, in other words, depends, in part, on the awareness of the nondramatic danger that forever threatens to engulf the arduously kindled dramatic spark. The apprehension of this threat heightens the complicity of the participants in the event and endows it with a compelling urgency.

In the "prelude" ["preludio"], the section before the beginning of *MR* proper, the author pays homage to these tenets of commedia art. He reveals his "[p]lay" ["Comedia"] to be a web of "beautiful lies" ["bellas mentiras"] (*MR*, 11) woven "Over the anguish of death" ["Sobre la angustia de la muerte"] (*MR*, 18).³¹ The tools of Arlequín's trade, the "jingle bells of my joy" ["cascabeles de mi alegría"], are like "graveyard roses. Under the laugh of Dyonisius / lies a sob!" ["las rosas del cementerio. ¡Bajo la risa de Dyonisos / Pasa un sollozo!"] (*MR*, 192). The laughter never quite dispells the sadness,³² for the pagan celebration (the troupe's activity) progresses with the knowledge of its own finitude—*carpe* ere the fete come to an end. "Oh, happy pagan memory!" ["¡Oh, alegre recuerdo pagano!"] (*MR*, 129) exclaims Arlequín in the midst of his travails. The elegiac note accompanies the nascent pagan vision. A world that is in the process of becoming is manifested as the recollection of a world that was. The dual perspective lies at the heart of the text. Theatrical resources are utilized in the presentation of a self-reflexive pagan world view.

---

30. Valle-Inclán uses the conventions of commedia art in *MR* to experiment with the inscription of the perspective of death in the aesthetic work. Arlequín is aware, though, of other traditions: "Let us hang our drapes / [our] heritage from Pedro Naharro" ["Colguemos nuestra bambalina, / Herencia de Pedro Naharro"] (*MR*, 72)—an indication of the array of theatrical conventions that Valle-Inclán will utilize in the development and expression of the famous deathlike "perspective from the other shore" ["perspectiva de la otra ribera"] (*Los cuernos de don Friolera*, 22).

31. See, in this text, chapter two, 33–34, where this passage is analyzed in more detail.

32. Arlequín, like the great farceurs of tradition, draws attention to the tragic presence behind the comic mask by situating his text (*MR*) on a limit. "Tragedy is at the limits of the probable. Beyond it, the play becomes laughable" ["La tragédie est à la limite du probable. Au-delà, le drame devient risible"] (Jean Mitry, *La Sémiologie en question* [Paris: Les Éditions Du Cerf, 1987], 243–44). Arlequín bridges the interstice that separates, and at the same time binds, the two modes that since antiquity have informed theatrical experience.

2
The Structural Consequences

The Symmetrical Frame

As indicated in the previous chapter, the opposition between pagan and nonpagan lends a special cast to *La Marquesa Rosalinda: Farsa sentimental y grotesca* [*MR*]. Arlequín's troupe struggles to bridge the gap separating the two positions and puts commedia dell'arte to the test.[1] The commedia method of making theatre falls under scrutiny: one moment the event functions as a theatrical occurrence while in another the event works to expose the theatrical characteristics of a preceding or forthcoming incident. As usual in Valle-Inclán, the disjunction between the actual presentation of the fictional world and the revelatory moment pointing to its fictive nature stands mediated. The characters pointing to the theatrical nature of their activity are themselves established representatives of theatre.[2] The interaction of perspectives becomes encased within a literary context. *MR* stands as one of the great *tours de force* of theatrical self-reference, "Making people aware of the world of the theatre—not of the outside world."[3] In this early masterpiece, the theatrical event is ceaselessly examined and observed.[4] The framework within which this examination takes place is studied in the remainder of this section.

    1. "Arte" in the sense of *mestiere* (craft or trade) and *abilità* (skill or craftsmanship).
    2. As a dramatic code, commedia dell'arte exudes the atmosphere of the stage: "It [commedia] has always presented itself as art and theater—with an almost self-conscious theatricality" (E. Kearn, "Beckett and the Spirit of the Commedia dell'Arte," *Modern Drama* 9.3 [1966]: 260).
    3. Peter Handke, "Nauseated by Language," an interview by A. Joseph, *Tulane Drama Review* 15.1 (1970): 57. Handke's importance in this context was indicated by Wladimir Krysinski in an engaging analysis of "textual theatricality," its components and codification, to whose insights this chapter is much indebted: "Changed Textual Signs in Modern Theatricality: Gombrowicz and Handke," *Modern Drama* 25.1 (1982): 3–16.
    4. The theatrical (self-) examination evident in *MR* is related, in part, to an incipi-

The Structural Consequences 33

The "Preludio" and the "Jornada Primera"[5] establish an outer and an inner frame. The distinction between the "Prelude" (with the members of the "farce cart" ["carro de la farsa"] (*MR,* 11) outside the palatial garden) and the first act (with the troupe and their cart inside the garden confines) betokens the gap separating performance from nonperformance time. Outside the garden, the commedia dell'arte troupe requests permission to perform: "The farce cart is already awaiting / your permission at the garden gate" ["Ya espera el carro de la farsa / Vuestro permiso en la cancela / Del jardín"] (11). The subject matter per se of *MR* has not yet begun: "And I will tell you the secret / of the Marquesa Rosalinda" ["Y he de contaros el secreto / De la Marquesa Rosalinda"] (13). The "Prelude" reveals the preparation for the fictional work to be presented, the gestures that will be employed, the poses that the troupe will utilize, and specifies their disposition: "Colombina should mix her laughs / with Pierrot's sobs [. . .] and the dignified pavane / should mix its rhythms to the young rhythm [. . .]" ["Mezcle sus risas Colombina / A los sollozos de Pierrot [. . . .] Y la pavana señoril / Mezcle su ritmo al ritmo joven [. . .]"] (12). Forthcoming attributes are glossed: "I will intertwine the fresh roses / with which vaudeville garbs itself / and the funambulatory rhymes / *à la* Banville [. . . .] A smell of rose and apple / both at the same time will my verses have: / as in a courtly farce / of Versalles or Aranjuez" ["Enlazaré las rosas frescas / Con que se viste el vaudeville / Y las rimas funambulescas / A la manera de Banville [. . . .] Olor de rosa y de manzana / Tendrán mis versos á la vez: / Como una farsa cortesana / De Versalles ó de Aranjuez"] (15–16).

One attribute in particular receives special attention—the fictive nature of the inner frame. The author of the "Prelude" refers to himself as "the poet who fills the stage / with love [affairs] and mockeries" ["el poeta que el tablado / Puebla de amores y de mofas"] (11). The play proceeds under his control: "In order to serve you, I weave

---

ent intellectual *malaise* with respect to theatre. Literary figures find reigning theatrical norms to be less then commendable in this period, and the burgeoning dissatisfaction leads to a veritable crisis in the following decade. (See Dru Dougherty, "Talía convulsa: La crisis teatral de los años 20," in R. Lima and D. Dougherty, *2 ensayos sobre teatro español de los 20* [Murcia: Cuadernos de la cátedra de teatro de la Universidad de Murcia, 1984]). Valle-Inclán, however, is one of the few dramaturges who actually explores the nature and the limits of his medium. The contrast with Jacinto Benavente's praised *Los intereses creados* (1907) is illustrative. Benavente uses commedia dell'arte conventions to garb a readily comprehensible moral message in an innovative fashion. Valle-Inclán makes the unsettling nature of the innovations the subject of dramatic expression.

5. *MR* has four subdivisions: a "Prelude" ("Preludio"), and three acts (entitled "Jornadas"). The English titles for these subdivisions will be used in the body of the text.

the scheme [plot] / of the Play in my strophes" ["Por serviros tejo el tramado / De la Comedia en mis estrofas"] (11). Immediately after revealing himself as poet/playwright, the author turns back to reflect on his poetic activity, characterizing it as the fabrication of "beautiful lies" ["bellas mentiras"] (11) and suggests how poets (among others) should undertake the fabrication process: "Lovers, Kings, and Poets / let us weave the beautiful lies / with the rythm of pirouettes" ["¡Amantes, Reyes y Poetas, / Tejamos las bellas mentiras / Con el ritmo de las piruetas!"] (11). Poetic and dramatic activity/writing ("I weave the scheme [plot]" ["tejo el tramado"]) and stage presence (on the poet's "stage" ["tablado"]) are simultaneous.

The author takes delight in underlining the poetic/dramatic features inherent in the soon to be revealed "secret of the Marquesa Rosalinda" (13). The world of drama ("beautiful lies") and performance time contrast with time in the nontheatrical world: "Let us weave the beautiful lies / over the anguish of death" ["Tejamos las bellas mentiras / Sobre la angustia de la muerte!"] (18). The theatre serves as a refuge—however illusory and false ("lies") the ensuing protection may actually be—from the anguish of death. The "garden gate" distinguishes merely talking about the fictive world from actually entering into and unfolding this world. At the same time, the distinction between "Armida's garden" (206) where the "secret of Marquesa Rosalinda" (13) is to be enacted and the "anguish of death" (18) surrounding this enchanted world of theatre heightens the theatrical import of the former. Attention is focused on the characteristics of the enchantment (the performance moment) as it eludes the encapsulating confines of the nonperformance world. This structure appears replicated inside the garden. The Abad's vigorous attempt to keep the troupe from enacting the "secret"—"Out of these gardens / [you] barnstormers and concubines / or by my gray beard / I will set the hounds on you!" ["¡Fuera de estos jardines / Los farandules y las barraganas, / O por mis barbas canas / Que os suelte los mastines!"] (26)—calls attention to the tenuousness (and the plight) of the dramatic moment struggling for existence. Throughout its entirety, *MR* will be speckled with indicators/reminders of theatrical presence— evidence of a fundamental *jouissance* as the play exposes its own theatrical nature. "[T]heatrical pleasure: it is scattered all over, it is never absent. Protean, obstinate, [and] lurking;"[6] it spurs the author of the "Prelude" to continue weaving (and expressing his fascination with the theatrical nature of) his lies.[7]

6. Anne Ubersfeld, "The Pleasure of the Spectator," *Modern Drama* 25.1 (1982): 127.

7. The audience (viewing the stage world) also participates in the revelation of the-

The "garden gate" serves as a bridge through which the passage from the outer frame to the inner work takes place. Arlequín establishes the link between what lies outside and inside the confines of the garden wall. He is at one and the same time the author of the "Prelude" as well as an actor playing the role of the character "Arlequín" in the play about to be performed. The author refers to himself as a member of the "farce cart" (11)—"I bring in my troupe / Pierrot and Polichinela" ["Traigo en mi comparsa / A Pierrot y Polichinela"] (11). Colombina is subsequently mentioned (12), so that all the essential commedia dell'arte members are introduced except Arlequín, suggesting that the speaker's mere presence, costume, and gait provide sufficient information to identify the speaker/author of the "Prelude." The first stage direction in the first act corroborates this supposition. The cart stops at the gate, and the entire troupe enters the garden. Arlequín remains the only member not named. The stage directions do not impart otiose information since the link between Arlequín, character in the inner work ("the secret of Marquesa Rosalinda" [13]), and Arlequín, speaker of the "Prelude" and the remaining member of the commedia dell'arte group, is already established. Arlequín further reinforces this correlation when, at the end of the "secret," he literally rips off his mask as character and returns to the cart in order to step outside the "garden gate" and return to the position shown in the "Prelude": "[Arlequín is speaking] The crazy chimeras of a barnstormer are over! [. . . .] I leave my mask hanging / on a laurel branch / and if I return to the cart / it is because my role is finished" ["¡Pasaron las locas quimeras / De farandul! [. . . .] Dejo colgada mi careta / En una rama de laurel, / Y si me torno á la carreta, / Es porque acaba mi papel"] (206). In this passage, Arlequín ceases to play the role of the commedia figure Arlequín in the inner work and, like the speaker of the "Prelude," comments on, or with reference to, this work. The show is over, and the troupe is ready to leave the theatre space (the garden) and resume their wandering. In addition to sharing an outsider's stance with respect to the "secret of the Marquesa Rosalinda," both the speaker of the "Prelude" and Arlequín are seen as leaders of the "farce cart"—Polichinela at the end exhorts Arlequín "[s]o that you may return, Arlequín, / to be the

---

atrical essence inasmuch as the revelation breaks "the invisible barrier of that once famous 'fourth wall' [. . . .] Abruptly, a closed play (embodying claustrophobia in a structural stasis) has been opened up [. . . .] From the little explosion that marks the collision of two planes—the scenic and the spectatorial—the corresponding explosion of laughter follows" (A. Kennedy, "The Theatre Breeds Comedy," *Modern Drama* 31.4 [1988]: 473). Comedy and theatricality, as the Galician well knows, couple in the most fertile of manners.

leader of the roost / in the penumbra of the garden / the cart awaits" ["Para que vuelvas, Arlequín, / A ser el amo del cotarro, / En la penumbra del jardín / Espera el carro"] (205)—a final indication of their mutual identification.

The structure of *MR* then proves to be that of a work within another work. The cart in its normal day-to-day life outside the garden with Arlequín commenting on the play about to be performed stands in contrast to the cart inside the garden with its occupants in the act of performing the "secret of the Marquesa Rosalinda." Moreover, the actors emerge from their roles at the end of the performed stage work, return to the cart, ready to leave the garden and to proceed with their offstage life. The play proper of *MR*—the "secret of the Marquesa Rosalinda"—is framed by an introductory commentary and a concluding reflection on the performance. This framing establishes a nascent tension between actor and character in the inner work. Indeed, throughout the inner frame a constant series of mock revelations ensue where the actor momentarily discards his/her fictive role as character only to scurry back under the protective covering of the fictional world. The duplicity resolves only at the end at which point the unsteady actor/character symbiosis (once again) comes clearly apart. The "play" ["comedia"] stands fully revealed as a "winged dream" ["alado sueño"] (206), and the fictional world is once again seen from the perpective of the "Prelude."

The inner work, "the secret of the Marquesa Rosalinda" (henceforth MR as opposed to *MR*), echoes the structural symmetry of *MR*—of a fictional work within a work. MR is a work about the preparation for another work. The Marqués orders the troupe to set up the stage space: "Erect your stage in the garden" ["Alzad en el jardín vuestro tablado"] (31). In view of these stage confines, the troupe simply engages in normal, day-to-day activity. By the second act, the Duenna confirms that the "stage" ["tablado"][8] stands erected (91). The troupe will offer to the Spanish court, in the Page's words, "the entertainment / of an Italian Farce" ["la diversión / De una Farsa Italiana"] (92). Arlequín characterizes the performance in more detail: "I have a Farce about my life / and it is so amusing / that when assembling [writing] it I also laughed" ["Tengo una Farsa de la vida mía, / Y es tan regocijada, / Que al componerla yo también reía"] (30).

The "tablado" and Arlequín's farce-to-be serve as mirrors, reflecting back on the outer frame of *MR* as an image in reverse. Seen in the light of the "tablado," the story of MR does not appear as the fiction-

8. "Tablado" will be used in the body of the text (in lieu of "stage") when referring to the Marquis's words: "Erect your stage in the garden" [Alzad en el jardín vuestro tablado"] (13).

al "beautiful lie" ["bella mentira"] the "Prelude" makes it out to be: the "tablado" serves as the indicator of the confines delimiting fictiveness. Arlequín and the troupe are not onstage and are not enclosed within theatrical space. As in the "Prelude," they are actors prior to or setting up for a production. When Colombina, angered beyond measure at Arlequín's continued affair with the Marquesa, announces the overtly theatricalized gesture of the distraught female—

> *Arlequín* — Where are you going?
> *Columbina*—I am going to that bench
>   in order to faint!
>
> [*Arlequín* — ¿A dónde vas?
> *Colombina* — ¡Voy á aquel banco
>   Para poderme desmayar!]

—Arlequín tells her to save the gesture for later: "Colombina, if I may be frank, / I believe that you should wait. / A fainting spell serves no purpose / when there are no people" ["Colombina, si he de ser franco, / Creo que debes esperar. / Un soponcio no tiene objeto / Cuando no hay gente"] (203). Arlequín emphasizes the fact that despite their intrinsic status as actors—figures of commedia dell'arte—in MR, they are not onstage. The episode is a private one. They are not before an audience; "there are no people."

Arlequín's need to clarify Colombina's apparent confusion regarding private and public personalities stems from the improvisatory characteristics of commedia. As a result of the priority accorded to the actor's *ad libitum* variations upon guidelines delineated in the character, the actor's dexterity and personal characteristics take precedence over the author's skill (manifested by the text the actor follows):

> The Commedia dell'Arte is above all the world of actors who were the creators and interpreters of their own parts. They selected the role for which they felt themselves to be best suited and identified themselves with it in such a way that the drama had to adapt itself to them and not they to the drama.[9]

In this type of performance, the boundaries marking the separation between stage (character) and nonstage (actor) presence blur:

> When a performer does not "play a character" what does he do? Stand-up comics play aspects of themselves. [. . . .] Disclosure is the heart of the comic's art. He carefully keeps to the edge—just a little too much and his act is embarrassing and painful. The audience teeters between knowing it is

---

9. Michele Scherillo, "The Commedia dell'Arte," *The Mask* 3 (1910–11): 115.

being put on and glimpsing brief, but deep looks into the "real man" [. . . .] One is never sure how much of the "star personality" is genuine and how much put on. The star is usually not sure either. A stereotyped mask thickens and freezes—this mask is worn publicly and privately throughout life.[10]

Commedia constantly shifts and combines disclosure and "stereotyped mask."[11] Life (offstage presence) invades the stage, and the stage extends beyond its confines to penetrate life. The fact that Arlequín has to point out to Colombina that they are not onstage ("there are no people") indicates the extent to which the stage infiltrates the ostensibly nontheatrical parameters of their daily life. Their behavior forms part of a tradition of "role-acting epitomised in the 'maskmaker' who cannot tear off the mask from his skin."[12] For indeed, MR resembles a montage that superimposes a play in the act of being staged onto the preparation for a play to be staged. Various elements composing this montage are now studied in the following sections.

Language

The characters of MR use a language abounding in the terminology of fictional works. The Page tells the Duenna of the Marquis's imminent vengeance on his wife's lover (Arlequín) and explains that the pair must now be on their guard: "[Marquesa Rosalinda] would be less stern if my lips / could make her aware of the plot / that the affronts of the Marquis are weaving against her" ["Menos adusta fuera, si mis labios / Pudiesen darle cuenta de la trama / Que tejen

---

10. Richard Schechner, "Actuals: Primitive Ritual and Performance Theory," *Theatre Quarterly* 1.2 (1971): 57.

11. Indeed, although Scaramouche (a stock character in commedia who does not wear a mask) was not created by the seventeenth-century actor Tiberio Fiorilli, he was virtually synonymous with this real life personage. Scaramouche was one of the several replacements born as a result of the demise of the character known as the Captain. "It was not, however, until Tiberio Fiorilli came on the scene that he [Scaramouche] was invested with real distinction and became a figure whose name developed into a by-word in seventeenth-century circles and whose interpreter found himself the centre of an elaborate myth" (Allardyce Nicoll, *The World of Harlequin* [Cambridge: Cambridge University Press, 1963], 103). The confusion between the actor and his role was sufficient to warrant a popular biography: *"Vie de Scaramouche"* (A. Nicoll, *The World of Harlequin,* 103). For an account of Fiorelli's ability to move the audience without using the mask so typical of commedia characters, see, among others, Pierre L. Duchartre, *The Italian Comedy* (New York: Dover Publications, 1966), 243.

12. Andrew Kennedy, "Mimesis and the Language of Drama: A Reply to Michael Anderson," *Drama, Dance and Music,* ed. J. Redmond (Cambridge: Cambridge University Press, 1981), 225.

contra ella los agravios / Del Marqués"] (94). When hiding from the Marquis, Arlequín states: "I will make myself safe / behind the [drop] curtains of the arbor" ["Me pongo en salvo / Detrás de los telones de la enramada"] (177). These references to the various parts of a fictive world serve as general atmospheric indices pointing to the theatrical ambience permeating the garden. When Dorotea, one of the chambermaids, addresses Colombina, the theatrical attributes of the latter come to the fore: "Do not have a fainting spell, Mrs. Barstormer! / Mrs. Barnstormer, do not make such a fuss! [. . .] Do not shed such lamentations / [because] the white powder is coming off your cheeks" ["¡No tome un soponcio, señora Farsanta! / ¡Señora Farsanta, no mueva alboroque! [. . .] no eche tanta planta, / Que de las mejillas se le va el revoque"] (156).

Alrequín, in particular, picks up on this ever-surfacing dramatic presence, turning discourse into the speech of an actor, an element that can be modified and corrected to better fit the contours of a stage world. Colombina has been eavesdropping while Arlequín has been courting the Marquesa:

> *Arlequín* — Why do you hide in the foliage?
> *Colombina* — Why do you cheat on me? [. . . .]
>   Lord! . . . Lord! . . . [How could] I have deceived Pierrot
>   with so much skill
>   for this villain!
> *Arlequín* — That is said in an aside
>
> [*Arlequín* — ¿Por qué te escondes en la fronda?
> *Colombina* — ¿Por qué me engañas? [. . . .]
>   ¡Señor!. . . ¡Señor!. . . ¡Que haya burlado
>   Con tanto arte,
>   A Pierrot, por este malvado!
> *Arlequín* — Eso se dice en una apart.]   (69)

The emotional substance of Colombina's outburst remains irrelevant. Her lamentation, like that of any actress, stands shorn of personal reference. Arlequín foregrounds "the act of expression, the act of speech [. . . .] used for its own sake."[13] By strictly acknowledging the exterior form of the utterance without concern for its content, the utterance becomes an object, a plastic entity to be molded from a purely theatrical point of view. As the leader of the cart (29), a professional *metteur en scène* responsible for the quality of the performance, Arlequín effectively halts the course of <u>MR</u> to admonish a member of the troupe for her behavior.[14]

13. Jan Mukarovsky, "Standard Language and Poetic Language," *A Prague School Reader on Esthetics, Literary Structure and Style*, ed. P. L. Garvin (Washington D.C.: Georgetown University Press, 1964), 19.

In essence, Arlequín recuperates the perspective of the "Prelude" wherein MR appears as pure fiction, a theatrical entity. These informative moments are constant in MR and, as only typical of dramatic discourse, are relayed "in a discontinuous fashion."[15] Nevertheless, a definite progression results. The indicators of theatricality well up in MR and intrude upon the fictive flow, gathering momentum, until finally they surge past the very parameters of MR and the whole "secret," not just particular moments, becomes a declared theatrical entity. To be more precise, Arlequín's revelation of the theatrical characteristics of Colombina's utterance forms part of an action that will not be completed until the very end of *MR*. The intervening arch of incompleteness whets desire for the termination of the action, drawing the two fiction-revealing moments (Alrequin's response to Colombina [69] and his uncovering—inasmuch as possible—the mask of his "role" [206] as character in MR) into close synchronic proximity. The two frameworks are bound by a common task, and the collaborative effort heightens textual unity.

As previously mentioned, in isolating Colombina's speech, Arlequín focuses attention not on the communicative aspects of standard language but on the speech act itself. This break, inscribed in the discourse matrix, points back to one moment and holds it still, in itself producing theatre:

> If theatricality is setting up of a scene (a *mise en scène*) rather than representation of a text, then in order that theatricality not fall into a succession of dramatic moments or poses leading to a climax within a logic of representation, the scene must be delayed or held—as a frozen frame or film still—to be dissolved [. . .] by the device of the *tableau vivant* (which collapses or decomposes itself under its own intertia of artificiality—its production is made evident, displayed as a representation).[16]

Arlequín's sudden stoppage of MR begets theatricality. The very arbitrariness of the detainment serves as a display of the artificiality encompassing the entire scene. By determining elocutionary presentation and deciding whether a speech should be an aside, the character Arlequín usurps, or at least claims a share of, authorial activity.

---

14. Arlequín responds in the same vein to many of Colombina's sallies: "Cry softly if you have to cry!" ["¡Llora bajo si has de llorar!"] (72). Various other commands (e.g., "Do not cry, for that makes you ugly" ["No llores, que te pones fea"] [158]) also appear to express Arlequín's concern for Colombina's stage presence.

15. Michael Kirby, "Structural Analysis/Structural Theory," *The Drama Review* 20.4 (1976): 58.

16. Philip Monk, "Common Carrier: Performance by Artists," *Modern Drama* 25.1 (1982): 164.

Arlequín's volitional imposition becomes, in effect, less a simulacrum of authorial control than a manifestation of theatre-in-the-making. Theatrical dynamism appears as such, as a mode of action in operation.

With regard to the status of MR, Arlequín's reaction to Colombina's statement remains ambivalent. From the perspective of the "Prelude," MR is a patently fictive "play": by revealing the theatrical nature of the speech being used, Arlequín attests to MR's fictional status and recovers the viewpoint of the "Preludio." Arlequín interrupts a play in order to make its playlike qualities more obvious: a "theatre which makes its audience conscious of the theatre's own element in order to work."[17] The incident proves itself a moment of (narcissistic) theatrical self-absorption. From the perspective of the inner frame, however, MR is not yet theatre but the preparation for theatre, for the staging of Arlequín's play. No interruption of a play occurs as such. Instead, the intermediary steps leading toward the emergence of theatre are shown. With the sudden irruption of theatricality, the troupe's activity becomes an enterprise conducive to the representation of Arlequín's play on the "tablado." The theatre-making apparatus is indeed bearing fruit, producing theatre (apparently) as practice for the troupe's presence on the "tablado."

Object

The status of the object bears witness to the steady theatrical encroachment onto the actions in MR. When Reparado and Juanco, the hooligans hired to frighten Arlequín from the garden, describe their victim, one of the particulars mentioned is his sword. Arlequín wears "a blade seven palms long at his side" ["hoja de siete palmos al costado"] (123). The sword constitutes an authentic threat, an instrument which Arlequín could wield in self-defense. Nevertheless, when Arlequín talks about using the weapon, he does so in terms of the theatre: "I / carry a sword in my sash, and I am used to / killing my friend Pierrot on the stage" ["Yo / Llevo al cinto una espada, y estoy acostumbrado / A matar al amigo Pierrot, sobre el tablado"] (144). Although not yet on the "tablado," Arlequín's action becomes a mere implementation of the more fundamental techniques of the stage. Action in the (to all appearances) nontheatrical world forever exudes theatricality.

Indeed, the sword retains its theatrical roots throughout MR and functions as a prime indicator of the ever-expanding stage presence in

17. J. L. Styan, "Pirandellian Theatre Games: Spectator as Victim," *Modern Drama* 23.2 (1980): 96.

the garden. When the sword comes to be invoked, it has evolved into a full-fledged stage object. Pierrot engages Arlequín in a duel in order to recover his gentleman's honor (197). The swords break. Arlequín exclaims "Mr. Pierrot, my steel is tin! [. . . .] a theatrical sword never kills" ["¡Señor Pierrot, mi acero es hojalata! [. . . .] espada de teatro nunca mata"] (198–99), while Pierrot muses, "You cannot kill me? [. . . .] Since I can not kill you, nor can I receive death / from your clown's hands / to philosophize over my fate / I return to the cart, step by step!" ["¿No me podrás matar? [. . . .] ¡Pues no puedo matarte, ni la muerte / Recibir de tus manos de payaso, / Para filosofar sobre mi suerte, / Me vuelvo á la carreta, paso á paso!"] (199). The stage has unambiguously come to the forefront. Arlequín and Pierrot become, despite their apparent intentions, actors feigning an action. The duel suddenly stands bereft of any significance other than as an exercise in theatrical gesture.

The object/character relationship, in consequence, reveals three intermingling levels. On one level, the object (sword) is simply indicative of itself as object—one more element constructing a possible fictional world. On another level, the character acts on the object and reveals the object's status as part of a fictional world. Arlequín will use the sword to kill potential attackers, yet the method by which he will do so is borrowed from the theatre. On the third level, the object changes what are nominally nontheatrical surroundings into theatrical moments. The object acts on the character, altering the perspective from which the character's desire to avenge his honor is to be viewed. The apparent reality of the duel disappears in its own imitation—the recreation of the duel generated by the use of theatre swords. The complete reciprocity and equivalence between the character and the object—"[props] are no longer the tools of the actor, we perceive them as spontaneous subjects equivalent to the figure of the actor"[18]—serve to highlight the concomitant existence of offstage/onstage presence.

Furthermore, the reciprocal interaction in which stage awareness transfers now from the characters to the sword, now from the sword to the characters,[19] exerts a profound effect on the manner in which the setting is viewed. The dynamic process establishes a web that binds the object/subject with its context, so that the relationship "is

18. Jiří Veltrusky, "Man and Object in the Theatre," *A Prague School Reader on Esthetics, Literary Structure and Style*, ed. P. L. Garvin (Washington D.C.: Georgetown University Press, 1964), 88.

19. The subject is not privilied *a priori* over the object. Valle-Inclán heightens the importance and relevance of all components of the stage world. See, in this text, chapter 3, footnote 22.

more than a spatial one, it is a relation of forces [. . .] that seem to be as physical as those which orient the compass needle toward its pole, [although they] really do not exist physically at all."[20] The interchange does not merely occur in or imply a spatial framework, but actually incorporates and includes the surrounding context in its actualization. The space of *MR* becomes "existential to the point of ceasing to exist as a setting and place. It no longer surrounds and encloses the performance, but [. . .] becomes part of the performance to such an extent that it cannot be distinguished from it. It *is* the performance."[21]

Character

Like other characters of MR, Polichinela purveys information at any given moment. At the same time, he manipulates his role and the characteristics through which this information is expressed in order to establish a perspective that contrasts with his immediate surroundings. In effect, Polichinela distances himself from his context and reflects on the various activities taking place in a commedia play.

Polichinela opens the second act with a series of statements on his characteristics as a hunchback: "Bam! Bam! Bam! / Everyone strikes my hump! [. . . .] Some come and others go / [. . . .] Everyone strikes my hump" ["¡Tan! ¡Tan! ¡Tan! / ¡En mi joroba todos dan! / [. . . .] Unos vienen y otros van / [. . . .] En mi joroba todos dan"] (85– 86). A source of good luck according to popular belief,[22] the presence of the protuberance is highlighted precisely in the second, the central of the three acts into which MR is divided. This structural accentuation itself emblematizes the fact that the hump continuously draws attention to itself. Polichinela's deformity marks the center of a movement that revolves around its presence. The characters of MR—Silvia, Dorotea, Urganda, The Duenna ["La Dueña"], The Page ["El Paje"]— desire the opportunity to touch the hunchback's protuberance.

---

20. S. Langer, *Feeling and Form* (New York: n.p., 1953), 175–76. Cited in Hollis Huston, "Dimensions of Mime Space," *Educational Theatre Journal* 30.1 (1978): 67. See also J. Honzl's comments on dramatic action in Frantisek Deák, "Structuralism in Theatre: The Prague School Contribution," *The Drama Review* 20.4 (1976): 92.

21. J. Feral, "Performance and Theatricality: The Subject Demystified," *Modern Drama* 25.1 (1982): 172–73.

22. Valle-Inclán pays particular attention to such popular beliefs, and the hunchback often appears in his works. See, for example, the second act of *Farsa y licencia de la reina castiza* where the "Hunchback" suspects the nature of Don Lindo's intentions: "I suppose / that you want to touch my hump / in order to change your luck?" ["Supongo / que pretendes tocarme la joroba / para mudar la suerte"] (266).

Polichinela goes through a long roster of individuals who come to strike his disfigurement: "The Beau strikes [. . . .] and the Captain [. . . .] and a vain don Diego [. . . .] and a musked dandy [. . . .] and spiteful cheats" ["Da el Galán, [. . . .] Y el Capitán [. . . .] Y un Don Diego presumido [. . . .] Y un petimetre almizclado [. . . .] Y fulleros despechados"] (85–86; 88–89). He carefully mentions that the people enumerated in his list are only a small portion of those that are actually drawn to his gibbosity: "Between my two humps flies humanity" ["Entre mis dos jorobas vuela la humanidad"] (88). No one escapes being drawn to the pervasive presence of the hump— "There is not a dolt / who does not touch / my hump" ["No hay bodoque / Que no toque / Mi joroba"] (89).

The contact that the characters of MR have with Polichinela's deformity repeats in the body of the play an element already stressed in the subtitle "Sentimental and Grotesque Farce" ["Farsa sentimental y grotesca"]—the omnipresence of deformation. A burlesque caricature counters the previous (sentimental) moment, in a doubling intrinsic to commedia dell'arte. Arlequín especially appears as a past master of parodic distortion, "When he was sentimental, on the verge of drawing tears from the audience, he parodied his own mawkishness" ["Cuando, sentimental, estaba a punto de arrancar lágrimas al público, hacía la parodia de su propia sensiblería"].[23] Polichinela's gibbousness concretizes the grotesque as a mode of writing in sensuously apprehensible terms.[24] Grotesque distortion itself, though, runs unmitigated throughout the play. Romantic and *fin de siècle* motifs and images stand wrenched from their original context. The "argonautic swan" ["cisne argonauta"] moves near the "cricket" ["grillo"] and the "toad" ["sapo"] (18). Arlequín presents the "metaphorical moon" ["luna metafórica"] (17), in a brutal distortion of the Romantic lover's distraught soliloquy, as a "[d]ivine quack" ["Divina curandera"] with a "snub nose" ["nariz chata"] (77–79). The poet José de Espronceda's sun, in an easily apprehensible reference to his poem ("*El sol: himno*"), becomes "The old man [. . . .] who makes mocking faces [. . . .] and is like a trampoline for the black flea" ["El viejo [. . . .] Que hace muecas burlonas [. . . .] Y es como un trampolín para la pulga negra"] (142). Polichinela's hump lies at the very center of the graceful contours molding the Versaillesque figures of speech:

23. María de la Luz Uribe, *La comedia del arte* (Santiago de Chile: Editorial Universitaria, N.D.), 50.

24. The concretization of the abstract lies at the very center of Valle-Inclán's artistic method. J. E. Lyon, for example, stresses the sensuous nature of his theatre in, "Valle-Inclán and the Art of the Theatre," *Bulletin of Hispanic Studies* 46.2 (1969): 132–52. See also, in this text, chapter 4, 96–99.

"[The Page remonstrates Polichinela] Courtesy requires that you offer your pompous [sumptuous] / back in the manner of a beau offering a rose" ["Pide la cortesía que ofrezcas tu pomposa / Espalda, como ofrece un galán una rosa"] (88). Base deformity tinges the courtly rococo gesture, elegant in style and sentiment, with a strange light.[25]

The two humps limit, to a great extent, Polichinela's comprehension of the view and the sentiments expressed by others. Colombina complains to Polichinela about Arlequín's unfaithfulness and hints at this circumscription: "Alas, Polichinela, you will never know, / because you do not have the figure of a beau, / what are loves sundered by fate / what are sighs gone to the wind!" ["¡Ay, Polichinela, tú no sabrás nunca, / Porque tú no tienes talle de galán, / Lo que son amores que el destino trunca, / Lo que son suspiros que en el viento van!"] (154). Yet, despite the seeming unity of the protuberances with his body, Polichinela does not remain completely identified with them. In the words of the author, "Polichinela runs through the gardens / between the two humps with which he celebrated" ["Corre por los jardines Polichinela, / Entre las dos jorobas con que hizo fiesta"] (90). The description implies a Polichinela who merely bears the "humps." Escape from the imprisoning confines of his physical deformation becomes a possibility. Polichinela finds refuge in the world of dreams—an ever-present yearning for the unattainable that pervades *MR* and runs so counter to the given circumstances. The Marquis tells Estrella that her fears are unfounded—her fears that convent walls and the rites of womanhood (marriage) will stymie living out her girlhood—"Always play [. . . .] Do not be prevented [from playing] by your coiffure, / nor your age, nor your husband. / There are grandmothers who thread their distaff / and rock a childhood dream / as if it were a doll / made of tulle and ivory" ["Juega siempre [. . . .] Que no te detenga el tocado, / Ni los años, ni tu marido. / Hay abuela que hila su rueca / Y mece un ensueño infantil, / Como si fuese una muñeca / Hecha de tul y de marfil"] (34). A dream, however illusory, can always be retained. When Rosalinda spins a tale of love and possible elopement with Arlequín, Amaranta continuously protests: "How your fantasy reels [out] sun rays! [. . . .] You are a raving lunatic!" ["¡Cómo devana rayos de sol, tu fantasía! [. . . .] ¡Estás loca de atar!"] (107). Yet, Rosalinda wants to ignore these interjections that belittle her reveries: "Do not become prosaic [. . . .] mocking Amaranta" ["No te pongas prosaica [. . . .] Amaranta burlona"] (106). "The world of dream [illusion]" ["El mundo del

---

25. The play of contrasts intrinsic to distortion is in itself of mystical import. See, in this text, chapter 1, section III.

ensueño"] (146), as Arlequín tells Rosalinda, stands open and Polichinela enters it ever so willingly: "Just now, I [Polichinela] was in the cart / dreaming that I was straight / when I discover lying in wait, / behind the brake, a wandering student / and behind him, a veiled woman / and a duenna and a premonstratensian, and [. . . .] Bam! Bam! / Everyone strikes my hump" ["Ahora estaba en la carreta / Soñando que era derecho, / Cuando descubro en acecho / Tras de la galga, á un bayeta. / Y tras él una tapada, / Y una dueña y un mostense, Y [. . . .] ¡Tan! ¡Tan! / En mi joroba todos dan"] (88–89). His dream world free of distortion, "I was straight," suddenly shatters—the people whom he discovers lurking behind the wagon confront him with the reality of his deformity, "Bam! Bam! / Everyone strikes my hump." Polichinela, like Arlequín at the end of MR, awakens from a "winged dream" (206). Whereas Arlequín's dream, the play MR ("the crazy chimeras / of a barnstormer" ["las locas quimeras / De Farandul"] [206]), is abruptly confronted with terminus in the figure of the "curtain stagehand" ["tramoyista del telón"] (207),[26] Polichinela's dream is confronted with the grotesque, lumbering commedia dell'arte figure of Polichinela in the play MR. The moments when he dreams "I was straight" ["que era derecho"] (88) are the critical instances allowing Polichinela the leeway to point at his role, the vantage point from which to regard the attributes of his own body as pertaining to a commedia play.

A vast throng intrudes upon Polichinela's dream and reaffirms its linkage with deformity (the hump). Among those Polichinela describes are the characters of MR (see 85–86): "concubines and sergeants in pairs" ["de par las coimas con los sargentos"] (86)—The Abbot refers to Reparado and Juanco as "two sergeants" ["dos sargentos"] (113), and a stage direction affirms that "Mari Sarmiento la Despenada and Ms. Galindo are jealous because of them [Reparado and Juanco]" ["Están celosas por culpa d'ellos / Mari Sarmiento la Despenada / Y la Galindo"] (127); the "ensign coming from Italy / struck by a gaullic arrow [of love]" ["alférez venido de Italia, / Que alcanzó una flecha de Galia"] (86) characterizes Arlequín, the self-confessed Italian "I was born in Italy" ["Vi la luz en Italia"] (30), who marries in Paris "Paris has given me what it most prizes: / debts, teachers, and a wife!" ["París me ha dado lo que más precia: / ¡Deudas, maestros, y una mujer!"] (63). Polichinela's list goes on (see 88–89): "A vain don Diego" ["un Don Diego presumido"] (88)—Amaranta refers to Arlequín as "the comely don Diego" ["el lindo

---

26. Later versions read "curtain assistant ["asistente del telón"] (*Obras completas de Don Ramón del Valle-Inclán* [Madrid: Plenitud, 1954], 312).

The Structural Consequences 47

Don Diego"] (49); "a willing cuckold" ["un cornudo consentido"] (89)—Marquesa Rosalinda explicitly states that the Marquis tolerated her previous lovers, "he knew how to respect my whims. / He would get sick entering my rooms, / he would strike his cane and heels on the dais, / he would kiss my hand" ["sabía respetar mis antojos. / Se constipaba entrando en mis habitaciones, / Sonaba en la tarima la caña y los tacones, / Me besaba la mano"] (101); "a musked dandy" ["un petimetre almizclado"] (89)—the Duenna calls the Page "a dandy / who utilizes all his brains trying to appear dainty" ["un petrimetre / Que en ser pulido pone todo el seso"] (92); "an excommunicated Abbot" ["un abate excomulgado"] (89)—the Abbot, as Colombina points out, "[i]s an abbot who does not say Mass" ["Es un abate que no dice misa"] (119).

Even when the descriptions Polichinela gives cannot be limited to one character, they are pregnant with connotative value regarding the world of MR. The phrase "Celestina Convent Gadabout" ["Celestina Trotaconventos"] (86), for example, alludes to the Duenna who will be the "matchmaker" ["casamentera"] between Estrella, locked up in the convent, and the Page (94), or to Amaranta, who (with a clergyman) manages to cement Estrella's marriage to Misia Rosa's son (169). "A camp follower" ["Una moza de partido"] (89) aptly describes Colombina's position—among the "concubines" ["barraganas"] (26) according to the Abbot because of her social position—she cuckolds Pierrot with Arlequín (69) and engages in a relationship with the Abbot (108–10). "Two [returning] landowners / from Peru / [. . . .] who seek marquisates / with ducats / from Peru" ["Dos encomenderos / Peruleros / [. . . .] Que pretenden marquesados / Con ducados / Del Perú"] (89) evokes the desire of the travel-weary Reparado and Juanco, who yearn to become "gentlemen of the court" ["señores en la Corte"] (115).

In an activity reminiscent of Max Estrella's near the end of his life (in *Luces de bohemia*), and as one of Max's predecessors in Valle-Inclán's roster of characters experimenting with distortion, Polichinela passes his world in review. His body, or rather one part of it—the humps—become the focal point drawing the members of MR together onto a common ground. Everyone, "humanity" (88) itself, desires contact with Polichinela's protuberances. As objects of desire, and as a result of the violence with which the desire comes to be manifested (Polichinela complains about "so much clubbing" ["tanto porrazo"] [91]), the humps in effect become separated from their bearer. Polichinela simply bears witness to their isolation, an observer distanced from the activity his own deformity sets in motion.

Moreover, Polichinela's observations detail characteristics of the play MR still to be revealed at the moment of their enunciation. The allusion to Reparado and Juanco, Mari Sarmiento la Despenada and la Galindo ("concubines and sargents in pairs") is not clarified until well into the second act. The phrase "Celestina Convent Gadabout" does not begin to be unraveled until after Polichinela exits. Even the allusions to earlier moments (e.g., "a vain don Diego," referring to Amaranta's characterization of Arlequín in the first act) recall scenes where Polichinela is not present. The information that Polichinela divulges trespasses the sequential order of MR. The commedia dell'arte character separates from the commeda dell'arte performer; Polichinela's role characteristics are the instruments allowing this "ex-trusion" to take place. In other words:

> No more than the spectator, is the performer implicated in the performance. He always keeps his viewing rights. He is the eye, a substitute for the camera that is filming, freezing, or slowing down, and he causes slides, superpositions, and enlargements with a space and on a body that have become the tools of his own exploration.[27]

Polichinela becomes this eye, a roving eye with the viewing lens turned inward. The protuberances become the ground whereon MR is viewed open, as Polichinela, recovering the perspective held by Arlequín in the "Prelude," glosses the characteristics of MR.

Self-Presence

The oscillatory movement between simply being onstage versus knowledge of being onstage, between the play MR and being outside the fiction-building paramaters of MR, reaches a dizzying intensity near the end of the piece.

> *Arlequín* — Where are you going?
> *Colombina* — I am going to that bench
>   in order to faint!
> *Arlequín* — Colombina, if I may be frank,
>   I believe that you should wait.
>   A fainting spell serves no purpose
>   when there are no people.
>   Because I am privy to the secret!
>   Naturally! [. . . .]
> *Colombina* — I faint because I feel like it,
>   Mr. Arlequín.
>   Or does etiquette prohibit
>   fainting in the garden?

27. J. Feral, "Performance and Theatricality: The Subject Demystified," 174.

The Structural Consequences 49

> *Arlequín* — Excuse an innocent jest.
> Do not be a little girl!
> And do not wrinkle your brow
> nor your pleated skirt so much.
> Dance, lovely, your tarantella
> in the gardens!
> But do not break the soles
> of your clogs!
>
> [*Arlequín*— ¿A dónde vas?
> *Colombina* — ¡Voy á aquel banco
> Para poderme desmayar!
> *Arlequín* — Colombina, si he de ser franco,
> Creo que debes esperar.
> Un soponcio no tiene objeto
> Cuando no hay gente.
> ¡Porque yo estoy en el secreto!
> ¡Naturalmente! [. . . .]
> *Colombina* — Me desmayo porque me peta,
> Seor Arlequín.
> ¿O es que prohibe la etiqueta
> Los desmayos en el jardín?
> *Arlequín* — Perdona una broma inocente.
> ¡No seas niña!
> Y no arrugues tanto la frente
> Ni la basquiña.
> ¡Baila, hermosa, tu tarantela
> En los jardines!
> ¡Pero no te rompas la suela
> de los chapines!] (203–4)

As previously indicated, Arlequín corrects Colombina's gesture (the elaborate self-consciousness about fainting), reminding her that her actions should not be guided by the gestures appropriate when there are "people." Arlequín, of course, knows MR's inherent duplicity, how it is fiction (seen in the light of the "Prelude") and nonfiction (a preparation for the fiction of Arlequín's play). The above cited "secret" resembling an aside and in its own right a conjurer of theatrical presence, bears witness to this duplicity. An apparent affirmation of nontheatricality slowly becomes attenuated by the attrition of the entire context in which it is situated. Merely positing the possibility that Colombina's gesture could be a theatrical gesture, that there could be "people" watching, lends, by negation, a latent theatrical cast to the elements of MR. The fact that Arlequín regards as a secret the information about the presence of "people"—about an audience and the consequent (theatrical) nature this onlooking bestows on the event in which Arlequín and Colombina participate—shrouds the entire issue in uncertainty.

Colombina reacts to Arlequín's insinuation that she is acting in a manner befitting an actress by immediately affirming the link between the gesture and a personal referent—"I faint because I feel like it." The fainting does not constitute an act in a representational sequence with observing "people," but rather the expression of a genuine desire. Yet, the very next lines attenuate the affirmation that she is not onstage. Colombina makes the garden a place where gesture falls under the strictures of an "etiquette"—a thinly disguised figure of speech for theatrical guidelines, as the next phrases make readily explicit. Arlequín actually apologizes for his previous statement (implying that they are not onstage), dismisses it as a puerile joke ("Excuse an innocent jest"), and picks up on the metaphor of the stage by becoming once more the *metteur en scène*. He treats Colombina as an actress who has to be directed ever so meticulously, every attitude controlled ("Do not be a little girl"), every gesture guided ("do not wrinkle your brow / nor your pleated skirt so much"), and every action detailed ("Dance, lovely, your tarantella"). Even in the midst of this triumphant resurgence of the stage, with the banner of theatricality prominently unfurled, the actual issue raised by Arlequín in the beginning of the passage—"there are no people," or is there an audience?, are they onstage?—still remains unanswered. These gestures, which Arlequín so minutely controls, could be part of a rehearsal session in preparation for the authentic onstage presence, when Colombina will indeed have a role in Arlequín's play to be performed in the garden.

The salient textual characteristic of MR, as emblematized in these two preceding instances, consists of an active foregrounding of the moment of theatre. The impetus driving toward the affirmation of nontheatricality returns MR to the constants of a theatrical world. The imperatives of the *metteur en scène* implicate MR in the theatre producing, theatre enactment process. As a drama text, MR experiments with the parameters of "drama" and "script," working to give a sense of immediacy and to infuse with theatricality the fonts that "pre-exist any given enactment, which act as a blueprint for the enactment, and which persist from enactment to enactment."[28]

Scripts (the basic code of the event) are in primitive enactments "patterns of doing, not modes of thinking," a "*manifestation* more than a communication," so that the actual deployment, the actualization of the event is not the "result of" but "contained in" the script

---

28. Richard Schechner, "Drama, Script, Theatre, and Performance," *The Drama Review* 17.3 (1973): 6. Schechner divides the total theatrical enterprise according to the four instances indicated in the title of his article and points out the links between the different elements. Further citations from this article include the pagination in the body of the text.

(Schechner, 7). In the course of time, however, drama arose as a specialized form of script:

> The potential manifestation that had previously been encoded in a pattern of doings was now encoded in a pattern of written words. The dramas of the Greeks, as Aristotle points out, continued to be codes for the transmission of action; but action no longer meant a specific, concrete way of moving/singing—it was understood "abstractly," a movement in the lives of men. Historically speaking, in the West, drama detached itself from doing. Communication replaced manifestation. (Schechner, 7)

The rise of drama as a specific form causes a rift of abstraction between words and "doing." The wedge of nonspecificity comes to be inserted between words as the codified vehicles for the transmission of action calling for *a* doing and the actual blueprint, the method by which *the* doing is to be enacted by the theatre group. The intimate unity of these two elements in the primitive script is sundered, as drama relegates to itself the temporal transference of action and increasingly subordinates the pattern of doing, so that it becomes, in effect, merely an illustration of the word's ability to call for action. The words are in a privileged position, but a position achieved by isolation—the call for doing is an abstraction divorced from and no longer containing a concrete doing:

> The script no longer functioned as a code for transmitting action through time; instead the doings of each production became the code for re-presenting the words-of-the-drama. Maintaining the words intact grew in importance; how they were said, and what gestures accompanied them, was a matter of individual choice, and of lesser importance. (Schechner, 7)

MR works precisely in this rift between words and doing—"the rupture between things and words."[29] The doing does not appear as an illustration of the words: it is actually a part of and contained in the text. The passive text, in other words, stands banished—the text does not allow itself to be represented:

> the stage *will no longer represent*, because it will no longer simply be added in the manner of a tangible [sensuous] illustration to a text that is already written, thought, or lived apart from it [the stage] and that it [the stage] would only repeat [. . . .] And non-representation, then, is original representation if representation also means the deployment of a volume, of a multidimensioned milieu, an experience that produces its own space [. . . .] A

---

29. Antonin Artaud, cited in Roger Copeland, "Brecht, Artaud and the Hole in the Paper Sky," *Theater* 9.3 (1978): 47.

closed space, that is to say, a space produced from within itself and not organized according to another absent place, a no-place, an alibi, or an invisible utopia.

> [la scène *ne représentera plus*, puisqu'elle ne viendra pas s'ajouter comme une illustration sensible à un texte déjà écrit, pensé ou vécu hors d'elle et qu'elle ne ferait que répéter [. . . .] Et la non-représentation est donc représentation originaire, si représentation signifie aussie déploiement d'un volume, d'un milieu à plusieurs dimensions, expérience productrice de son propre espace [. . . .] Espace clos, c'est-à-dire espace produit du dedans de soi et non plus organisé depuis un autre lieu absent, une illocalité, un alibi ou une utopie invisible.][30]

MR originates a "closed space" produced from within. The text not only calls for, but participates in, the deployment of a theatrical doing. The words of the drama—as transmitters of the "secret of the Marquesa Rosalinda" through time—are accompanied by and interspersed with the moments showing when the words beget theatricality. Unlike the complacent subservient text willing to serve as the basis for a theatrical representation outside its own bounds, MR partakes of the action by which the elements of the drama are galvanized into the actual production of theatre.

Near the beginning of MR, Arlequín goes through the instruments of his trade: "I carry in my cart / a crown of paper, a reed scepter, / and another dried crown of laurels [. . . .] An old trunk, all covered with tinsel, / that I call the Ossuary of History / and a bundle of jingle bells" ["Llevo en mi carreta / Corona de papel, cetro de caña / Y otra corona seca de laureles [. . . .] Un cofre viejo, todo de oropeles / Al que llamo el Osario de la Historia, / Y un haz de cascabeles"] (30–31). All the resources that the commedia dell'arte cart and its coffer have to offer are indeed deployed throughout MR. At the same time, Arlequín's promise to present a play about his own life comes true. He avails himself of the "History" of his craft to make MR the play (the "Farce of my own life" ["Farsa de la vida mía"] [30]) referred to in conversation with the Marquis. When Arlequín removes his mask and resoundingly evidences the theatrical nature of MR, the play about his life does not simply stand revealed—it has been shown performed. The Marquis (among others), initially a mere spectator, becomes engulfed by a "devouring theatricality"[31] and converted into one of the figures presenting the play. The moments when theatrical presence was detected and then seemingly swept away,

---

30. Jacques Derrida, "Le Théâtre de la cruauté et la clôture de la représentation," *L'Écriture et la différence* (Paris: Editions de Seuil, 1967), 348–49.

31. See, in this text, chapter 1, footnote 20.

these doubts and hesitations, are all steps in the production of the play MR, a progressive depiction of the uncertain ground upon which an engendered theatricality struggles to develop.

The context surrounding MR is likewise fertile in theatre-making activity. As previously noted, the outer framework (*MR*) reveals the troupe before MR (the inner frame) actually begins as an event, and the fictive characteristics of this event are detailed at some length. The inner frame (MR) takes this situation and doubles it, evincing, as Barrault points out, that "The unique phenomenon of dramatic representation, the final objective of all theatre, is the artificial re-creation of an Act."[32] The cart stays in the garden, and the troupe stands outside the confines of the "tablado" where Arlequín's play is to be enacted. Nonetheless, although the troupe's activity (apparently) takes place before the representation of this play, the fictional import of their behavior is constantly highlighted. Like an image before its mirror, MR reenacts the essential attributes of the outer frame. MR, swathed in artificiality, reflects back a patent recreation of the "Prelude." The "Act" and its double are constantly viewed in and around MR—the reproduction manifests its fictiveness while knowing full well its status as re-creation, as an image.

When Arlequín rips off his mask, the evident objective of his action is MR—Arlequín the actor denuded of his role points to the fictionality of MR. The implications of the revelation, however, extend beyond the immediate confines of MR. As an image of the outer frame, MR partakes of an inherent unreality, "the reflected image is unreal" ["l'object en image est un irréel"].[33] This presence of the "unreal" ["irréel"]—the exploitation of the double—broadens the effect of Arlequín's action, for "the reflected object is a *defined lack*: it takes the shape of a cavity" ["l'objet en image est un *manque défini*: il se dessine en creux"] (Sartre, 163). The actor (in *MR*) serves as the model delimiting the contours of the character (in MR) and the reflection betokens what it desires to become. The character needs or feels impelled to become the actor. The movement is not unidirectional, however. Both feel "the attraction of the abyss" ["l'attrait du gouffre"][34]—the gap separating/uniting the object and its reflection. This gap, emphasized time and again by the structure of the play, remains at the center of the narrative movement. The character's magic world ("Armida's gar-

---

32. Jean-Louis Barrault, "On Stanislavski and Brecht," *Theatre Quarterly* 3.10 (1973): 3.
33. J. P. Sartre, *L'Imaginaire* (Paris: Gallimard, 1948), 162. The pagination of the following quotation from this text is given in the body of the text.
34. The term is cited in Robert Storey, *Pierrots on the Stage of Desire* (Princeton: Princeton University Press, 1985), 138. See also pages 95–98.

den") leads to the nonmagical world where the actor is forced to recognize the "disillusionments" ["desengaños"] dispelling his "winged dream" ["alado sueño"] (206). Although Arlequín admits that "flocks are flocks / and my Pegasus, Clavileño" ["los rebaños son rebaños, / Y mi Pegaso, Clavileño"] (206), the tain still holds an imprint of the dream. The dreamer never ceases to yearn for his dreamed counterpart. Arlequín the actor needs Arlequín the character. The actor realizes that the stage is necessary for self-expression and invokes the audience to witness his affirmation of this need ("I must leave for tomorrow / showing you my heart" ["he de dejar para mañana / El mostraros mi corazón"] (207). The distance extant between the outer and the inner frames, in other words, both separates and binds. The doubling assures unity: MR implicates MR. Arlequín bridges the gap between the two perspectives and thus stresses their link: the action that deems MR a theatrical event carries over to MR. The nontheatrical position of the outer framework is undermined by the very gesture that was to separate it from the theatrical—Arlequín's unmasking. An ever-vigilant theatricality reigns supreme. In MR, "theatre is the real, the stage spills over, going beyond its space" ["le théâtre est le réel, la scène déborde son espàce"].[35]

35. André Helbo, "Le Discours théâtral: une sémantique de la relation," *La relation théâtrale*, ed. Régis Durand (Lille: Presses Universitaires de Lille, 1980), 98.

3
The Dynamics

Mise en scène/Authorial Interplay

Valle-Inclán's experiments with theatricality studied in the second chapter are an important contribution to the innovative theatre of the period. The present chapter is a further examination of Valle-Inclán's revitalization of then prevalent Spanish notions of things dramatic. The Galician writer rebels against the stifling strictures of a "psychological or bourgeois theatre that we call specialised or partial in contrast to complete theatre" ["le théâtre psychologique ou bourgeois que nous appelons spécialisé ou partiel par opposition au théâtre complet"][1]—"partial" because the searing focal point on which the theatrical elements converge is the text at the expense of the performance.

Valle-Inclán constructs a "special theatrical code"[2] that fuses both text and performance. The popular forms of drama are central to this fusion. In the province of vaudeville, melodrama, and in the acting and the puns of the *zanni*, emphasis rests on the immediacy and effectiveness of stage impact and presentation, rather than on the timeless value of the text. Improvisation stands equal to the written word. As a result, Valle-Inclán makes extensive use of farce and slapsticklike elements in his theatre. *La Marquesa Rosalinda: Farsa sentimental y grotesca* and *La cabeza del dragón: Farsa* are cases in point. The "prodigal son" of his generation[3] expands literary horizons with the

---

1. J. L. Barrault, "Du théâtre total et de 'Cristophe Colomb,'" *Cahiers Renaud-Barrault* 88 (1975): 27.
2. Erika Fischer-Lichte, "Theatrical Communication," *Degrés* 29 (1982): f-3. For a brief discussion on how textual and performance appreciation are integrated into a "single coherent and unified approach to the complete dramatic entity," see Michael R. Booth, "Theatre History and the Literary Critic," *The Yearbook of English Studies* 9 (1979): 15.

recovery of the popular (stage) and its characteristics. Oral culture—the whole culture of Séptimo Miau (*Divinas palabras*), of Maese Lotario (*Farsa italiana de la enamorada del rey*), of the wandering bard (*Voces de gesta*), of the group of barnstormers (*La Marquesa Rosalinda*)[4]—becomes an essential and integral part of Valle-Inclán's desire to privilege performance per se apart from performance as a representation of the word.[5]

Within this context, Valle-Inclán exploits the parodic force latent in theatre: "*the theatre always shows up the artificialities hidden in literature. When placed on the stage, even in intelligent fashion, facile sentimentality, the trivialities of the daily round and mere abstractions must drop their mask.*"[6] Valle-Inclán uses the theatre's ability to unmask—the particular vigor with which "artificialities" can be shorn of their allure on the stage—to inscribe his own dramatic perspective. The text/*mise en scène* comes to be bridged with the distanced and distancing perspective so clearly developed in *Los cuernos de don Friolera* (*Cuernos*)—the perspective that views the world from "the other shore" ["la otra ribera"] (*Cuernos*, 22). Valle-Inclán adopts an "in the air" ["en el aire"] rather than a "standing" ["en pie"] position with respect to the characters.[7] He separates the

3. The term is from P. Salinas's essay, "Significación del esperpento o Valle-Inclán, hijo pródigo del 98" (reprinted in *Literatura española siglo XX* [Madrid: Alianza, 1972], 86).

4. Valle-Inclán's interest in various aspects of popular culture derives, in part, from his desire to recover a *true* Spanish—a Spanish different from the Calderonian dominated expression of the literary establishment. Popular language and slang are a means to linguistic authenticity: "Another statement [of Valle-Inclán's] that elicited surprise, if not protest, was to the effect that the upper classes, including the aristocracy (I do not recall whether he included the royalty), spoke very poor Spanish, or he may have said Castilian. He noted that it was only the middle class, and especially the lower fringe thereof, that used pure Spanish" (Olav K. Lundeberg, "An Evening with Valle-Inclán," *Hispania* 13.5 [1930]: 401). For the role of theatre in Valle-Inclán's search for a *new*, contemporary Spanish, see, in this text, chapter 4, section 1.

5. Popular dramatic forms in themselves stem from a particular theatrical tradition: "Tragedy, such as we conceive it, implies a text. This text [. . . .] is what the poet 'teaches', *didaskei,* to his[/her] actors and to the chorus. In contrast to oral poetry, little place is left for improvisation. Every part of the representation is organized, at least partially, by the writing beforehand [. . . .] Comedy, as commedia dell'arte [will] later, allows for improvisation" ["La tragédie, telle que nous la concevons, implique un texte. Ce texte [. . . .] est ce que le poète 'enseigne', *didaskei,* à ses acteurs et au choeur. Contrairement à la poésie orale, peu de place est laissée à l'improvisation. A l'avance, chaque partie de la représentation est organisée, du moins partiellement, par l'ecriture [. . . .] La comédie, comme plus tard la *commedia dell'arte*, admet l'improvisation"] (Charles Segal, "Tragédie, Oralité, Ecriture," *Poétique* 50 [1982]: 136).

6. Jean Vilar, "The Director and the Play," *Yale French Studies* 5 (1950): 22–23.

7. The reference is to Valle-Inclán's famous aesthetic formulation (as chronicled by G. Martínez Sierra): "I will begin by telling you [Valle-Inclán is speaking] that I

author from the stage world, to a great extent, by making the play's own construction the subject of the drama. The author unmasks theatrical construction, mocking the characters' world in laying out for perusal the literary foundations on which it rests.[8] At the same time, the author cannot vaunt his "in the air" viewpoint unchecked. The restraints are imposed by the theatrical text itself, a text that is incomplete, constantly demanding the stage:

> writing and reading are subordinated to what is specifically theatrical: the performance. The activity of the writer looks for its realization in the activity of the actor, which in turn looks for its realization in the spectator.[9]

Valle-Inclán now cedes authority, now asserts authority, over features pointed out time and again as "specifically theatrical." The conflict-

---

believe that there are three ways to see the world artistically or aesthetically: kneeling, standing, or up in the air. When one looks from a kneeling position [. . .] the characters [and] the heroes are endowed with a condition superior to the human condition [. . . .] There is a second way, which is to look at the novelistic protagonists as if they had our own nature [being], as if they were our brothers, as if they were ourselves [. . .] with our own virtues and our own defects [. . . .] And, there is a third way, which is to look at the world from a higher plane [. . .] and to consider the characters of the plot as inferior to the author with a touch of irony" ("Comenzaré por decirle a usted que creo hay tres modos de ver el mundo artística o estéticamente: de rodillas, en pie o levantado en el aire. Cuando se mira de rodillas [. . .] se da a los personajes, a los héroes, una condición superior a la condición humana [. . . .] Hay una segunda manera, que es mirar a los protagonistas novelescos como de nuestra propia naturaleza, como si fueran nuestros hermanos, como si fuesen ellos nosotros mismos, [. . .] con nuestras mismas virtudes y nuestros mismos defectos [. . . .] Y hay otra tercer manera, que es mirar al mundo desde un plano superior [. . .] y considerar a los personajes de la trama como seres inferiores al autor con un punto de ironía"] (R. Cardona and A. Zahareas, *Visión del esperpento* [Madrid: Castalia, 1970], 236–37).

8. The examples are many. In *La Marquesa Rosalinda*, when Arlequín asks the Marquesa for permission to replace her lost slipper, the directions include the following stanza: "In the foam of the silk lace / the mythical doric siren sings. / A hand shipwrecks in the waves. . . / Such is the moral of rhetoric!" ["Canta en la espuma de las blondas / La mítica sirena dórica. / Naufraga una mano en las ondas. . . / ¡Es la moral de la retórica!"] (62). The last line reflects back on the preceeding lines. The fact that the third line ends with the word "ondas" stems from "the moral of rhetoric"—the rules of versification require the third line to rhyme with the first line of the quatrain. The stage direction reveals its own construction. The art of playwriting turns inward to focus momentarily on the methods that ensure dramatic progression. See W. Nigel Dodd, "Metalanguage and Character in Drama," *Lingua e Stile* 14.1 (1979): 137, for the thematization "of the rhetorical conventions of theatrical communication." For the pleasure inherent to metaphors deriving from such theatrical thematization, see Sidney Homan, "When the Theatre Turns to Itself," *New Literary History* 2.3 (1971): 408.

9. Robert Champigny, "Theatre in a Mirror: Anouilh," *Yale French Studies* 14 (1954): 57. See also P. Larthomas, "Le Langage dramatique," *L'Information littéraire* 24.4 (1972): 166.

ing mesh of authorial give-and-take sets in motion (or simply reveals) an activity revolving around the relative control over the play's components. Various aspects of this activity are studied in the remainder of this section.

The passage of time remains conspicuously absent in the dialogue, and the exchange between the characters demands the situational context of the stage of which it is deprived. In the second part of *La Marquesa Rosalinda* (*MR*), Colombina leaves Arlequín to his solitary musings:

> *At this point a retainer enters. He approaches the actor [Arlequín]. He speaks to him in secrecy for a moment.*
>
> *The Retainer [to Arlequín]* — Excellency, a noble lady who is veiled
>   begs you to approach the footboard of her carriage.
> *Arlequín* — Lady, raise a corner of your veil
>   even though the sun of your sky may blind me.
>
> [*Aquí un rodrigón Sale. Al comediante Llega. Le habla con Sigilo, un instante.*
>
> *Rodrigón* — Excelencia, una noble dama, que se reboza,
>   Os ruega que al estribo lleguéis de su carroza.
> *Arlequín* — Señora, levantad una punta del velo,
>   Aunque haya de cegarme el sol de vuestro cielo]   (*MR*, 138).

The dialogue proceeds instantaneously, apparently without regard for the spatial context. Indications as to the time it takes Arlequín to go from where he is to the carriage from whence (most probably) the Retainer proceeds are missing. Arlequín addresses the Lady immediately after the Retainer's demand and reveals a missing element—the pause indicating the occurence of the event. The incompleteness points directly toward the representation, revealing the insufficiencies inherent to the text.

By means of such moments, the gaps stretching between the text and the performance are revealed. Valle-Inclán, as a consummate playwright, molds the text to make these interstices ubiquitous. The dialogue demands—or in its more subdued moments evinces the desire for the collaboration of—the *mise en scène*. In the first section of *MR*, for example, an extensive episode centered around Marquesa Rosalinda's lost slipper ends with Rosalinda and Amaranta's celebration of Arlequín's verbal dexterity:

> *Rosalinda* — Gallant wit!
> *Amaranta* — As in France
>   and in the Court of King Louis!

> A court in gardens whose fragrance
> of love, [the court] sends over Paris.
>
> [*Rosalinda* — ¡Galante ingenio!
> *Amaranta*- ¡Como de Francia
>   Y de la Corte del Rey Luis!
>   Corte en jardines que su fragrancia
>   De amor, envía sobre París.] (*MR*, 63)

Arlequín continues immediately after Amaranta's gloss with an autobiographical revelation: "I am from Bergamo, I lived in Venice, / but I have spent some years now wandering at will" ["Soy de Bergamo, viví en Venecia, / Pero años hace vuelo á placer."] The dialogical construction itself does not indicate any transition. Nonetheless, when Arlequín begins to speak, the interaction between the characters, which thus far consisted of comments on Rosalinda's "marvelous foot of illusion" (62), takes a turn. The text presents an unresolved tension that can only be dissipated by the actor's accentuation—a slight hesitant pause indicating the search for words with which to continue the conversation, an emotional emphasis to greet the commencement of the new topic (especially since the conversation takes a personal, revelatory turn), and so forth. The text calls for the technical prowess of the actor, who now stands associated with and implicated in the dialogue.

Finally, the audience joins the figures of the director[10] and the actor elicited by the text. *La cabeza del dragón* (*CdD*) reveals the superimposition of the two different axes along which dramatic information comes to be distributed during performance: the internal axis of dramatis personae to dramatis personae, and the external axis of dramatis personae to audience.[11] In the third scene, Verdemar, disguised as a clown, has been encouraging the distraught Infantina:

> *The Princess leaves and Prince Verdemar watches her move away through the tortuous paths of the labyrinth as if lost or enchanted in it* [the labyrinth]. *In the hollowed out base of an old oak, the Elf sings.*
> *Prince Verdemar* — Princess of my dreams, I will die in the attempt or I will triumph over the Dragon!
> *The Elf* — You gave me liberty
>   my royal dove!
>   Oh dove that flies so high
>   without fearing the hawk!
> *Prince Verdemar* — Ah! The Elf! I will call him for help. For-

---

10. As used in this section, "director" is largely synonymous with *mise en scène*.
11. See Paola Gulli Pugliatti, "The Distribution of Implicit Information in the Opening Scenes of Dramatic Texts," *Lingua e Stile* 16.3 (1981): 481.

tunately, I kept the ring which he gave me when I opened the door of the tower for him.
The Elf — Here I am, my Prince. What is your wish?
Prince Verdemar — Your help to triumph over the Dragon.
The Elf — Come with me. You will have the diamond sword.

[*Se va La Infantina, y El Príncipe Verdemar la mira alejarse por los tortuosos senderos del laberinto, como perdida ó encantada en él. En el fondo escavado de un viejo roble, canta el Duende.*
El Príncipe Verdemar — ¡Princesa de mis sueños, moriré en la demanda ó triunfaré del Dragón!
El Duende — ¡Me diste libertad
mi paloma real!
¡Palomita que vuelas tan alto,
sin miedo del gavilán!
El Príncipe Verdemar — ¡Ah! ¡El Duende! Le llamaré en mi auxilio. Afortunadamente, conservo el anillo que me dejó cuando le abrí la puerta del torreón.
El Duende — Aquí estoy, príncipe mío. ¿Qué deseas?
El Príncipe Verdemar — Tu ayuda para triunfar del Dragón.
El Duende — Ven conmigo. Tendrás la espada de diamante.]
(*CdD*, 87–88)

The Prince does not seem to realize, much less acknowledge, the presence of the Duende until after the Duende's song. Nonetheless, the communicative interaction between the two dramatis personae is (however faintly) posited. The song appears to exert some insinuative power, bringing out Verdemar's sudden exclamation, "Ah! The Elf! I will call him. . . ." The stage directions, to be sure, are sparse in details: they lay the responsibility of evincing the probable link between the two characters on the director.[12] The overlap between the song and the Prince's action effectively recovers and acknowledges the Duende's existence. Nevertheless, as previously indicated, Verdemar's expressed unawareness of the Duende's presence attenuates the firmness of this link. The song postulates a recipient and the text ultimately confers this function, this acknowledgment of the Duende's intervention, on an audience. The recoverableness of the song depends on the presence of a spectator extrinsic to the dialogue

---

12. The suggestive role of the Elf's song, as well as many of his other appearances (e.g., "Suddenly, the Elf becomes invisible" ["De pronto el Duende se hace invisible" *CdD*, 156]), bring to mind the scenic problems in *The Tempest* caused by the often invisible Ariel with his songs and the influence they exert. Valle-Inclán often names Shakespeare in his aesthetic disquisitions and indeed confesses that "I have done theatre taking Shakespeare as my teacher" ("He hecho teatro tomando por maestro a Shakespeare") (R. del Valle-Inclán, in J. Antonio Hormigón, *Valle-Inclán, cronología y documentos,* [Madrid: Ministerio de Cultura, 1978], 103).

but, at the same time, guaranteed by the dialogue's structure. The interchange between dramatis personae does not suffice. The audience as overhearer is implied. Valle-Inclán's constructs his texts so as to assist in and lead to "the performance [. . . .] the intrinsically poetic moment; the moment when, with the spectators' presence contributing the final drop, the chemical precipitate appears."[13]

The *mise en scène*, then, receives paramount importance. The play facilitates, as well as incorporates, the passage from text to stage. Actor, stage director, and audience are continually summoned, making evident that the affirmation and divulgence of these summons are a self-set goal that mark the texts as specifically

> theatrical with respect to "real" [. . . .] [T]he desire to represent [. . .] and, on the other hand, the awareness of this desire on the part of the receiver as well as the emitter appear to be probably the only universal characteristic of the theatrical act [. . . .] The theatrical act is intentional and it offers itself as such.
>
> [théâtral par rapport au "réel" [. . . .] [L]'intention de représenter [. . .] et d'autre part la reconnaissance de cette intention par le récepteur aussi bien que par l'émetteur apparaîtraient comme probablement la seule caractéristique universelle du fait théâtral [. . . .] L'acte théâtral est intentionnel et il s'offre comme tel.][14]

The author has relinquished the text and delivered it to the participants in the stage world activity. The relaxation of authorial power pays due homage to dramatic presence. At the same time, however, the text bears the unique stamp of the Valle-Inclanesque perspective.

While perhaps a commonplace, "One obvious method by which the dramatist may try to control the action is the stage direction."[15] Valle-Inclán's directions regulate not only the action, but the viewpoint with regard to this action. The text betrays the author's firm intention to consolidate his presence. The Elf, in *CdD*, tells Prince Verdemar how to obtain the key to his cell: "*The Elf* — Approach your mother and ask her to look into your right ear because it hurts. And while she looks, stick your right hand carefully into her pouch and take the key" ["*El Duende* — Llega á tu madre, y dile te mire en la oreja derecha, porque te duele. Y mientras ella mira, mete la mano con tiento en su faltriquera y saca la llave"] (*CdD*, 30). These instructions are in actuality stage directions emitted from the dialogical

---

13. J. L. Barrault, "The Rehearsal: The Performance," *Yale French Studies* 5 (1950): 3.
14. Milan Bunjevac, "La Marque de la théâtralité," *Degrés*, 32 (1982): e-4.
15. Arnold Hinchliffe, "Literature in the Theatre?" *The Yearbook of English Studies* 9 (1979): 10.

interchange of the characters in preparation for the scene wherein the Queen, the Prince's mother, joins her son:

> *Prince Verdemar* — Look into this ear, mother.
> *The Queen* — What is wrong?
> *Prince Verdemar* — A wasp entered and is buzzing around inside.
> *The Queen* — I don't see anything.
> *Prince Verdemar* — Leave it, mother, it will come out.
>
> [*El Príncipe Verdemar* — Miradme en este oído, madre.
> *La Reina* — ¿Qué tienes?
> *El Príncipe Verdemar* — Una avispa se me ha entrado y me zumba dentro.
> *La Reina* — No veo nada.
> *El Príncipe Verdemar* — Dejadlo, madre, ya saldrá]
> (30–31).

The Elf indicates the course of action to be followed, and his fellow characters obey. Yet, the author remains unsatisfied with and consequently takes part in this directing that does not proceed unambiguously from his space. After the encounter between Prince Verdemar and the Queen takes place, the stage direction glosses what has already occurred: "The queen was stooping down to look into the Prince's ear. The young man, winking an eye, was pilfering the key from the pouch." ["Señora Reina se agachaba para mirar en la oreja del Príncipe. El muchacho guiñando un ojo le hurtaba la llave de la faltriquera"] (31). Eminently superfluous from the viewpoint of the *mise en scène*, the repetition simply imparts a stamp of legitimacy to the stage directions provided by the characters. The author insists on exercising his prerogative to command, makes evident his desire to rule, and reaffirms, however slightly, his position of authority. In essence, the stage direction forestalls delegating the power evidenced in direct speech, since the character is played by an actor:

> The I-narrator of the actor constructs with voice and gesture: 1) the conditions of discourse (time-space); 2) the discourses of various characters; 3) the narrative as such. It is the I-actor who is the subject of the enunciation and who says as much; however, this is the fundamental situation in all theatre, not only in the theatre of the narrator: the position of the narrator always underlies all the activity of the actor, [and is] implicit in his work and [is] visible or made evident at intervals in this or that particular form of representation (epic theatre): but even in the case where he only assumes one of the voices of the narrative enunciation, he can at moments return to his function as subject of this narrative enunciation and say implicitly; *I will narrate something to you* or *I am narrating to you.*

[Le Je-narrateur du comédien construit par la voix et le geste 1) les conditions du discours (l'espace-temps), 2) les discours des divers personnages, 3) le récit proprement dit. C'est le je-acteur qui est le sujet de l'énonciation et se dit comme tel; or c'est dans tout théâtre et pas seulement dans le théâtre de conteur, une situation fondamentale: la position du conteur est toujours sous-jacente dans toute pratique de comédien, implicite dans son travail et visible ou mise en lumière par moments dans telle ou telle forme particulière de représentation (théâtre épique): mais même dans le cas où il n'assume qu'une des voix de l'énonciation narrative, il peut par instants revenir à sa fonction de sujet de cette énonciation narrative et dire implicitement: *je vais vous raconter ou je vous raconte.*][16]

Onstage, the character/actor[17] affirms "I am narrating to you." The Elf may assume the posture of the story teller, tell the events of the *mise en scène*, and direct their appearance. Nevertheless, this posture remains under the vigilant shadow of the author. Stage actions—the fact that the Prince leans over, allows the Queen to look in his ear, and otherwise perfectly follows the Elf's instructions—are executed in accordance to the author's will.

Similarly, the author affirms his presence vis-à-vis the director. The opening stage direction of *CdD* reads as follows:

Three young princes play ball in the Arms Patio of a castle with many towers like those [castles] in the adventures of Orlando: It can be of diamond, bronze, or mist. It is a fantasy castle, like the ones children know how to dream. It has large walls covered with ivy and it has not yet been restored by the King's architects. Praise be to God!

[Tres príncipes donceles, juegan á la pelota en el Patio de Armas de un castillo muy torreado, como aquellos de las aventuras de Orlando: Puede ser de diamante, de bronce ó de niebla. Es un castillo de fantasía, como lo saben soñar los niños. Tiene grandes muros cubiertos de hiedra, y todavía no ha sido restaurado por los arquitectos del Rey. ¡Alabemos á Dios!] (13).

The director enjoys a large margin of freedom. The castle can be of this or that material. The author, in fact, asks for the stage world constructor's collaboration, for his annotations are more a suggestive point of departure than a list of specifications.[18] The rather ambigu-

16. A. Ubersfeld, "Le Discours de comédien," *Degrés* 30 (1982): a4–a5.
17. The duality is inherent to scenic discourse: "Torn between the character (the other of the text) and the actor (the other of the game), the subject cannot find its *proper* place other than in its own rent, in the oscillatory movement of its own irresolution" ["Déchiré entre le personnage (l'autre du texte) et le comédien (l'autre du jeu), le sujet ne trouve alors sa place *propre* que dans sa propre déchirure, dans le mouvement oscillatoire de son irrésolution"] (Albert Dichy, "Objets, acteurs, personnages dans le discours scénique," *Littérature* 43 [1981]: 98).

ous "fantasy castle" stands concretized by the phrase "like the ones children know how to dream" as rich in significative value as the first phrase it purports to specify. Yet, the apparent lack of precision in the actualization of the *mise en scène* is of such nature that, in its further development, it permits the author to reaffirm and apply his power over the characters' world.

The author's directions reveal the stage world to be constructed of the remnants of literary codes. Orlando's adventures elicit Italian epics replete with enchanted knights and magic swords. The Elf in the character list suggests fairy-tale worlds and dragons. The author even evokes momentarily the atmosphere of the "minstrel" ["juglar"] reciting Spanish epic poems "Praise be to God!" ["¡Alabemos a Dios!"].[19] The substratum underlying the characteristics depicted in the world of *CdD* comes to be seen in an unabashedly fictional light. Moreover, the whole fictional construction stands in grave danger of being destroyed. The author gives thanks that the crenelated castle of the fairy tale has not been brought up to date and "restored by the King's architects." The destructive intent heightens the very artificiality of the essential framework structuring the text—the world and features of the fairy tale.[20] The fairy tale continuously recoils against

18. "[W]hile the *didascalies* can be considered as a series of directives, they are not necessarily imperative directives. Indeed, it is obvious that very often they indicate 'entreaty directives' [. . . .] which demand that the practitioners fill in a gap, that they co-operate in the imagined scenic fiction [. . . .] as though the author were asking the director to choose an appropriate signifier for the imprecise signified which he has suggested" (J. Laillou Savona, "*Didascalies* as Speech Act," *Modern Drama* 25.1 [1982]: 31). *Didascalies* signify "everything which comes to us directly from the playwright" (J. L. Savona, 26). The *didascalies* can assume, then, a variety of functions in the structure of the play (narrative, the act of naming, and so forth) of which stage directions per se are a subset. In this text, stage directions are often synonomous with *didascalies*.

19. The constant praise and mention of "God" ("Dios"), even in what are apparently incongruous situations characterizes the Spanish medieval epic. Valle-Inclán selects and repeats such characteristics to stress the literary sources underlying his own text, as in his recreation of the epic poem in *Voces de gesta* (*VdG*): v.g., "A drum is heard. My God, what could it be!" ["Se oye un atambor. ¡Mi Dios, que sería!"] (*VdG*, 44). A. Risco considers the "minstrel" ["juglar"] to be a "mythic projection (on behalf of a primitivist cult that is very *modernista* and in itself of romantic origins) of the bohemian and rebel artist of the beginning of the century" ["proyección mítica [a favor de un culto primitivista muy modernista y ya de origen romántico] del artista bohemio y rebelde de principios de siglo"] ("El juglar en la obra de Valle-Inclán," in M. Criado de Val, *La Juglaresca* [Madrid: Edi-6, 1986], 471).

20. The literary codes used and evoked by Valle-Inclán in *CdD* are as wide-ranging as they are distinctive. *CdD* exemplifies the literary work "as a kind of *hypercode*, bringing together within itself a host of subcodes, some of which exercise a dominance and enjoy a stability with respect to others, which are nascent, wanting or 'repressed'

the intrusion of an author who in some manner belittles or undermines the very foundations (the "fairy-taleness") on which the play stands. The modifications have not been realized "yet," but admitting the possibility leaves the castle in a precarious state.

The stage directions form part, then, of a constant interchange. At first, with the call for co-participation in the definition of the theatrical world, the author seems to dissipate his control over its characteristics, as if this world were in the hands of the director. The apparent relaxation of control, however, is deceptive. The author first highlights the literary background on which his work stands: its inherent artificiality (e.g., "like [. . .] in the adventure of Orlando") comes to the fore. Second, the author points out the severe and radical limitations to which the elements of the play's world are subject. The lurking threat of re-modernization betokens the permutability hanging over the fairy tale and the radical uncertainty surrounding its very existence in relation to an author/evocator/manipulator of a kaleidoscope of literary quotations constituting/constructing the work. Both as commentator and as constructor, the author reveals the play's innate artificiality and fragility. The revelation momentarily, in the instance and in the revelatory context, places the author in a position of relative superiority. Authorial space, in other words, separates the creator from the created, a separation antithetical to Shakespearean theatre where "Creator and created are of the same human clay" ["Creador y criatura son del mismo barro humano"] (*Los Cuernos de don Friolera*, 38). Valle-Inclán presents the play, to a great extent, as a diversion, a game of which the object is to control the interplay of a whole gamut of literary snippets.

Mocking: Mechanical Entrenchment

At any given instance, the author of *La cabeza del dragón* (*CdD*) undermines the preceding moment. The Queen's entrance merits considerable description: "The Queen enters with her crown: A

---

through various formal mechanisms" (Thomas A. Lewis, "Notes Toward a Theory of the Referent," *PMLA* 94.3 [1979]: 462). The attempt to determine and label a dominant code in Valle-Inclán's text which gathers the others under its organizing fold constitutes a difficult, if not impossible, task. Nonetheless, for practical purposes, and with due recognition of its limitations, the label "fairy tale" will be used with reference to *CdD*. For a study of the extent to which "the audience can respond to the play as a parody of its genre and at the same time appreciate its qualities of fairy-tale enchantment," see D. Nicholson, "Valle-Inclán's *The Dragon's Head*: Symbolist Fairy Tale and Satyr Play," *Modern Drama* 29.3 (1986): 461.

page holds the train of her mantle, a whippet springs at her side, on her wrist she maintains a hawk" ["Sale Señora Reina con su corona: Un paje le recoge la cola del manto, un lebrel le salta al costado, en el puño sostiene un azor"] (*CdD*, 30). Each element later reappears in a different—a sarcastic, mocking, ridiculous—fashion: "The Queen arrives crying. As a result of her hiccoughs, her crown dances around her head. The hawk she carries on her wrist opens its wings, the whippet at her side starts barking profusely. And the page who holds the train of her royal mantle wheezes, sticking out his tongue" ["Señora Reina acude llorando. Con el hipo que trae, la corona le baila en la cabeza. El azor que lleva en el puño abre las alas, el lebrel que lleva al costado se desata en ladridos. Y saca la lengua, acezando, el paje que le sostiene la cola del manto real"] (35). The audience confronts two radically different views of the same element without a transitional ground mediating between the two images. They are simply presented as such: the clash and resulting stridency left unresolved.

When an attitude, object, or feature does not face its faithfully recorded distorted image, the theatrical elements begin a caustic interplay with other elements. Seemingly laudatory phrases are conjoined to elements that render the ensuing entity ridiculous by the sheer disparity of the parts. The fairy-tale castle appears time and again with storks: "The Elf appears once again between the merlons, and, in the highest parts of the sharp-pointed towers, the storks change legs" ["Aparece otra vez el Duende entre las almenas, y en los más alto de las torres puntiagudas, las cigüeñas cambian de pata"] (23). These animals inflict an unexpected and deflationary jolt on the connotative value of the castle, accrued in the innumerable tales in which it plays so preponderant a part: "The echoes of the castle bear the song, and in the upper reaches of the towers, the storks listen with one leg up in the air. The storks' attitude foreshadows the admirers of Richard Wagner" ["Los ecos del castillo arrastran la canción, y en lo alto de las torres las cigüeñas escuchan con una pata en el aire. La actitud de las cigüeñas anuncia á los admiradores de Ricardo Wagner"] (17). The storks incorporate a Wagnerian gesture that bestows a ridiculous and affected presence on the fairy-tale world: "The [Elf's] song is heard once again, and the storks change legs in order to rest before falling into musical ecstasy" ["Vuelve á oírse su canción, y las cigüeñas cambian de pata, para descansar antes de caer en el éxtasis musical"] (21).

The Valle-Inclanesque trait of uniting elements in unresolved clashes effectively disrupts any possible linear continuity in the development of the atmosphere, plot, characterization, and other features of the stage world. General Fierabrás receives high praise at one point: "The heroic General Fierabrás" ["El heroico general Fierabrás"] (138). A moment later, the stage direction reduces him to a caricatured and cruel extreme: "He is a palsied old man with a chest full of crosses and a cropped skull. The end of his nose drips without mercy like a gargoyle" ["Es un viejo perlático, con el pecho cubierto de cruces, y la cabeza monda. La punta de la nariz le gotea sin consideración, como una gárgola"] (138). Here, the conception of the heroic is effectively presented, but not allowed to develop; the previous moment does not serve as a basis from which to further explicate or draw out the traits inherent to it. In this aspect, *CdD* shares an essential feature of comedy: "comedy regulary denies us the 'constant illusion of an imminent future' [. . .] to produce comedy, the comic playwright must necessarily thwart the futurity inherent in any act."[21] The play becomes a concatenation of these "thwarted instances" in all aspects and at all levels. Specifically though, the contradictory juxtapositions and the turmoil provoked by the continuing oppositions create a tension-filled atmosphere that underscores authorial presence.

The "in the air" position (see, in this chapter, footnote 7) removes the author from sharing and participating in the travails of the characters. Even apparently neutrally phrased stage directions—"King Mangucián sits down at the right hand of King Micomicón and yawns with delectable sloth, as if this were the best appetizer to get ready to eat" ["El Rey Mangucián toma asiento á la diestra del Rey Micomicón y bosteza con deleitable largura, como si ello fuese el mejor aperitivo para disponerse á comer"] (157)—provide a distancing/separating breach. The "as if this were," an interpretation of the king's action (the yawn), allows for the possibility of a mistaken analysis that establishes and emphasizes the presence of an interpreter.

From his vantage point, the author commences an undisguised negative barrage. The King, in royal anger after hearing of the Elf's escape, "has a red face, as if he had just got up from eating" ["lleva la cara bermeja como si acabase de abandonar los manteles"] (36). When the character acts in a certain fashion, the manner of execution reminds the author of an unflattering homologue: "With a hop like those made by frogs and toads, [the Elf] disappears" ["De un salto como los dan las ranas y los sapos, desaparece"] (109). These unfavorable interpretations of the characters and their world, the disparaging attitude manifested, are symptomatic of the superior/inferior relationship existing between author/character. A

---

21. D. E. Gruber, "The Imperfect Action of Comedy," *Genre* 10.1 (1977): 118.

phrase, even the use of a single word, destroys the prevalent emotional tone, runs counter to the situation which the characters confront, and allows the whole context to be viewed dispassionately from a position distinct from the atmosphere built up by the preceding moments. In detailing the circumstances surrounding the duel between the Prince and Espandián, the leader of the bandoleers, the author's last phrase completely disrupts the preceding description:

> Espandián stands up knocking down his chair, and with his cape wrapped around his arm, in the manner of a buckler, and sword in hand, he stands guard in the middle of the kitchen. The Prince also draws his sword. They fight making a lot of noise and Prince Verdemar wounds Espandián. The blind man's dog, in a fit of laughter, bites his tail.

> [Derribando la silla se levanta Espandián, y con la capa revuelta al brazo, á guisa de broquel, y la espada en la mano, toma campo en mitad de la cocina. El Príncipe pone también mano á su espada. Riñen con mucho estruendo, y El Príncipe Verdemar hiere á Espandián. El perro del ciego, en un rapto de risa, se muerde el rabo] (64).

The dog's laugh in the midst of the disarray and movement of the battle becomes the de facto point of reference from which the entire scene comes to be judged.[22] The unharmonious mirth stands not as a fortuituous inclusion, a slip of the authorial pen, but as a fully intentional commentary indicative of the author's attitude toward the character's world. The duel elicits an outburst of farcical laughter.

The above-mentioned duel stems from an ever more violent quarrel between the bandit Espandián and his companion Geroma. Yet the terms used to describe the altercation between the couple are those more commonly reserved for a merry prank: "The inn becomes happy with ruckus" ["Se alegra la venta con tumulto"] (62). Any sort of transcendence to the incident, of possible repercussions arising therefrom, stand abruptly curtailed, forestalled by the innocuous language used in the description. The actual consequences of the quarrel (the duel and Prince Verdemar's narrow escape from the hands of Espandian's group intent on revenge) are a source of merriment for the author. The stage world—its contradictions and slapsticklike

---

22. As a theatrical sign, the animal is charged with semiotic value. The intent to increase the importance of each theatrical element, an integral part of Valle-Inclán's innovations (see, in this text, chapter 2, section III) forms part of a more general reaction against the theatre's exclusive concern with the character as the primary and fundamental source of significance. For the role of farce in the Surrealists' (particularly Apollinaire's and René Daumal's) attempt to make of the object a coequal force on par with the subject, see A. Bermel, *Farce* (New York: Simon & Schuster, 1982), 28.

nature—elicits Valle-Inclán's derisive tone and, at the same time, this tone further accentuates and contributes to the affirmation of the stage world's laughable and inconsequential nature. The stage world becomes the butt (or the cause) of a continual authorial mocking. The *didascalies* reveal an absolute dearth of sympathy for the characters and share common cause with "black humor":

> Black humor is bounded by too many things such as stupidity, skeptical irony, the joke without any transcendence . . . (the list would be long) but it is, above all, the mortal enemy of that sentimentality which gives the impression of being perpetually at bay—the sentimentality always [presented] against a blue backdrop.
>
> [L'humour noir est borné par trop de choses, telles que la bêtise, l'ironie sceptique, la plaisanterie sans gravité . . . (l'énumération serait longue) mais il est par excellence l'ennemi mortel de la sentimentalité à l'aire perpétuellement aux abois—la sentimentalité toujours sur fond bleu.]23

The many sources informing the author's sardonic mirth are part of an effective distancing lever that the author uses throughout the play. The derision contributes to isolating the stage world by stymying identification or emotional involvement with this world.24 Nevertheless, the author's mocking laughter does not completely assure nor entirely establish the singularity of the stage. As expressed by don Estrafalario, "Tears and laughter are born from the contemplation of things similair to ourselves" ["Las lágrimas y la risa nacen de la contemplación de cosas parejas a nosotros mismos"] (*Los Cuernos de don Friolera,* 19). In view of a faint, yet lingering, emotive presence, the distancing intent manifested by the mocking comes to be corroborated by the progressive concretization of what Bergson calls "[t]he mechanical encrusted [tacked] on the living" ["*Du mécanique plaqué sur du vivant.*"].25 *CdD* exemplifies the French philosopher's definition of the comic as the continuing vacillation between the human and the rigid: "The comic effect is all the more striking [. . . .]

---

23. A. Breton, *Anthologie de l'humour noir* (Paris: Éditions du Sagittaire, 1950), 15–16.

24. A dispersal of interest away from the characters constitutes one of the principal effects spurred by the constant belittling of the stage world. Attention focuses elsewhere: "The eye is on the discourse rather than on the individual, on the intellect as well as on the emotions." (E. Brater, "Brecht's Alienated Actor in Beckett's Theatre," *Comparative Drama* 9.3 [1975]: 204). The emphasis on language, for example, a constant in the work of Valle-Inclán, is highlighted through the downplaying of empathic response.

25. Henri Bergson, *Le Rire* (Paris: Felix Alcan, 1911), 39. The pagination of the following citation from this work is cited in the body of the text.

because these two images, that of a person and that of the mechanical, are precisely integrated the one into the other" ["L'effet comique est d'autant plus saisissant [. . . .] que ces deux images, celle d'une personne et celle d'une mécanique, sont plus exactement insérées l'une dans l'autre"] (Bergson, 31). The play, however, heightens the mechanical presence accompanying the characters as such, quite apart from its use in comic instances—the momentary surprise and shock resulting when the graceful or agile stands unmasked and reveals a mechanical rigidity. Valle-Inclán stresses the ubiquity of automatism per se. Machinelike characteristics crop up in all places and serve as a distancing instrument slowly eroding the possibility of empathic, emotive reaction. The stage is distinct both in degree and kind, a step toward the aesthetic of don Estrafalario, "going beyond pain and laughter" ["una superación del dolor y de la risa"] (*Los cuernos de don Friolera*, 21).

The royal entourage in *CdD* plays an essentially subordinate ceremonial role:

> King Micomicón appears with an ermine mantle, crown and scepter. The attendants appear after him. Ladies and courtiers exchange smiles and puerile looks [. . . .] They know how to courtesy and smile with their eyes as quiet, round, and brilliant as the beads of a necklace.
>
> [Aparece el Rey Micomicón con manto de armiño, corona y cetro. Los cortesanos aparecen tras él. Damas y galanes cambian sonrisas y miradas pueriles [. . . .] Saben hacer cortesías y sonreír con los ojos quietos, redondos y brillantes como las cuentas de un collar.] (123, 92)

The author spares no opportunity to stress that the entourage is confined to the realm of the gesture and describes their movement in some detail: "The attendants let out a cry and remain frightened: Their mouths open, morsels in the air, and cup in hand" ["Los cortesanos dan un grito y quedan espantados: Las bocas abiertas, el bocado en el aire y la copa en la mano"] (158). All the connotative possibilites of ballet are elicited by these perfectly coordinated figures. Specifically, "The ballet is one of the surest means of attaining to caricature, to a world of fairy enchantment, to a comic stylization, to a poetic transcription of sentiment."[26] The ceremonial courtesies of the retinue contribute to a fairy-tale charm and a delicate poeticality, attributes adroitly exploited by Valle-Inclán, Copeau, and others intent on expanding theatrical vocabulary. At the same time, however, stylization can be brutally foregrounded, so that "poetic transcription"

---

26. Wallace Fowlie, "Mystery of the Actor," *Yale French Studies* 5 (1950): 8.

becomes a caricature. This latent comic/caricaturesque force surfaces time and again, so that with respect to the balletlike figures

> who leave, come, dance, move together, adopting at the same time the same poses, gesticulating in the same fashion [. . . .] we think distinctly of marionettes. Invisible strings appear to link hand to hand, leg to leg, every muscle of one physiognomy with the analogous muscles of the other: the inflexibility of the correspondence makes the softness of the forms itself solidify before our eyes and [makes] everything harden mechanically [into a mechanical structure].
>
> [qui vont, viennent, dansent, se démènent ensemble, en prenant en même temps les mêmes attitudes, en gesticulant de la même manière [. . . .] nous pensons distinctement à des marionnettes. Des fils invisibles nous paraissent relier les bras aux bras, les jambes aux jambes, chaque muscle d'une physionomie au muscle analogue de l'autre: l'inflexibilité de la correspondance fait que la mollesse des formes se solidifie elle-même sous nos yeux, et que tout durcit en mécanique.][27]

The author ensures that the palatial retinue's calculated movements become the gestures of so many puppets:

> The Princess appears among a long entourage of ladies and young ladies-in-waiting, pages and chamberlains. The Master of Ceremonies walks between them all striking the floor with his silver club. In moments of silence, young ladies-in-waiting and pages, ladies and chamberlains move with the puerile air of puppets whose movement is governed by a string.
>
> [La señora Infantina aparece entre un largo cortejo de damas y meninas, pajes y chambelanes. El Maestro de Ceremonias anda entre todos batiendo el suelo con su porra de plata. En los momentos de silencio, meninas y pajes, damas y chambelanes accionan con el aire pueril de los muñecos que tienen el movimiento regido por un cimbel.] (91–92)

A plethora of suggestive procedures help "fix" the machinelike nature of the stage. The simple accumulation of epithets, a most common Valle-Inclanesque trait, imparts a mechanical, automated tinge. In the example cited above, the reiterated use of "Ladies and young ladies-in-waiting, pages and chamberlains" exerts an incantatory effect. The rhythmic, musical, strictly sensuous qualities of words are exploited in order to convey, as well as to take part in, the expression of the authorial distancing perspective. The words mimic ceremonial patterns. *La Marquesa Rosalinda* (*MR*) constantly evokes balletlike rhythms:

27. H. Bergson, *Le Rire*, 36.

And Polichinela jumps to the beat
of [those] marionettes a string sets dancing

[Y Polichinela salta en el compás
De las marionetas que baila un cimbel]

(*MR*, 83)

The Page and Miss Estrella enter,
two figures in a minuet

[Salen el Paje y Doña Estrella,
Dos figuras de minué]

(170)

Arlequín pirouettes,
greeting as they do in France,
and evokes an operetta rhythm
with the elegance of his rhythm

[Arlequín hace la pirueta,
Saludando al modo de Francia,
Y evoca un ritmo de opereta
Con el ritmo de su elegancia]

(188)

Arlequín greets in a mocking fashion
with a grotesque pirouette.
Funambulatory Colombina
appears gesticulating.
She does one whirl through the garden
with the rhythm of a marionette
that brings to mind the little comedy
of Fagotín's [puppet] show

[Arlequín saluda burlando,
Con una pirueta grotesca.
Colombina funambulesca,
Aparece manoteando.
Hace un vuelo por el jardín
Con un ritmo de marioneta,
Que recuerda la comedieta
Del retablo de Fagotín]

(131)

An evident musicality guides, indeed rules, the characters' movements.[28] The apprehension of this rhythm becomes the self-set goal of

---

28. Valle-Inclán considers dance in a special, quasi-mystical light: "Dance is the highest aesthetic expression [. . . .] Only in dance do the subtle paths of beauty, sound, and light join in a supreme comprehension" ["El baile es la más alta expresión estética [. . . .] Solamente en el baile se juntan los sutiles caminos de la belleza, sonido y luz, en una suprema comprensión"] (*La lámpara maravillosa* [*Lámpara*], 95). As playwright, Yeats shares these sentiments, likewise utilizing dance and stylized movement to attain "those collective archetypal experiences that give art a quasi-religious function and authority" (A. Koritz, "Women Dancing: The Structure of Gender in Yeat's Early Plays for Dancers," *Modern Drama* 32.3 [1989]: 388). Given the interpenetration of the mystic with the sensual throughout *Lámpara*, it comes as little suprise that in the Galician writer's drama, "dance becomes the favored mechanism for giving plastic, theatrical form

the play's strophes, as the author states at the onset: "As in the flageolet of the Galician / sheperd [. . .] dances [should dance] the charm of the trochaic / verse" ["Como en la gaita del galaico / Pastor [. . .] Salte la gracia del trocaico / Verso"] (12). Plot development depends on the dance: in order to narrate Marquesa Rosalinda's secret, Arlequín has to place "in my strophes the flounces / of a dancing skirt" ["en mis estrofas los caireles / De una falda de medio paso"] (15). More precisely, the words interweave with the dance's rhythm: "In order to serve you, I weave the scheme [plot] / of the Play in my strophes [. . . .] Let us weave the lovely lies / with the rhythm of pirouettes" ["Por serviros tejo el tramado / De la Comedia, en mis estrofas [. . . .] Tejamos las bellas mentiras / Con el ritmo de las piruetas"] (11). In addition to their value as blocks constructing the plot of the play, the words serve as containers of its rhythmic vitality. The verses are of choreographical import to the "operetta rhythm" ["ritmo de opereta"] (188) and the "hurdy-gurdy beat" ["compás de organillo"] (137). The movement that propels Colombina's "marionette rhythm" ["ritmo de marioneta"] (131) is not simply ordered, but comes to be interiorized and reflected in the rhythm of the verse. On the one hand, the strophes permit the author to interpenetrate the words with the action they order or describe—the words are saturated with vitality. This interpenetration breaks through the limitations circumscribing language as a mere information bearer: "Could it be that the transmission of information [. . . .] is merely one of 'the most specialized and most unimportant' functions of language [?]" ["La transmission de l'information ne serait-elle [. . . .] qu'une des fonctions 'les plus spécialisées et les plus secondaires' du langage[?]"][29] On the other hand, the fact that the verses aptly incarnate

---

to sexual desire" (D. Dougherty, "Theater and Eroticism: Valle-Inclán's *Farsa y licencia de la reina castiza*," *Hispanic Review* 55.1 [1987]: 19). See also J. Amor y Vázquez, "Valle-Inclán y las musas: Terpsícore," in D. Kossof and J. Amor Y Vázquez, eds., *Homenaje al profesor William L. Fichter* (Madrid: Castalia, 1971), 11–31.

29. André Guimbretière, "Approche du référent," *Degrés* 3 (1973): f-3. The musical characteristics latent in words and the role of rhythm and rhyme are indispensable means to the mystic/aesthetic comprehension described in *La Lámpara maravillosa* [*Lámpara*]: see the section entitled "Milagro musical," especially the third section. Indeed, *Lámpara* counsels: "Let us make our entire life in the manner of a strophe" ["Hagamos de toda nuestra vida á modo de una estrofa"] (52) in order to overcome temporal limitations and grasp eternal intuitions. The experimentation with the plastic nature of the word and the desire to draw out its possible rhythmic potential evidenced in Valle-Inclán's theatre form part of the broad-ranging endeavor set forth in *Lámpara* (see chapter 4 of this text, especially section three, where the various means by which Valle-Inclán's plays garner an "intuition of eternity" ["intuición de eternidad"] [Lámpara, 53] are examined). At the same time, using the sensuous, physical import of words

the movements and the beat, which make of the characters puppets that a "string sets dancing" ["que baila un cimbel"] (83), provides the author with an adequate means with which to make manifest his distanced/distancing view differentiating the stage.

Subversive Mirroring

Valle-Inclán presents characters shrouded in uncertainty, manipulated by the author in an act of literary montage, and accentuates the distancing latent in the author-as-manipulator of the stage world by adopting a negative, derisive stance. The characters respond to this pervasive authorial perspective in a similar fashion. They rise up against their manipulated status, implying a moment nonconforming with the literary code used by the author. Both author and characters are immersed in a constitutive display/exemplification of literary codes and a derision/subversion of these codes where, ironically perhaps, the Text stands as the constant around which the author/character activity revolves, the de facto substratum on which their dual interplay rests.

In his essay "De rodillas, en pie, en el aire," Buero Vallejo maintains that the *esperpento* transcends light farce precisely because it does not attain the complete and total distortion inherent to an "esperpentic" aesthetic.[30] The aesthetic position by which the characters are regarded entirely from "the air" (see, in this chapter, footnote 7), in perfect detachment, certainly defines the *esperpento*, but in masterworks such as *Los cuernos de don Friolera* or *Luces de bohemia*, this position appears alongside a Shakespearean posture in which the author considers himself to be on an equal footing with his creations. A continuous alternation ensues: on the one hand, a tragic figure stands in comically grotesque surroundings and situations; and, on the other hand, a tragic world is populated with grotesquely comic figures. The unique appeal of the *esperpento* derives from the gaps, the moments not forming part of the prevailing situation, that

---

—"Where words can not reach with their meanings, the waves of their music reach" ["Adonde no llegan las palabras con sus significados, van las ondas de sus músicas"] (*Lámpara*, 69)—opens new possibilities for theatrical expression, as recognized by such figures as J. L. Barrault: "Thus the word, by its imitative essence that can go through onomatopeia, then jumblement, is a *sonorous dance*" ["Ainsi par son essence imitative qui peut passer par l'onomatopée, puis la fatrasie, la parole est une *dance sonore*"] ("Le Corps magnétique," *Cahiers Renaud-Barrault* 99 [1979]: 76).

30. A. Buero Vallejo, "De rodillas, en pie, en el aire," *Revista de Occidente* 15.44–45 (1966): 132–45.

establish a difference allowing the surrounding atmosphere to be judged and contrasted. "Nonesperpentic" elements are in the process of pathetically or bathetically succumbing to or emerging from "esperpentic" deformity. Witness, for example, the emergence of don Friolera in *Los cuernos de don Friolera*, his ranting against those people who impose the Calderonian imperative (the first scene); how he relegates the Calderonian imperative, in its incarnation doña Tadea Calderón, to a ball-toss arcade (scene nine), although p(b)athetically powerless in the sway of the code of honor. Similarly in *La cabeza del dragón* (*CdD*), an important part of the characters' behavior consists of an ever-present struggle against the monolithic imposition of a set frame. Violence and strife are the bywords. The characters are at odds with their immediate context and are forever attempting (and forever failing) to stand entirely free of their surroundings.

The characters remain unable to function without reference to the code according to which the author actualizes their movement. In taking the Princess to the fountain to be sacrificed—the fairy-tale stricture requiring the immolation of the Princess to save the kingdom from the fury of the monster—the Master of Ceremonies does not actually know where the fountain lies: "I can not tell you for sure" ["Yo no puedo decíroslo con certeza"] (*CdD*, 92). The fountain always remains in the distance, "the run of a whippet" ["la carrera de un galgo" (93) away. Nevertheless, the Rules must be obeyed:

> *[The Master of Ceremonies is speaking to the Princess]* Etiquette rules that you be handed over to the Dragon at the Fountain of the Dwarfs! This has been customary for the past two thousand years! The Court of the King your father maintains in vigor the practices of the good King Dagoberto, and according to the fifteenth [practice], it is established that every time the Dragon requests a princess, she must be brought to it [the Dragon] at the Fountain of the Dwarfs! We can not break such an old tradition!
>
> [¡La etiqueta establece que seáis entregada al Dragón en la Fuente de los Enanos. ¡Es el uso desde hace dos mil años! La Corte del Rey vuestro padre mantiene en vigor las prácticas del buen Rey Dagoberto, y por la décimaquinta se establece que cada vez que el Dragón se presente á reclamar una princesa, ésta le sea llevada á la Fuente de los Enanos! ¡No podemos romper una tradición tan antigua!] (94)

In spite of his uncertainty and confusion over the actual presence of the fountain—an uncertainty that reflects the distance/differentiation of the "etiquette,"[31] the rules to be imposed, from the characters' actu-

---

31. In *La Marquesa Rosalinda,* Colombina also refers to the strictures of an "etiquette." See in this text, Chapter 2, 48–50.

al situational context—the Master reiterates the obligation to comply with superior dictates. Despite the Princess's revolt against the Code's imposition, the Master refuses to alter its application and to "modify any of the good King Dagoberto's ordinances" ["modificar una pragmática del buen Rey Dagoberto"] (102). In fact, the Princess only rebels against the ceremony surrounding the sacrifice, not the fairy-tale sacrifice itself: "But I am a girl who only knows how to die in order to save everyone. I have never read King Dagoberto's ordinances" ["Pero yo soy una niña que sólo sabe morir por salvaros á todos. Nunca he leído las pragmáticas del Rey Dagoberto"] (97). The destiny of the fairy-tale princess remains unchanged: the Princess conforms to her role-identity. The Princess's refusal to follow the Master's rules and search for the fountain—the violence wrought on the Code by separating the manner in which to enact the ceremony from the enactment itself—instances an ongoing process in the play. The fairy-tale structure imposes itself, appears to be overthrown, only to be imposed again: even as a result of the rebellion, the Text stands reinforced. The Dragon's severed head is verified as *real* (as the one which Verdemar faced) because it corresponds to the Text: "Seven rows of teeth as narrated in the chronicle of the good King Dagoberto!" ["¡Siete hileras de dientes como relata la crónica del buen Rey Dagoberto!"] (130). The Text imparts authenticity, establishing and consolidating the parameters within which the characters move.

The omnipresence of the Text and the mocking tone of the author effectively institute a superior/inferior relationship with respect to the characters that provides a "centre of gravity,"[32] an initial ground or frame from which to apprehend the play:

> To understand a performance text element, then, means to match it against a frame statement. A frame statement may be viewed as an element of a network of frames guiding the construction of reasoning chains. To understand coherently a text, then, means: recognizing the relevant frame elements, determining their senses using frame presuppositions, completing causal chains, elaborating statements or questions according to events or objects in focus.[33]

---

32. Andrew Kennedy, "Natural, Mannered, and Parodic Dialogue," *The Yearbook of English Studies* 9 (1979): 54. His study of a natural language as the standard from which deviations proceed proved especially applicable to the use of the Text in *CdD* and the successive integrative/separatist modulations developed throughout the play.

33. C. Tindemans, "Coherence. Putting 'Pieces' Together," *Degrés* 31 (1982): i-4. See also: Irving Goffman's pioneering study of the frame and the frame perspective in "The Theatrical Frame," *Frame Analysis* (New York: Harper & Row, 1974), 124–55; J. O. Urmson's analysis of the background conditional required to interpret the actor's phatic act as a full-scale speech act, in "Dramatic Representation," *The Philosophical Quarterly* 22.89 (1972): 333–43.

CdD's dual organizational pattern, however, as previously noted, confronts a continuous violence on both fronts. The characters struggle to attenuate authorial power and question their (con)textual limitations.

By contrast, in several of Valle-Inclán's other plays, *Divinas palabras* (*DP*) for example, the ambiance is different. In this text, the author provides details, "A peasant couple with a sick daughter" ["Un matrimonio de labriegos con una hija enferma"] (*DP*, 7), that do not appear in the character's own dialogue (103; 172–76). Moreover, the author clearly specifies the various names that one character will use—"Lucero, who at times is called Séptimo Miau and buddy Miau" ["Lucero, que otras veces se llama Séptimo Miau y compadre Miau"] (*DP*, 7). In *La cabeza del dragón* (*CdD*), on the other hand, the characters take the lead in detailing characteristics more commonly found in the list of characters. King Micomicón presents "The Princess" ["La Señora Infantina," in the author's description], as "Blanca Flor" (*CdD*, 105; 123). Similarly, the dialogical interaction concretizes and names "The Blind Man" ["El Ciego"] as "Zacarías" (50). The Blind Man reveals "The Buffoon" ["El Bufón"] to be "Bertoldo" (50). The characters participate fully in an activity generally reserved to the author. Only after the complete revelation of the characters' identity takes place within the dialogue does the author incorporate the nomenclature, using "Bertoldo" in the first stage direction of the last scene (151).

The tone struck by the usurpation or intended usurpation of an authorial function forms part of a general trend in which the characters struggle against their own patently manipulated status as quasi-puppets. An everpresent affirmative/repudiative dialectic is firmly established. In subverting or contradicting the position of the author, the characters attempt to reduce in some measure the distance that separates them from the author. The *didascalies* are subject to an undisguised erosive onslaught. The author describes the Queen's "pouch" ["faltriquera"] as "[t]he ornate pouch sewn with golden thread, made from the satin of a doublet [in which] the King sweated thirty battles!" ["¡La rica faltriquera cosida con hilo de oro, hecha con el raso de un jubón que en treinta batallas, sudó Señor Rey!"] (31). Subsequently, however, the Princes comment on the gifts received from their father and mock the King's courage in battle, casting doubt on the fact that the "pouch" is indeed woven from one of the King's battle worn "doublets":"

> *Prince Pompón* — Some gift my father has given me! [. . . .]
> *Prince Ajonjolí* — And me, with his mantle sweated in a hundred royal parties!

> *Prince Verdemar* — I am happy with my sword.
> *Prince Pompón* — Since it doesn't have a dent!
> *Prince Ajonjolí* — It could hardly have one since it never left its sheath.
>
> [*El Príncipe Pompón* — ¡Buen regalo me ha hecho mi padre! [. . . .]
> *El Príncipe Ajonjolí* — ¡Pues á mí, con su manto sudado en cien fiestas reales!
> *El Príncipe Verdemar* — Yo estoy contento con mi espada.
> *El Príncipe Pompón* — ¡Como que no tiene ni una mella!
> *El Príncipe Ajonjolí* — Mal podría tenerla no habiendo salido de la vaina.]
>
> (36–37)

The characters have stretched the crediblity and authority of the *didascalie*.

From the "classic inn" ["venta clásica"] (43) to the presence of "Maritornes," Cervantian texts form the background to the Second Act. Although the characters evoke, in turn, this literary precedent, they are not bound by a "Cervantian imperative." The Buffoon, to cite an example, couples immigration to the "Indies" with the revelation that the automobile chauffeurs in the kingdom have been instructed to run over the "old people" (54–55). The *didascalies* are not the sole textual *locus* harboring a display of contradictions. These contradictions—characteristics marking the author's distancing intent—proliferate outside the *didascalies* as well. The characters undertake to share in and to imitate, however weak the end result, the activity of the author, attempting to appropriate in some measure the methods that permit and establish his superiority.

A constant violence within the characters' world accompanies the tension between the author and the characters. A particular action denies or mocks the past or future movement of another character, at times indirectly, more often than not directly:

> *Prince Pompón*— I never saw elves, nor did I think there ever were any. Elves, witches, goblins, spells are no longer things of our age, my brothers. This [thing] that the gardener has caught in the forest is probably not an elf.
> *Prince Ajonjolí* — I saw it, and it has all the characteristics of an elf, Prince Pompón.
> *Prince Pompón* — [Your] eyes can be so misleading, Prince Ajonjolí!
>
> [*El Príncipe Pompón* — Yo nunca vi duendes, ni tampoco creí que los hubiese. Los duendes, las brujas, los trasgos, las hechicerías, ya no son cosa de nuestro tiempo,

hermanos míos. Ese que el jardinero ha cazado en el
bosque, no será duende.
El Príncipe Ajonjolí — Yo lo vi, y tiene de duende toda la
apariencia, Príncipe Pompón.
El Príncipe Pompón — ¡Mucho engañan los ojos,
Príncipe Ajonjolí!]

(18)

Elements intrinsic to the fairy tale ("elves") are rebuffed. They remain something alien, foisted upon, rather than part of, the characters' world. Fairy-tale norms may have to be accepted, but the characters chafe at the imposition. Verdemar renders the soliloquy of the prince cursed by his father and forced into banishment by the plotting of his brothers as: "My brothers will inform on me, and my father will eat my heart raw and without salt [. . . .] I will have to flee from this palace where I was born. I only regret not being able to kiss the hand of my mother and say goodbye to her. . . And ask her for some doubloons for the trip!" ["Mis hermanos me delatarán, y mi padre se comerá mi corazón crudo y sin sal [. . . .] Tendré que huir de este palacio donde he nacido. Sólo siento no poder besar las manos de mi madre, y decirle adiós. . . ¡Y pedirle algunos doblones para el viaje!"] (39). The last line, with the emphasis accorded by the exclamation marks, ends the lamentation with a farcical touch that subverts the soliloquy's integrity.

Instances similar to the one described in the preceding paragraph, which parody the most solemn moments of the fairy-tale structure, are evident throughout the text. The sacrifice of the Princess who will commit suicide rather than allow her father (the King) to renege on his royal word (the King has promised the Princess in marriage to whoever slays the dragon and Espandián, the bandit, lays claim to the feat) indicates, at the same time, the depth of the Princess's love for Prince Verdemar, who has actually killed the dragon but remains in disguise (she prefers death rather than marriage to the impostor Espandián). Yet, this most solemn of moments receives a laughable and parodic twist. The Princess determines to take hemlock and the Duchess preparing the potion exclaims: "Oh! What a tragedy! And I who cannot cry! Do you want the hemlock with a lot of sugar, my child?" ["¡Oh! ¡Qué tragedia! ¡Y yo que no puedo llorar! ¿Queréis la cicuta muy azucarada, niña mía?"] (141).

The characters distance themselves from the conventions regulating the situation in which they are found. The Princess's reaction upon receiving the "clogs" from Verdemar instances one moment of a pervasive trend: "Oh! How pretty! Only fairies in stories have them like this" ["¡Oh! !Qué lindos! Sólo las hadas de los cuentos los tienen así"] (109). The Princess effectively casts doubt on the "fairy taleness" of the context, for the connotative power of her negation implies that her surroundings are not part of a fairy tale—the "clogs" have been inserted in her world.

The success of the characters' rebellion remains short-lived: they achieve only momentary independence from governing conventions. The play's final moments demonstrate the two sides of the interplay. The penultimate moment destroys the Elf's stature as the representative (only equalled, perhaps, by the dragon) of fairy-tale characteristics:

> [*The Elf addresses the King*] What I have just finished serving you in this plate of gold, oh powerful King Mangucián, is raw lamb heart without salt. Was it not in this fashion that you once clamored to eat the heart of that prince, your son, who had released the Elf? Now you see that the dish is not very tasty! Dogs, lions, tigers, wolves, and cats eat raw and bloody meat because they have in their stomachs an enormous amount of hydrochloric acid that makes it easy for them to digest it. But even if in some remote time in the past, kings could have done the same thing, today, as a result of species evolution, they no are longer able to do so. As they lost in prerogatives, they lost in stomach potency. Constitutional kings can only be vegetarians.
>
> [Lo que en este plato de oro acabo de servirte, poderoso Rey Mangucián, es corazón de cordero crudo y sin sal. ¿No era así como clamabas un día por comerte el corazón de aquel príncipe, hijo tuyo, que había dado libertad al Duende? ¡Ya ves que el plato no es muy sabroso! Los perros, los leones, los tigres, los lobos y los gatos se comen la carne cruda y sangrienta porque tienen en sus estómagos una gran cantidad de ácido clorhídrico que les hace fácil digerirlas. Pero los reyes, si un tiempo remoto pudieron hacer lo mismo, hoy, por la evolución de las especies, ya no pueden. Al perder en regalías, perdieron en potencia estomacal. Los reyes constitucionales sólo pueden ser vegetarianos.] (158–59)

The phrases about constitutional monarchies and hydrochloric acid, so completely out of context, distance the Elf from the fairy-tale setting. In the following moment, those characters, who had at times (although to a much more limited extent and with much more reserve than other fellow characters) rebelled against and ridiculed the conventions, submit themselves to fairy-tale mandates:

> *Prince Verdemar and the Princess, holding hands, go to kneel in the presence of the two Kings. Their voices rise together.*
> *The Two* — Bless us!
> *The Kings* — May the Heavens also bless you, extending our dynasties for ever and ever!
> *All The Guests* — Amén!

> [*El Príncipe Verdemar y la Señora Infantina, cogidos de las manos, van á ponerse de rodillas en la presencia de los dos Señores Reyes. Sus voces se levantan hermanadas.*
> Los Dos — ¡Bendecidnos!
> Los Reyes — ¡Qué los altos cielos igualmente os bendigan, dilatando nuestras dinastías por los siglos de los siglos!
> Todos Los Invitados — ¡Amén!]
>   (159–60)

CdD ends with the triumphant affirmation of the fairy tale. The characters affirm its power, completely enveloped in its fold. Yet the affirmation merely *appears* triumphant, standing as it does on the shoulders of the Elf's immediately preceding undermining gesture.

The ever-present duality, the affirmative/repudiative movement in the characters' world, runs parallel to the constructive/destructive activity evident in the *didascalies*. A specular inverted symmetry takes hold: the two reflecting halves set in motion a recurrent, complementary, caustic interplay wherein the affirmations of the characters are mockingly derided by the *didascalies*, and wherein the constructive intent of the *didascalies* is undermined by the characters. The all-encompassing net of reciprocal subversive activity, a constant distancing with regard to (and in the context of) the Text, brings to the forefront a fundamental unsettling Valle-Inclanian characteristic: the doubling of the mirror splinters the stable perspective, the elements constituting the "many shades of gay and comforting laughter."[34] The laughter has no one source, the mocking tone proceeds to no one target. A radical uncertainty wears away any putatively dominant perspective. Distancing is ubiquitous in a play constituted by the perpetuation of an erosive mechanism at work at all levels, active in all moments.

De-Hierarchization

Valle-Inclán typically unites elements pertaining to semantic fields poles apart:

> What first strikes one about Valle-Inclán's language, more than the great richness of the vocabulary and the abundance of neologisms of all types, is the intentional inappropriate use, the semantic changes that he imposes even upon very common words, according to his will and whim.
>
> [Lo que primero sorprende en el lenguage de Valle-Inclán, es más que la

---

34. Auréliu Weiss, "Truth and Theatre," *Comparative Drama* 4.1 (1970): 66.

gran riqueza de vocabulario y que la abundancia de neologismos de todo orden, la impropiedad intencionada, los cambios semánticos que impone incluso a vocablos muy comunes, según su capricho y gusto.]³⁵

In *La cabeza del dragón* (*CdD*), such disruptions of *standard* hierarchal order between words become the norm. Moreover, the play heightens an alteration and distortion within the word. Discourse incorporates, indeed interiorizes, the attritive and caustic atmosphere of the play.

The interchange between the Princes in the first act, symptomatically enough, reveals the significance accorded to the word in *CdD*. The Elf places the emphasis squarely on "the word" ["la palabra"]— the ability to join the word with its signified, the promise with its realization. Each of the three Princes, in turn, places his "word" on show, and the action revolves around situations that exhibit (put to the test) each Prince's affirmation. Prince Pompón, as the eldest, becomes the first to disassociate his word from the action to which it is bound. He promises the Elf freedom:

> *Prince Pompón* — Give me back the ball and I will open the door for you.
> *The Elf* — Do you swear to do it?
> *Prince Pompón* — My word is a king's word
>
> [*El Príncipe Pompón* — Devuélveme la pelota y te abriré la puerta.
> *El Duende* — ¿Me lo juras?
> *El Príncipe Pompón* — Mi palabra es de Rey.]
> (*CdD*, 19)

Yet when the Elf returns the ball, the promise is broken (a similar affirmation and retraction occurs with the second Prince, Ajonjolí, in a passage to be commented upon shortly). The word, the statement of intentions, stands divorced from any significance in terms of causal linkage. The word has value only in itself, not for the signified it so seductively, yet deceptively, insinuates.

Prince Verdemar points out this state of affairs to the Elf: "I regret that the deceitfulness of my brothers makes you doubt my word" ["Me duele que el engaño de mis hermanos te haga dudar de mi palabra"] (29). In many instances throughout the play, Verdemar attempts to unite the signifier with the signified. When the King bestows gifts on the three Princes, for example, Pompón and Ajonjolí

---

35. A. Risco, *La estética de Valle-Inclán en los 'esperpentos' y en el 'Ruedo Ibérico'* (Madrid: Gredos, 1966), 163–64.

immediately undermine the integrity of the royal gesture by attempting to exchange their respective presents with Verdemar's. Only Verdemar maintains the gift's symbolic unity: "My father gave it [the sword] to me, and I will not exchange it for anything in the world" ["Me la dió mi padre, y no la cambio por nada del mundo"] (38). More eloquent perhaps, in this context, is the manner in which Verdemar restores the title of hero (dragon slayer) to its rightful proprietor (himself). The revelation of Espandián as an impostor takes place as a result of the dragon's severed tongue (136–41). Verdemar alone possesses the instrument that maintains gestural integrity: his insertion of the tongue into its rightful place lets the act *speak* for itself in all clarity.

The interchange occurring between Verdemar and the Buffoon aptly brings out the relation of the communicative sequence, whether word or gesture, with respect to its meaning. When Verdemar asks the Buffoon why he does not commit the "madness" ["locura"] of killing the dragon, since he lives from his ability to "say mad things in the court" ["decir locuras, en la Corte"] (46), the Buffoon responds in a categorical fashion: "[I live] from saying such [mad] things, but not from doing them" ["[Vivo] De decirlas ["locuras"], pero no de hacerlas"] (46). Subsequently, the Buffoon clearly and distinctively outlines a definition of the poetic/buffoonish activity:

> Buffoons are like poets [. . . .] A poet finishes a sonnet replete with amorous complaints, a great subtle and lachrymose madness, and he has his wife in bed with her leg broken by a blow with a stick. He appears demented in his verses and in real life he knows how to be more sane than a clerk.
>
> [Los bufones somos como los poetas [. . . .] Un poeta acaba un soneto lleno de amorosas quejas, la mayor locura sutil y lacriminosa, y tiene á la mujer en la cama con la pierna quebrada de un palo. Aparenta una demencia en sus versos y sabe ser en la vida más cuerdo que un escribano.] (46–47)

Verdemar, however, remains fundamentally perturbed with the poetic and buffoonish lack of concern for the discrepancy between word and meaning (or between stated purpose and subsequent action). He cannot adopt the buffoonish outlook. When Verdemar, much later, finally dons the Buffoon's attire, he finds the role imitation impossible: the Princess points out: "your words have a far away sound that does not match with your buffoon's hood" ["tienen tus palabras un son lejano que no cuadra con tu caperuza de bufón"] (84–85).

Despite Verdemar's basic incomprehension, the Buffoon's exposition of the ties extant between buffoonish (farcical) and poetic (dramatic) activity proves to be highly revelatory.[36] Here a character of *CdD* comments, ever so gently, on *CdD*'s characteristics. The dramatic language serves as the crucible wherein the fusion of the buffoonish and the poetic activities occurs, with the consequent incorporation of the split between "say mad things" ["decir locuras"] and "do mad things" ["hacerlas [locuras]"]. Language registers a loss of the bond linking the assertion to what is actually asserted, a separation of the utterance from the implications of the uttered statement. Consequently, the dialogical interchange is *loosed* from its situational context. The dialogue proceeds, in part, by the interaction of the signifiers themselves, not by the action or meaning entailed or implied by the signifiers. The following passage exemplifies the characteristics of this process:

> [the dialogue is part of an intense quarrel between Espandián and his concubine, Geroma, in the inn]
> *Espandián* — Geroma, you can scratch me. A man of my standing knows what ladies are like. But, careful not to say a single word that slights my honor!
> *Geroma* — Give me back the plate!
> *The Buffoon* — You can kill a woman, but you can not be disrespectful to her. I am sure that Mrs. Geroma would be more in agreement if you had killed her.
> *Geroma* — What are you saying, carnival face!
> *The Buffoon* — I am speaking in your defense, Mrs. Geroma.
> *The Bully [Espandián]* — I suffice for her defense. Geroma, stay within the bounds of words; since they are yours, they do not offend me. But a wife owes obedience to her husband, and if you forget, I will [must] remind you.
>
> [*Espandián* — Geroma, á mí puedes arañarme. Un hombre como yo conoce lo que son señoras. ¡Pero cuida de no decir una sola palabra ofensiva para mi honor!
> *Geroma* — ¡Vuélveme el plato!
> *El Bufón* — A una mujer se la mata, pero no se la falta. Seguro estoy de que se hallaría más conforme con que le hubieses quitado la vida, la Señora Geroma.
> *Geroma* — ¡Qué hablas tú, cara de antruejo!
> *El Bufón* — Hablo en vuestra defensa, Señora Geroma.
> *El Bravo* — Yo basto para su defensa. Geroma, quédate

---

36. A burlesque, farcical laughter makes its presence felt throughout the play. The Buffoon himself "[j]umps [. . .] rousing and [acting in a] farcical [manner]" ["Salta [. . .] embullando y farsando"] (77). His ostentatious use of farce strengthens the bond relating the buffoonish and the farcical, corroborating the respective links between buffoonish/poetic and farcical/dramatic activities.

siempre en las palabras, que por ser tuyas no me ofenden. Pero la mujer debe obediencia al marido, y si lo olvidas, he de recordártelo.] (62–63)

Espandián's utterances reveal that his position on words suffers a reversal. In the beginning, he insists that Geroma not utter a "single word that slights [. . . his] honor," ["una sola palabra ofensiva para [. . . su] honor] but at the end, Espandián affirms that her words, "since they are yours, they do not offend me" [que por ser tuyas no me ofenden"]. The status of words per se diminishes, their importance suffers a slight. Moreover, words and action appear in flux. Espandián stresses now one element, now the other. In more detail: a) Espandián, in addressing Geroma, stresses that words are important, not actions—Geroma cannot offend his honor, but she can strike him ("careful not to say a single word that slights my honor" ["cuida de no decir una sola palabra ofensiva para mi honor"]), yet, "you can scratch me" ["ámí puedes arañarme"]; b) The Buffoon agrees with Espandián that words are important, not action—Geroma would prefer death to being offended; c) Geroma reacts negatively to the Bufoon's statement and its implications, in the surprised "[w]hat are you saying, carnival face!" ["¡Qué hablas tú, cara de antruejo!"]; d) The Buffoon stresses that he applies Espandian's statement to Geroma for a purpose ("I am speaking in your defense" ["¡Hablo en vuestra defensa"]). The application, however, magnifies the action/words import of Espandián's statement: to prefer death rather than insults is simply an exaggeration of Espandián's preferring Geroma to scratch rather than to slight his honor; e) As a reaction to the Buffon's exaggeration of Espandián's previous statement, Espandián completely reverses his position: "stay within the bounds of words [. . .] they do not offend me [. . . .] a wife owes obedience" ["quédate siempre en las palabras [. . .] no me openden [. . . .] la mujer debe obediencia al marido"]—what matters are actions, not Geroma's insults.

Espandián establishes mutually exclusive parameters in both affirmations, in which either words or actions are the pivotal influential factors. Yet the first affirmation, as is only typical of Valle-Inclán's continuous play of opposites, has its reverse image in the second affirmation that upsets the postulate of the first with two principal consequences. First, the causal coherency of the dialogical structure within a given context is broken: Espandián can affirm a statement and totally ignore its implications, directly contradicting it a moment later. The dialogue proceeds by bypassing a cohesive structural development with one unit conforming to the previous unit in a successive logical movement. The dialogue is not bound to its past, as a general rule, not solely within a given interchange. The moment before the passage analyzed above, Geroma has insulted Espandián—"Drunk, ruffian, womenbeater" ["¡Borracho, rufián, apaleamujeres!"] (61)—as well as actively assaulted him—"Mrs. Geroma shows her nails, scratching his face" ["La Señora Geroma saca las uñas, arañándole la cara"] (62). In this context, Espandián warns Geroma to desist from undertaking what she has already explicitly commited. The threats of Espandián, already contradictory in themselves, are incongruous with, and indeed are uttered without recognition of, preceding events. The logical seams between the different segments of the play prove to be conspicuously loose.

Second, the reverse image duplication (the affirmation of an opposite) wears away the difference extant or previously held with respect to the two elements of the opposition (Geroma's words or her actions): the affirmation of each opposite cancels the affirmation of the other. The actual message and the different signifieds in Espandián's counterpoint are inconsequential—the characters can affirm as well as deny them. Attention is focused on the elements in their interchange, seen as an exercise in expression; their anterior lingering significations are (relatively) unimportant to the dialogue. The units composing language are exchanged for their value *qua* units: emphasis rests on their ability to be manipulated and on the manipulation itself. The notion of language as the sacrosanct carrier of meaning, the bearer of an ulterior significance that structures the play, is being worn away.

Valle-Inclán experiments with and fully exploits an essentially nonbinding dialogue. With the importance of the transmitted sidelined, language leaves the full weight of its emphasis on the transmitter, on the vehicles bearing the information. In fact, dialogue eschews placing valuational importance on anything except continuity. Valle-Inclán presents a kaleidoscopic range of elements in an impressive display, without a hierarchical conception of order or of sequential coherence. The language has no particular onus. "[W]ord play of facile comicity, of a *sainete* character, such as proliferates in the *esperpentos*" ["juegos de palabras de fácil comicidad, de carácter sainetero, como los que tanto abundan en los esperpentos"][37] alternates quite freely with elements drawn from a Cervantian vocabulary, Ariostan sources, and so forth. Any and all elements can be used to impel further expression. This blurring of hierarchies and their binding parameters—an ever-present free play—has an effect

---

37. A. Risco, *La estética de Valle-Inclán en los 'esperpentos' y en el 'Ruedo Ibérico* (Madrid: Gredos, 1966), 93.

similar to that of a continual witticism or unexpected quip: "The wisecrack is pulled in two directions: it is a pause for laughter and functions at the same time as one more step forward in the constant progression of the dialogue."[38] The shock provoked by bringing together two contradictory elements causes a momentary pause, a short hiatus. The import of the resulting collision, though, remains largely ignored and plays a minimal role as an element of further elaboration. Attention comes to rest on the pause itself, on the ability of language to cause the unexpected. The seriousness of dialogue as a revealer of consequent information, as perceived in traditional theatre, is waived. Dialogue can be a mere happening, unaware of its past, disregarding its own immediate, situational context and unconcerned with future consequences.[39] The momentary interplay between the elements takes precedence. The movement of the dialogue is self-serving; the language does not remit to and remains unpreoccupied with elements exterior to the moment's particular occurrence. The Abbot in *La Marquesa Rosalinda* (*MR*), for example, waxes eloquent in subterfuge:

> *Amaranta* — Mr. Pandolfo [the Abbot]
> They say Mrs. Colombina
> is learning how to translate Ovid with you.
> *The Abbot* — Calumnies of a vipered tongue!
> Venom of an ophidian!
> *Rosalinda* — And they say that in the sovereign speech
> of Ovid and Actium Plautus
> you have devised a [an allegorical] play
> where she appears as a pagan deity.
> *Amaranta* — Does she appear as Venus?
> *The Abbot* — Oh! . . . The sinful
> quill pen of mine sweetens the apple.
> *Amaranta* — Does she appear dressed?
> *The Abbot* — [Dressed] As a lady!
> She appears as a huntress
> with the bow and the hounds of Diana.
> *Rosalinda* — I know, dear Abbot, the dress. She is not
> wearing a thread!
> *The Abbot* — It is not a costume, my lady, for cold
> [weather]!
> *Rosalinda* — Nor long to sew.
> *Amaranta* — Have you had a full rehearsal of the role?

---

38. F. Jameson, "The Laughter of Nausea," *Yale French Studies*, 23 : 27.
39. For an analysis of how the "slippage of signification and the intrusion of one universe of discourse into another [. . . .] makes possible the phenomenon of linguistic cannibalization" (in another context, but suggestive nonetheless), see Leonard Wilcox, "Modernism vs. Postmodernism; Shepard's *The Tooth of Crime* and the Discourses of Popular Culture," *Modern Drama* 30.4 (1987): 560–73 (the citation is from 563).

> *The Abbot* — A rehearsal without everything, not yet, my lady.
>
> [*Amaranta* — Señor Pandolfo,
> Dicen que la señora Colombina
> Con vos aprende á traducir á Ovidio.
> *El Abate* — ¡Calumnias de una lengua viperina!
> ¡Veneno de un ofidio!
> *Rosalinda* — Y dicen que en la parla soberana
> De Ovidio y Accio Plauto
> Habéis compuesto un Auto
> En donde sale de deidad pagana.
> *Amaranta* — ¿Sale de Venus?
> *El Abate* — ¡Oh!. . . La pecadora
> Péñola mía, endulza la manzana.
> *Amaranta* — ¿Sale vestida?
> *El Abate* — ¡Como una señora!
> Sale de cazadora,
> Con el arco y los perros de Diana.
> *Rosalinda* — Conozco, caro Abte, el atavío. ¡No lleva un alfiler!
> *El Abate* — ¡No es traje, mi señora, para el frío!
> *Rosalinda* — Ni largo de coser.
> *Amaranta* — ¿Hicisteis del papel cumplido ensayo?
> *El Abad* — Un ensayo sin todo, aún no, señora.]
>
> (*MR*, 109–10)

Informational disclosure suffers a *rallentando* effect, so that language can indulge in a simple frolic. Dexterity and artifice are on exhibit. The incident becomes an excuse for a virtuoso display of expressive form. Each sally focuses attention on linguistic manipulation and constitutes, as well, (in Jameson's words) "one more step forward in the constant progression of the dialogue." Of particular interest are the penultimate lines,

> *Rosalinda* —[. . .] She is not wearing a thread!
> *The Abbot* — It is not a costume, my lady, for cold [weather].
> *Rosalinda* — Nor long to sew

> [*Rosalinda* — [. . .] ¡No lleva un alfiler!
> *El Abate* — ¡No es traje, mi señora, para el frío!
> *Rosalinda* — Ni largo de coser],

wherein the divulgence of additional information is reduced to an absolute minimum. Wit and the resources of language are paraded for their own effect, one element leading to the next under no obligation other than that of nontermination; and precisely in this feature lies a major factor contributing to the vigor, the immediateness, of Valle-Inclán's dramatic language. Like the spider drawing the thread from its own body, the moment's own impetus spins the dialogical matrix. Liberating language from an external burden, from its capacity to service other elements (especially the psychological development of the characters) leaves a denuded language with the need to forge its own links. The result is the institutionalization of unexpectedness: the sheer (and unpredictable) multiplicity of elements bandied about indicates the effort exerted in pulling the linguistic moment from the abyss of terminus—death.[40] Virtuoso effects are drawn out, all possible resources are called upon, for language, in its display of freedom, has to overcome the looming taunt of termination—a taunt given by and deriving from the presupposition of an audience, regardless of origin, whether inside the dramatic world (other characters), or outside the confines *stricto sensu* of the stage (the spectators). The audience, "the spectator *turned witness*" ["le spectateur *devenu témoin*"][41] of the stage interaction, demands a succession of dramatic moments. Language has to prove its ability to satisfy. The immediacy of the challenge is patent, the tension high, as the audience (actor/character/spectator) stays riveted to the means by which linguistic continuity will be achieved—language (progression) becomes the sole measure of dramatic existence. The circumscribing delimitation of termination draws together the elements involved in the dramatic into a common front and reaffirms their unity.

Constant reminders of an intrinsically theatrical nature accompany linguistic vividness—as if the emphasis on *CdD*'s dramatic characteristics were to add force to the conservation of its identity. In the previously cited example wherein the Elf tests the three Princes and the veracity of their "word" ["palabra"] (see in this chapter, page 82), the discourse reaffirms the status of Prince Ajonjolí as "Prince":

> *The Elf* — Will you open the door for me?
> *Prince Ajonjolí* — I will open it.
> *The Elf* — Do you swear to do it?

40. See in this text, chapter 1, section IV.
41. A. Ubersfeld, "Notes sur la dénégation théâtrale," *La relation théâtrale*, ed. Régis Durand (France: Presses Universitaires de Lille, 1980), 22. See pages 21–23, where the investigation centers on the constant superimposition of the "I actor, you actor, he spectator, [and] character ["je comédien, tu comédien, il spectateur, personnage"]. These elements of the dramatic communication undergo constant interchange. B. States offers an analysis of the "self-expressive, collaborative and representational modes" (actor, audience, and character respectively) in "The Actor's Presence: Three Phenomenal modes," *Theatre Journal* 35.3 (1983): 359–75. (The citation is from 360.)

Prince Ajonjolí — [I give you] the word of a King.

The Elf — No! Not the word of a King.

Prince Ajonjolí — Well, what [other] word would you like? I cannot offer you any other. If I am not King, I was born to be one, and my word is according to my station.

The Elf — And could you not give me the word of an honest man?

Prince Ajonjolí — You are slighting the respect that is my due as Prince of lineage. Honest man, this is applied to a peasant, a vinegrower, an artisan, but no one is so insolent as to say it of a Prince. Man of honor is applied to a captain, a noble, a duelist, and to certain rogues who fight each other with cardboard swords.

The Elf — I know that cardboard swords and sabers are the best ruse to act like a gentleman.

Prince Ajonjolí — You cannot call a Prince an honest man nor a man of honor. It is derogatory.

The Elf — For whom?

Prince Ajonjolí — For my blue blood.

The Elf — Prince Ajonjolí, then I will have no choice but to resign myself to your royal word. Here goes the ball.

[*El Duende* — ¿Me abrirás la puerta?

El Príncipe Ajonjolí — Te la abriré.

El Duende — ¿Me lo juras?

El Príncipe Ajonjolí — Palabra de Rey.

El Duende — ¡No! Palabra de Rey, no.

El Príncipe Ajonjolí — ¿Pues qué palabra quieres? Yo no puedo empeñarte otra. Si no soy Rey, nací para serlo, y mi palabra es conforme á mi condición.

El Duende — ¿Y no me podrías dar palabra de hombre de bien?

El Príncipe Ajonjolí — Me estás faltando al respeto que se me debe como Príncipe de la sangre. Hombre de bien, se dice de un labrador, de un viñador, de un menestral, pero nadie es tan insolente que lo diga de un Príncipe. Hombre de honor se dice de un capitán, de un noble, de un duelista y de algunos pícaros que se baten con espadas de cartón.

El Duende — Ya sé que las espadas y los sables de cartón son la mejor tramoya para presumir de caballero.

El Príncipe Ajonjolí — A un Príncipe no se le puede llamar ni hombre de bien, ni hombre de honor. Es depresivo.

El Duende — ¿Para quién?

El Príncipe Ajonjolí — Para mi sangre azul.

El Duende — Príncipe Ajonjolí, tendré entonces que conformarme con tu palabra real. Ahí va la pelota.]

(24–26)

The character indicated by the name Ajonjolí is absolutely adamant in his refusal to give a word other than that of Prince, "my word is according to my station ["mi palabra es conforme á mi condición"].

Nevertheless, the identification bears within it the seeds that begin to deconstruct its own affirmation. Ajonjolí completely separates royal characteristics from those of an "honest man" ["hombre de bien"] and a "man of honor" ["hombre de honor"]. The vehemence of his affirmation, however, betrays an intrinsic unease. Actors are among those included as "men of honor." In the actor's realm, "cardboard swords and sabers" ["las espadas y los sables de cartón"] are used in order to "act like a gentleman" ["para presumir de caballero"]. Although Ajonjolí vows not to belong to this theatrical world, much like his elder brother Pompón, he essentially reneges on his promise (26–27). As the Elf insinuates, the "word of a King" ["Palabra de Rey"] does not bind its enunciator. A split appears that posits using the name Prince Ajonjolí in the manner of the actor using "cardboard swords and sabers"—as a "trick" ["tramoya"] to make one appear to be a Prince. The language reflects the fact that, onstage, the actors are distinct from their role:

> As he is acting, he [the actor] appears to us as a sum of gestures, attitudes, intonations which we identify as signs aiming at the fulfillment of the referential function; but, paradoxically, we identify them as such only when they fail in that function, i.e., when, for various reasons, we lose contact with the referent elsewhere, say Hamlet in Elsinore, and return to the signifier on the stage, the Actor here and now.[42]

Ajonjoli's revelation of a breach is further confirmed by Verdemar, who shows the actor to be an ever-stalking presence in *CdD*. In asserting the integrity of his word as Prince—"Elf, give me the ball and I will behave [fulfill my word] as an honest man, as a gentleman, and as Prince" ["Duende, dame la pelota, y cumpliré como hombre de bien, como caballero y como Príncipe"] (28)—Verdemar uses the "word" of the three levels earlier distinguished by Ajonjolí. In so doing, Verdemar incorporates the word of the actor into his own. The enunciation shows how it is distinct from its enunciator: "Discourse no longer has the form of a homogeneous block."[43] The marks of stage identity are constantly reaffirmed to allay, in part, the effects of a violence that threatens the very nature of dramatic identity.

---

42. Jean Alter, "Performance and performance: On the Margin of Theatre Semiotics," *Degrés* 30 (1982): d-9.

43. Patrice Pavis, "On Brecht's Notion of Gestus," *Languages of the Stage* (New York: Performing Arts Journal Publications, 1982), 45.

4
Dissemination

Provenance

In the closing days of 1922, Valle-Inclán responds to Cipriano Rivas Cherif's query concerning theatre:

> I sincerely believe that the shame of the theatre is a consequence of the total disaster of a people, historically. Theatre is not an individual art, it still maintains some of the religious effusion that raised the cathedrals. It is a result of the liturgy and architecture of the Middle Ages. Without a great people infused with common ideas or sorrows, there cannot be theatre. There can be poets, philosophers, critics, novelists and painters. But not dramaturges nor architects. They are collective arts. First the Pharaohs and afterwards the pyramids. First gentlemen's honor, afterwards don Pedro Calderón. The feelings of the spectators create comedy and preempt the dramatic author.

> [Seriamente, creo que la vergüenza del teatro es una consecuencia del desastre total de un pueblo, históricamente. El teatro no es un arte individual, todavía guarda algo de la efusión religiosa que levantó las catedrales. Es una consecuencia de la liturgia y arquitectura de la Edad Media. Sin un gran pueblo, imbuído de communes ideas o dolores no puede haber teatro. Podrá haber líricos, filósofos, críticos, novelistas y pintores. Pero no dramaturgos ni arquitectos. Son artes colectivas. Primero los Faraones y las Pirámides después. Primero el honor caballeresco, después Don Pedro Calderón. El sentimiento de los espectadores crea la comedia, y aborta al autor dramático.][1]

The sentiments expressed in this letter are gestating in the period 1909–16. Valle-Inclán is not simply a renovator of theatrical lan-

---

1. In José Caamaño Bournacell, "Valle-Inclán y el concepto del teatro," *Mélanges à la mémoire d'André Joucla-Ruau*, 1 (Aix-en-Provence: Editions de l'Université de Provence, 1978), 506–7.

guage. The progressive mechanization of the characters, the role of the *didascalies* in the attritive movement against aesthetic codes and the unmasking of theatricality studied in the previous chapters are, of course, a few of the many characteristics heralding the emergence of the most innovative dramaturge in twentieth-century Spanish letters. Yet, this molder of dramatic language is acutely aware of the links between personal and collective expression. The dramaturge stands inseparable from his "people," bound to "common ideas or sorrows" by dint of his medium—language.

Valle-Inclán is at one with those who believe that language bears within its parameters the characteristics of a people: "the Gallic spirit is entirely present in the intricacies of its grammar [. . . .] Every language contains the past of its people, and the French language carries with it, along with the note of the Carmagnole, the cries of a king's agony" ["el espíritu galo está todo en los giros de su gramática [. . . .] Cada lengua contiene el pasado de su gente, y la lengua francesa lleva en sí, con las notas de la Carmañola, los gritos de la agonía de un rey"] (*La lámpara maravillosa* [*Lámpara*], 74–75). This specificity determines and limits, to a great extent, the nature of future development. "Words impose norms on thought, they chain it, they guide it, and show it unexpected paths [. . . . languages] open the rivers the emigrations of Humanity will take" ["Las palabras imponen normas al pensamiento, lo encadenan, lo guían y le muestran caminos imprevistos [. . . . los idiomas] abren los ríos por donde han de ir las emigraciones de la Humanidad"] (*Lámpara*, 78–79).

Mankind, though, does not remain a simple pawn moved by language: "Words are always a creation of the multitudes" ["Las palabras son siempre una creación de multitudes"] (61). The "original flight" ["vuelo originario"] of a certain people gives way as a "new conscience" ["nueva conciencia"] (79) evolves. Language incorporates this new consciousness, chronicling in a slow, aggrandizing fashion the ever-expanding concentric circles of a "past" ["pasado"] (75). Language, then, always stays in flux. "Languages make us" ["Los idiomas nos hacen"] while, at the same time, "we undo them" ["nosotros los deshacemos"] (79) as part of a process:

> The clashing struggle of the human soul enlarges the language prison, and, at times, its combats are so arduous that it breaks it [the prison]. And at times, languages are so entrenched in their confines that our poor souls do not find space to open their wings and other select, mystic, and subtle souls, given that they could fly, cannot express their flight.
>
> [El encontrado batallar del alma humana agranda la cárcel de los idiomas, y á veces sus combates son tan recios, que la quiebra. Y á veces los idiomas

son tan firmes en sus cercos, que nuestras pobres almas no hallan espacio para abrir las alas, y otras almas elegidas, místicas, y sutiles, dado que puedan volar, no pueden expresar su vuelo.] (79–80)

The expression of the "human soul," in particular of "select, mystic, and subtle souls"—an apt description of the superior status that Valle-Inclán accords the artist (see, for example, 48–49; 51; 91)—takes place within the "confines" of a language and, indeed, has to wage a taxing battle to expand already established delimiting frontiers. The new expansion, once incorporated, becomes the past, the "confines" confronting future generations. Expression remains entirely inseparable from previous expression. The past is linked to the future, as Valle-Inclán is wont to say throughout *Lámpara*—"the memory of what [all things] were and the embryo of what they are to be" ["el recuerdo de lo que [todas las cosas] fueron y el embrión de lo que han de ser"] (52).

When language-as-process freezes, when its prisonlike nature comes to be imposed on a people, change—the expression of the "human soul" (79) in its new "flight" (80)—is stifled and a "new conscience" (79) cannot take root.

> Sad destiny that of those races buried in the hermetic castle of their old languages like the mummies of remote Egyptian dynasties in the hollow sonority of the Pyramids. Sad are you, sons of the Latin She-Wolf on the shore of so many seas, if your lyres do not break all the chains with which the tradition of Speech imprisons you.
>
> [Triste destino el de aquellas razas enterradas en el castillo hermético de sus viejas lenguas, como las momias de las remotas dinastías egipcias, en la hueca sonoridad de las Pirámides. Tristes vosotros, hijos de la Loba Latina en la ribera de tantos mares, si vuestras liras no quebrantan todas las cadenas con que os aprisiona la tradición del Habla.] (80)

Valle-Inclán lambastes time and again Spain's fossilization of the dynamic relationship between language and expression. Spain had effectively locked herself in the parameters of a "traditional [pure] prose" ["prosa castiza"] (86). The "century that they call golden" ["siglo que llaman de oro"] (82) had become the "prison" that new expression which felt the "imperative of the hour" ["imperio de la hora"] (86) could not break. Tradition and innovation had reached a critical and fundamental impasse. The phrase, "we have to undo them [languages]" ["nosotros hemos de deshacerlos"] (80), is as much a description of the linguistic evolution of a people as a formulation of the aesthetic/ethical imperative Valle-Inclán espouses in the midst of the Spanish cultural scene. Valle-Inclán sounds the battle cry, railing against a Spanish language in radical isolation from its "people," a language that was no longer "the unanimous voice, summation of all, and the expression of a collective conscience" ["la voz unánime, suma de todas y expresión de una conciencia colectiva"] (82).

Lámpara's call for a new language—"Let us go back to living in ourselves and to create for ourselves an ardent, sincere, and cordial expression" ["Volvamos á vivir en nosotros y á crear para nosotros una expresión ardiente, sincera y cordial"] (85)—goes hand in hand with indications as to Valle-Inclán's own role in the creation of this new contemporary language: "For many years now, day by day, in that which concerns me, I work digging the cave to bury this hollow and pompous traditional [pure] prose that can no longer be ours when we write" ["Desde hace muchos años, día á día, en aquello que me atañe yo trabajo cavando la cueva donde enterrar esta hueca y pomposa prosa castiza, que ya no puede ser la nuestra cuando escribamos"] (85–86). The Galician writer consciously and purposefully links a personal aesthetic to the travails of the Spanish "collective conscience" ["conciencia colectiva"] (82). "In the first place—says [Valle-Inclán]—I believe that the supreme aspiration of art, and especially of Theatre, should be to collect, to reflect, to give the life-sensation of a people or of a race" ["En primer término—dice—yo creo que la suprema aspiración del arte, y especialmente del Teatro, debe ser recoger, reflejar, dar la sensación de la vida de un pueblo o de una raza"].[2] The interest and the need for a peculiarly Spanish aesthetic expression surface time and again (the following interview dates from 1911):

> I believe that within the weakness and atony of the national character, scenic work should revolve around invigorating our theatre. French art has excessively infiltrated the customs of the Castillian stage: in our heroic past, and more than anything, in [our] glorious tradition, there are more than enough elements to reconstruct the glorious past of the *National Art*.

> [Creo que dentro de la debilidad y atonía del carácter nacional, el laborar escénico debe girar en sentido de vigorizar nuestro teatro. El arte francés se ha infiltrado demasiado en las costumbres de la escena castellana; en nuestro hazañoso historial, y más que nada en la gloriosa tradición, hay sobrados elementos para reconstruir el pasado glorioso del *Arte Nacional*.][3]

---

2. R. del Valle-Inclán, in D. Dougherty, *Un Valle-Inclán olvidado: entrevistas y conferencias* (Madrid: Fundamentos, 1983), 61. This interview dates from 1 January 1915.

3. Dru Dougherty, *Un Valle-Inclán olvidado*, 34. Unamuno makes a telling observation in this context of the ivory tower versus the committed *Spanish* Valle-Inclán:

The theatre's singular compenetration with a "people infused with common ideas or sorrows," as indicated in the quote at the beginning of this chapter, suggests the reason behind Valle-Inclán's concentration on theatre as opposed to the novel and to lyric forms in this period—an indication of the Galician writer's commitment to remedying the fact that "Castillian does not create from its intimate substance the link with the moment that the world [now] lives" ["El habla castellana no crea de su íntima substancia el enlace con el momento que vive el mundo"] (*Lámpara*, 83).

Theatre occupies a privileged position as a vehicle for those artificers of language, who, as Valle-Inclán, "feel the imperative of the hour" (86)—those artificers who desire to break through the "language prison" (79) and have an effect on the prevalent Spanish *Weltanschauung*: "Any substantial change in language is a change in conscience, and the collective soul of [a] people is more a creation of the word than of race" ["Toda mudanza substancial en los idiomas es

---

"And above all, and before anything else, Valle-Inclán was very Spanish. Spanish above all other things" ["Y sobre todo y ante todo, Valle-Inclán fue muy español. Español por encima de todas las cosas"] (*Ahora* 7 January 1936: 9). Even such early works as *Las sonatas* evince the self-conscious awareness of Spanish identity and crisis with their constant juxtaposition of past and present, glory and debacle—the steward's pitiful need to befriend bandits in order to return the Indies to Spain and "to make Charles V Emperor" ["hacer emperador a don Carlos V"] (*Sonata de estío*, 224–27). In 1915, Valle-Inclán considers Galdós as the "redeemer of our theatre" ["redentor de nuestro teatro"]: "No one before him [Galdós] had brought to the stage the vast problems of the author of the *Episodios*" ["Nadie antes que él había traído a la escena los vastos problemas que el autor de los *Episodios*"] (D. Dougherty, *Un Valle-Inclán olvidado*, 61). Valle-Inclán regards the *Comedias bárbaras* as a historical chronicle and confesses, "I have participated in the changes of a caste society (the nobles that I knew as a boy) and what I saw, no one will see. I am the historian of a world that ended with me" ["He asistido al cambio de una sociedad de castas [los hidalgos que conocí de rapaz], y lo que yo vi no lo verá nadie. Soy el historiador de un mundo que acabó conmigo"] (in C. Rivas Cherif, "La comedia bárbara de Valle-Inclán," *España* 16 February 1924: 8). *Cuento de abril* "has its origen in a historical reality of the Galician people [....] it narrates an incident in one of the Galician Suevic king's life" ["tiene su origen en una realidad histórica del pueblo gallego [....] cuenta un episodio de uno de los reyes suevos de Galicia"] (E. González López, "*El cuento de abril* de Valle-Inclán: sus fuentes y su arte," *Revista Hispánica Moderna* 32 [1966]: 189). Valle-Inclán's theatrical discourse in this "pre-esperpéntico" period not only evinces, but works within and stands committed to (an admittedly *sui generis* conception of) Spanish concerns. In 1910, Valle-Inclán describes *Voces de gesta* as "a book of legends, of traditions, in the manner of *Cuento de abril*, but stronger, more important. I will collect the voice of an entire people. Only those books that collect wide plebeian voices are great" ["un libro de leyendas, de tradiciones, a la manera de *Cuento de abril*, pero más fuerte, más importante. Recogeré la voz de todo un pueblo. Sólo son grandes los libros que recogen voces amplias plebeyas"] (D. Dougherty, *Un Valle-Inclán olvidado*, 26).

una mudanza en las conciencias, y el alma colectiva de los pueblos, una creación del verbo más que de la raza"] (78). At the same time, the particular status of theatre within the literary hierarchy does not obscure for the Galician writer its situation in the overall context of aesthetic creation: "The arts of the eyes are simple and pleasant to know while the literary ones are exceedingly arcane. Always fleeting, always in spectres! [. . . .] Literary arts give the impression of not being defined yet, of struggling for existence" ["Son las artes de los ojos de un conocimiento fácil y placentero, y las literararias arcanas por demás. ¡Siempre alejándose, siempre en espectros! [. . . .] Las artes literarias dan la sensación de no haberse definido aún, y de luchar por ser"] (93–94). The senses are the primary means allowing the apprehension of an entity as an entity of aesthetic magnitude.[4] In particular, "All beautiful and mortal things that we create are for the eyes or for the ears alternatively" ["Todas las cosas bellas y mortales que nosotros creamos, son para los ojos ó son para los oídos, alternativamente"] (94–95). Valle-Inclán endeavors to overcome the arcaneness of literature[5] by means of these two halves of what might be denominated a "sensuous imperative." Spanish theatrical renovation begins with an adequate comprehension of "sovereign eyed eagles and listening moles [. . . .] the animals that symbolize the ways of human knowledge" ["Aguilas de ojos soberanos, y topos auditores [. . . .] las bestias que simbolizan los modos del humano conocer"] (105). For Valle-Inclán:

4. Valle-Inclán scorns the intellect time and again. See *Lámpara* 65–66, and, in this text, chapter 1, footnote 15.
5. Art must lie outside temporal limitations. As such, literature stands at a disadvantage with respect to other art forms "executed on hard, firm, almost eternal substances that through the centuries retain a matutinal grace full of evocations and of light" ["realizadas sobre substancias duras, firmes, casi eternas, que á través de los siglos perduran en una gracia matinal llena de evocaciones y de luz"] (*Lámpara*, 93). The oft-repeated image of the "crystals" ["cristales"] embodies the aesthetic/mystic symbiosis Valle-Inclán so values: "We find that things are what they are because of what they have in them that is most durable, and we love that which hoards a strength with which to oppose Time. Of all things beautiful to the eye, none more so than crystals. The eye's joy at looking at them is a sacred sentiment, because for the eye crystals do not have an age. When we think that their yesterday is a thousand years ago and that they will remain unchanged for another thousand, we feel the religious emotion of considering them outside of Time. The light of crystals has something of a prayer" ["Hallamos que las cosas son lo que son, por lo que tienen en sí de más durable, y amamos aquello donde se atesora una fuerza que oponer al Tiempo. De todas las cosas bellas para los ojos, ninguna tanto como los cristales. El goce de los ojos al mirarlos, es un sentimiento sagrado, porque para los ojos los cristales no tienen edad. Cuando pensamos que su ayer es de mil años y que permanecerán sin mudanza al cumplirse otros mil, sentimos la emoción religiosa de considerarlos fuera del Tiempo. La luz de los cristales tienen [sic] algo de oración" (45–46).

the great problem of the Spanish dramaturge consists in creating scenes, combining new forms of spectacle for the pleasure and solace of the eye. Going back to *La Celestina*, we find the variety of scenes that would be needed today [. . . .] But this is not all. The salvation of theatre in Spain depends, in addition, on another factor that is not less important [. . . .] The spirit of a language is another aspect that the dramaturge should bear in mind [. . . . a discussion follows in which French is described as a language of half-tones capable of all subtle grades of expression. In contrast to this delicate dialogue full of wit stands] the harshness of our language [. . . .] It is the character of our language that imposes these absolute and definitive forms: judgement, imprecation, insult, shout [. . . .] Two actors, from the moment they meet, speak shouting by a natural impulse [. . . .] This is, then, another of the capital terms under which definition any genuine creation desirous of touching the soul of the people must labor in our theatre. To the importance accorded to the scene, previously mentioned, it is now necessary to add that of the shout. Both demands are rooted in our most legitimate tradition and are today more imperative than ever, if our efforts at renovation are to prosper among us. Let us concretize the formula that the Spanish dramaturge has before him: scenes and shouts.

[el gran problema del dramaturgo español consiste en crear escenarios, combinar nuevas formas de espectáculo para regalo y solaz de los ojos. Remontándonos a *La Celestina* hallamos esa variedad de cuadros que hoy convendría [. . . .] Pero esto no es todo. La salvación del teatro en España depende además de otro factor no menos importante [. . . .] El espíritu de la lengua es otro aspecto que el dramaturgo debe tener muy presente [. . . .] la aspereza de nuestra habla [. . . .] Es el genio de nuestro idioma el que impone esas formas totales y definitivas: la sentencia, la imprecación, el denuesto, el grito [. . . .] Dos cómicos tan pronto se encuentran hablan a gritos por natural impulso [. . . .] Es éste pues otro de los términos capitales a cuyo régimen debe someterse en nuestro teatro toda creación genuina que aspire a tocar el alma del pueblo. A la importancia que asume el escenario, antes referida, es preciso ahora añadir la del grito. Ambas exigencias entroncan con nuestra tradición más legítima y son hoy más imperiosas que nunca, si es que madura el esfuerzo renovador entre nosotros. Concretemos la fórmula que tiene por delante el dramaturgo español: escenarios y gritos.][6]

These observations lie at the basis of the ceaseless conflicts structuring *La cabeza del dragón*. One moment denies or in some manner opposes or foils another in a pattern of complex shifts. A theatre of linear development is eschewed in favor of a theatre of constant, intricate movement, reflecting even on an intrascenic level the variety and contrast that Valle-Inclán regards as essential for a theatre that touches "the soul of a people." More precisely, these series of sharp,

---

6. D. Dougherty, *Un Valle-Inclán olvidado*, 185–86.

stark contrasts evince the peculiarities of the Spanish language: "Our theatre cannot deny that it is born in Castille" ["Nuestro teatro no puede negar que nace en Castilla"],[7] and the Castillian language requires "absolute and definitive forms."[8] Insinuation, the gradual development and revelation of a characteristic, remains anathema to Valle-Inclán. "[I]mprecation, insult, shout"[9] comprise the crucial factors to be considered when determining the form of the *new* theatre. The continuous unsettling contrast that stamps Valle-Inclán's production reveals the extent to which his theatre is shaped by and bound to the Spanish context.

Proposition and Development

The Galician's commitment to theatrical change[10] goes hand in hand with a detailed grasp of the obstacles to this change: the conventions regulating Spanish dramatic discourse. *El Embrujado: Tragedia de Tierras de Salnés* (*Embrujado*) is eloquent in this regard. This work, judging from the little critical attention it has received, would at first appear to be of a traditional nature and of scant importance and repercussion in Valle-Inclán's oeuvre.[11] Nevertheless, Valle-Inclán's 1927 return to the work originally published in 1913 (its inclusion in *Retablo de la avaricia, la lujuria y la muerte,* published in 1927) as well as the rigor and interest with which Valle-Inclán oversees its pro-

---

7. R. de Valle-Inclán, in John Lyon, *The Theatre of Valle-Inclán* (Cambridge: Cambridge University Press, 1983), 207.
8. See also, in this text, chapter 1, footnote 25.
9. See D. Dougherty, *Un Valle-Inclán olvidado,* 156, for an interview with Valle-Inclán in which these characteristics are again mentioned in the context of Catalan and Castillian differences.
10. As Valle-Inclán admits to C. Rivas Cherif, "I am always a young revolutionary" ["Yo soy siempre un joven revolucionario"] (J. Caamaño Bournacell, "Valle-Inclán y el concepto del teatro," 506).
11. M. Bermejo Marcos, for example, takes the view: "Half a century later, and judging the work with all objectivity, one must recognize that if it is true that Galdós rejected it solely on critical grounds [*Embrujado* was rejected for the repertoire of the Teatro Español and a polemic with Galdós ensued. See D. Dougherty, *Un Valle-Inclán olvidado,* 37–44], he was not lacking in justification: the tragedy is not of the quality its author assumed [. . . .] all that the author wants to be tragic does not go beyond melodrama, and not infrequently, [appears] false [. . . .] the dramatic result is poor" ["A medio siglo de distancia, y juzgada la obra con toda objetividad, hay que reconocer, si es cierto que Galdós la rechazó solamente por su juicio crítico, que no le faltó razón: la tragedia no tiene la calidad que su autor le suponía [. . . .] cuanto el autor quiere que resulte trágico no pasa de ser melodramático y no pocas veces falso [. . . .] El resultado dramático es pobre"] (*Valle-Inclán; introducción a su obra* [Salamanca: Anaya, 1971], 178–79). See also, in this chapter, footnote 31.

duction in 1931, years after the *esperpento*,[12] suggest another aspect to *Embrujado*: the work's continued relevance and (potential) variance with regard to prevailing theatrical practices. An innovatory essence comes guised in a semblance of traditional garb.[13]

A clear societal framework prevails in *Embrujado*. Don Pedro presides, semifeudally, over a group of servants and tenants. Duty and function are determined by a rigid class division.[14] The evasion or the inability to fulfill one's societal role has fateful consequences. Don Pedro, for example, wants descendants, a desire that leads him to bow before the exigencies of Rosa Galana[15] and accept her illegitimate son as his grandchild. Yet class pride comes to the fore, overriding at times his need for a grandchild: as don Pedro states to Rosa, "[o]ur blood cannot mix [. . . .] I had proposed either my blood or yours. Yours has won, Rosa Galans. You take your son and I bury all the love of an old man" ["Nuestra sangre no puede mezclarse [. . . .] Había propuesto que mi sangre ó la tuya. La tuya ha vencido, Rosa Galans. Te llevas á tu hijo y yo entierro todos mis amores de viejo"]

---

12. I. López Heredia, in D. Dougherty, *Un Valle-Inclán olvidado*, 217. See also, on the same page, J. Romero Cuesta's observation that Valle-Inclán went to the rehearsals "daily, always worried about the most minute detail, or what could appear to be minute" ["diariamente, siempre preocupado por el detalle más nimio, o que pudiera parecer nimio"].

13. The disjunction between the actual staging (according to the conventions of the period) and the *mise en scène* potential implicit in Valle-Inclán's plays, *Embrujado* in this case, is particularly evident, of course, in *La Marquesa Rosalinda* (*MR*). The review of a 1912 production comments that *MR* "opened successfully" ["[fue] estrenada con éxito"] and attributes an important part of the play's success to "the direction and presentation" ["la dirección y presentación"] of María Guerrero and Fernando Díaz de Mendoza (F. Alonso, *Nuevo Mundo* 7 March, 1912: N.p.). The auspicious reception of the work contrasts with Valle-Inclán's negative assessment: the interviewer states that *MR* "opened" ["se estrenó"], while Valle-Inclán reticently admits, "Yes . . . it was . . . staged. I think that neither Díaz de Mendoza nor any of his colleagues understood it. María Guerrero hardly recited the verses as I wrote them. // And the audience, don Ramón? // I think that what happened to the director happened to the audience. Well, one should not put the blame on the spectators. They did not hear my work. That is why I am hoping for the book to come out. I do not enjoy looking like a maker of absurdities" ["Sí . . . se puso . . . en escena. Creo que ni Díaz de Mendoza ni ninguno de sus compañeros la entendió. Apenas si María Guerrero dijo los versos como yo los escribí. // Y el público, don Ramón? // Al público creo que le sucedió lo mismo que al director. Bueno, no hay que echar el sambenito sobre los espectadores. Ellos no oyeron mi obra. Por eso estoy deseando que salga el libro. No me es grato aparecer como hacedor de disparates"] (D. Dougherty, *Un Valle-Inclán olvidado*, 46).

14. J. P. Borel remarks that on one level *Embrujado* "is a struggle between two social classes as represented in Rosa and in don Pedro" ["es una lucha entre dos clases sociales, representadas en Rosa y en don Pedro"] (*El teatro de lo imposible* [Madrid: Ediciones Guadarrama, 1966], 208).

15. Notice that the characters frequently refer to Rosa Galana as Rosa Galans.

(*Embrujado*, 60 – 61). Class consciousness and psychological needs clash, causing don Pedro's torment.

When The Blind Man's Girl urges Anxelo to adhere to Rosa's scheme and to dupe don Pedro, she stresses the possibility of becoming a gentleman: "You are to look like a gentleman with your tobacco pouch full and your silver watch" ["Tú á estar hecho un caballero con tu petaca llena y tu reloj de plata"] (83). Anxelo does indeed flee the strictures of his class, that of a common worker tilling the land. The possibility of changing social classes, then, is formulated, yet the rigid distinctions are conserved. Ignoring his duties marks the beginning of Anxelo's plunge into the demonic, leading him into contact with Rosa:

> *The Blind Man's Girl* — Singing and laughing were never sins.
> *Anxelo* — That is what the Devil says. But to laugh and to sing, one must be idle and leave the ground untilled. And from not sowing comes not having bread, and stealing, and killing.
>
> [*La Moza del Ciego* — Cantar y reír nunca fué pecado.
> *Anxelo* — Eso dice el Demonio. Pero para reír y cantar hay que holgar y dejar la tierra sin cavar. Y del no sembrar viene el no tener pan, y el robar y el matar.] (78)

The social order resembles, to a striking degree, the order depicted in *Comedias bárbaras* (*Comedias*), as critics have noted:

> [*Embrujado*] Belongs in Valle-Inclán's theatre to the series of works with a Galician milieu that gather primitive feelings from the farmland [. . .] and bring to the dramatic stage a play of elemental passions, barbaric greatness, and base instincts, between which the spark of tragedy jumps, over which the most inflexible tradition gravitates, with all its weight, like fate.
>
> [Corresponde en el teatro de Valle-Inclán a esa serie de obras de ambiente gallego, que recogen del agro los sentimientos primitivos [. . .] y traen al retablo dramático un juego de pasiones elementales, de bárbaras grandezas y bajos instintos, entre los cuales salta la chispa de la tragedia, sobre la que gravita con todo su peso, como una fatalidad, la tradición más inflexible.][16]

Yet, although *Embrujado* takes place within the confines of a strict and inflexible tradition, it does not share the rampant primitiveness and arbitrariness of passions found in the *Comedias*. An emphatic stress on the aristocracy and the intrinsic superiority of the aristocratic mode pervades the *Comedias*. Don Juan Manuel's three sons,

---

16. E. Díez Canedo, *Artículos de crítica teatral. El teatro español de 1914 a 1936*, vol. 4 (México: Joaquín Mortiz, 1968), 28.

for example, who are a shame to their lineage, put to flight a large crowd of commoners (*Romance de lobos*, 172–82)—the difference between the two classes is evident even in the context of "unworthy" aristocrats. In *Embrujado*, on the other hand, don Pedro's haughtiness in dealing with Rosa—"Our blood cannot mix" (*Embrujado*, 60)—derives as much from his pride ("he always was very zealous of his priviliges" ["siempre fué muy celoso de su fuero"] [116]) as from his greediness. Pride as a motive for the protection of his priviliges ["fuero"], terms with a somewhat alien resonance to a bourgeois mentality, come to be replaced by a universally comprehensible motive—the desire to hold on to one's possessions. More pointedly, references to don Pedro as a "peasant" ["labrador"] [35, 62]) thwart any aristocratic notion of innate distinctiveness; lineage does not determine don Pedro's class stature. Whereas don Juan Manuel makes his own laws, scorning the legalities of courts as "an invention good for women, for children, and for old men whose hands tremble" ["una invención buena para las mujeres, para los niños y para los viejos que tienen temblonas las manos"] (*Aguila de blasón*, 146–47), don Pedro's reaction when confronted with the probable assassins of his son is "I will ask for justice" ["Pediré justicia"] (*Embrujado*, 132). His respect for the legal code resembles that of an entrenched bourgeois, in complete distinction to don Juan Manuel. Only after Juana de Juno insinuates a questionable relationship between Rosa and the "court" ["curia"] (31) and after La Navora indicates the impossibility of obtaining justice through a legal system controlled by this "court" (133) does don Pedro threaten to take justice in his own hands (133). Don Pedro remains very much an accessible character, malleable, in spite of the Galician ambience he inhabits, to bourgeois strictures. Valle-Inclán opens the impenetrable Galician primitivism of the *Comedias bárbaras*, rendering it more comprehensible to an urban audience. Although still within the confines of a semifeudal social and moral order, don Pedro's behavior, his reactions and his desire for children are an onstage manifestation of what the bourgeois order largely condones.

The active desire to elicit (bourgeois) empathic reaction translates into the play's foregrounded emotional overtones—the pity aroused by don Pedro's suffering as a result of Rosa's schemes. The pathos stands marked by the change from what he was: "Don Pedro Bolaño is unrecognizable! That generous smile he had for poor and rich, he buried it with the the son they killed!" ["¡No es conocido Don Pedro Bolaño! ¡Aquella risa tan liberal para los pobres y ricos la enterró con el hijo que le mataron!"] (27–28). After his son's death, the Abuela and the Cabezalero attribute stinginess to don Pedro (16–19).

That don Pedro's miserliness stems from his constant caviling, doubts, and grief becomes evident when he combines stinginess— threatening one of his tenants for not paying on time (124)—with generosity—exchanging the Abuela's two meager corncobs (16, 123–24) for a whole bread (125), or taking pity on a hard-pressed family (128–29). Rosa Galana's effort to deprive him of descendants lies at the basis of the erraticism. The urge for a fruitful procreation (after many failed efforts [138]) drives don Pedro. He rebukes doña Isoldina for adopting "the manners of a printed book" ("los modos de libro impreso" [45]) with respect to don Miguel (don Pedro's son). Against the stock responses of doña Isoldina, "You never love more than once in your life" ["No se quiere más que una vez en la vida"], don Pedro presents a more elemental force: "One loves always: The young woman [loves] the young man and the old man [loves] the child" ["Se quiere siempre: La moza al mozo, y el viejo al niño"] (120). Don Pedro makes explicit that the right to offspring is being denied him. Though he claims the status of grandfather, both Juana de Juno and Mauriña go out of their way to state quite explicitly that Anxelo, not don Miguel, fathered the child (32; 71; 75). In reality, the child's paternity matters little, as don Pedro admits near the end: "What does it matter if it was a hoax" ["Qué importa que fuese engaño"] (138).[17] He would have married Isoldina "with another man and raise[d] your children as my grandchildren. . . That is what should have been!" ["con otro hombre y criar vuestros hijos como mis nietos. . . ¡Eso debió ser!"] (120). The psychological axis on which don Pedro functions remains fixed, and it is in the broad terms of offspring—"one loves always [. . .] the old man [loves] the young child" (120)—that he speaks. Don Pedro, incarnating the good, natural desire to have and claim descendants stands against Rosa, the evil, unnatural force opposing this desire. The readily condoned and *sosegante* elements binding society in a unit are pitted against a destructive, unwanted, and *desasosegante* presence.

Valle-Inclán's experimentation with the features of conventional theatre—the use and manipulation of elements easily allowing an audience presence/identification—is, in the context of the demonic, witchlike attributes that Rosa brings to the stage, particularly significant in Valle-Inclán's evolution. There are precedents, of course, for an onstage supernatural presence. The bewitchment of the pregnant woman and the midnight ritual performed by Sabelita in order to break the spell cast in the apple (*Aguila de blasón*, 199–210) show the effects of witches' power. Moreover, the likelihood that such a

17. See also *Embrujado,* 33, where don Pedro appears to know of the hoax concerning the child's paternity according to the other characters.

demonic world may reveal itself comes to be voiced. The Marquis is advised not to sit outside at night under the moonlight because of witches (*El Marqués de Bradomín*, 104 –5). Nonetheless, these allusions to the supernatural, in spite of their relative frequency, are relegated to one basic function: they constitute the ambience, the pseudo-mythical Celtic atmosphere of the plays.[18] The extent to which the supernatural forms a background is highlighted in *El Marqués de Bradomín* by the figure of the outsider, the Marquis. Galicia and its feudal lore interest the aristocrat in a contemplative fashion, as part of a static, yet piquant, picturesque. The earlier *Comedias bárbaras* (*Aguila de blasón* and *Romance de lobos*) play on the dichotomy of the servants/masters in a similar fashion. Goblins, devils, and witches are invoked in the servants' world and aristocratic activity, to a great extent, merely remains on the borders of this world. The role of the supernatural remains ancillary, the center of dramatic interest is elsewhere.

The treatment of the demonic in *Embrujado* differs substantially from that in previous works, with two main effects. First, the supernatural ceases to be confined to the realm of the merely ambience-creating backdrop. The demonic, up until this moment closely tied to Galician tradition, stands distanced from its Galician moorings. Rosa simply incarnates a terrifying supernatural and her function is to manifest this as clearly and as visibly as possible onstage. *Embrujado* constitutes the first and the essential step that allows the demonic to be linked to the mystic, transcendent overtones Valle-Inclán later utilizes in *Cara de plata* (*Cara*), for example and the whole motif of the *Comedias bárbaras*—don Juan Manuel's quest for spiritual salvation.[19] *Cara* reunites and overwhelmingly affirms the satanic overtones implicit in the characterization of don Juan Manuel ("I am afraid of being the Devil!" ["¡Tengo miedo de ser el Diablo!"]

---

18. E. S. Speratti-Piñero, "Los brujos de Valle-Inclán," *Nueva Revista de Filología Hispánica* 21.1 (1972): 40–70, gives a thorough account of the correlation between Galician superstitions and the witchlike in Valle-Inclán's works. See also: D. McGrady, "Elementos folclóricos en tres obras de Valle-Inclán," *Thesaurus* 25.1 (1970): 49–58; R. Seeleman, "Folkloric Elements in Valle-Inclán," *Hispanic Review* 3.2 (1935): 103–19.

19. "The *Comedias bárbaras* narrate the history of the spiritual disintegration and reintegration of the feudal hero [. . . .] Valle-Inclán wants to beget a new conscience, seeking man's redemption, incarnated in the transgressor [. . .] don Juan Manuel Montenegro" ["Las *Comedias bárbaras* cuentan la historia de la desintegración y reintegración espiritual del héroe feudal [. . . .] Valle-Inclán quiere engendrar una nueva conciencia, buscando la redención del hombre, encarnado en el transgresor [. . .] don Juan Manuel Montenegro"] (W. Williamson, "Las *Comedias bárbaras* de Valle-Inclán: estudio temático, estructural y estilístico," diss., Indiana University, 1972: 139, 89–90).

[*Cara*, 275]), thus infusing new significance to his earlier pronouncement, "God orders me to repent for all my sins... An entire life! An entire life!" ["Dios me ordena que me arrepienta de mis pecados... ¡Todo una vida! ¡Todo una vida!"] (*Romance de lobos*, 69), as well as to his pilgrimage to Doña María's manor. The issue is not only repentance, but purification—the transformation from sin to an exalted state, from an intrinsically satanic self to a new, redeemed self. The demonic in *Cara* endows the quest motif of the *Comedias bárbaras* with profound implications, and as Díaz Plaja points out:

> all this conception of the demonic has nothing—or very little—to do with the belief in ghosts, characteristic of the Galician other world. It is a transcendent conception that proceeds conjointly from the most unsettling Romantic sources and cabalistic fonts
>
> [toda esta concepción de lo demoníaco no tiene nada que ver—o muy poco—con la creencia de lo espectral, característica del ultramundo galaico. Es una concepción trascendente que, procede a la vez de los fondos más inquietantes del Romanticismo unidos a las fuentes cabalísticas].[20]

Second, as the projection of a *desasosegante* supernatural, Rosa Galana undermines the *sosegante* and indicates the theatre's right to its own privacy. This proclamation of a slowly affirmed autonomous stage is symptomatically revealed with the child's death at the end of *Embrujado*, for without descendants, the entire semifeudal order represented by don Pedro Bolaño collapses. Rosa's triumph implies the complete ascendancy of the destructive, the rejected, and the feared over the *sosegante*. Audience presence, in the elements, desires and order exemplified or espoused by don Pedro, succumbs, crushed by the one part of the stage world that remains irreducible, imposing its own unwantedness.

Valle-Inclán thus makes use of the unsettling presence Rosa imparts to the stage, in other words, to assert that the theatre operates within its own functional parameters. Conventional drama highlights the importance of female characters:

> But it is possible that with reference to the "character" sign, the decisive codes were those of masculine and feminine. The first governed the

---

20. G. Díaz Plaja, *Las estéticas de Valle-Inclán* (Madrid: Gredos, 1965), 120. Romantic fonts are tapped with great effect in the opening scene of *Romance de lobos*: The "Holy Brotherhood of the souls in penance" ["Santa Compañía de las ánimas en pena"] vividly reminds don Juan Manuel of his sins and of his need to repent in a manner reminiscent of Espronceda's *Estudiante de Salamanca* or of the *Miserere* ending the Duque de Rivas's *Don Alvaro o La fuerza del sino*.

woman-house-intimacy correspondence and the attributes of the woman as mother, wife, and daughter; the second associated man with the exterior and with authority [. . . .] The less conventional theatre never failed to present a conflict without resolution between characters and space, between woman and house [. . . . yet even] the most daring works recovered in some way, in the last analysis, the old gender paradigm with its consequences of family, home, masculine functions and feminine functions.

[Pero es posible que, en lo referente al signo "personajes", los códigos decisivos fueran el de lo masculino y el de lo femenino. El primero dictaminaba la correspondencia mujer-casa-intimidad y los atributos de la mujer como madre, esposa e hija; el segundo relacionaba al hombre con el exterior y la autoridad [. . . .] El teatro menos convencional presentaba infaliblemente un conflicto sin restauración entre personajes y espacio, entre la mujer y la casa [. . . .] las obras más atrevidas recuperaban de algún modo, en último término, el antiguo paradigma de los géneros, con sus consecuencias de familia, hogar, funciones masculinas y funciones femeninas.][21]

Even in such works as the *Comedias bárbaras*, so unacceptable to contemporary stage practices, "feminine functions" still remain essentially conventional. Doña María plays an especially revelatory role in this regard, serving as the traditional center, the axis around which the actions of her husband, don Juan Manuel, to a certain extent, revolve.

These conventions are undermined, however, in *Embrujado*.[22] Only doña Isoldina embodies the familiar values associated with the home (117–18), even though her (unconsummated) role as wife remains usurped by Rosa's illegitimate affair with don Miguel. Rosa breaks with the traditional stage conception of the feminine. Not once does she appear indoors. The intimacy of the home is replaced by the "small inn" ["ventorrillo"] (92)—Rosa's house—a public abode where rest is transitory. Her obligations, even as an illegitimate wife, are scorned when she betrays her putative husband don Miguel, and in all likelihood knew of or even contributed to his death (52–53; 144–45). As mother, she shows only unconcern and the desire to turn maternity into a source of income. Rosa not only breaks the feminine paradigm and contravenes the (expected) actions of the ordinary evil-doer, she

---

21. Luis Fernández Cifuentes, "García Lorca y el teatro convencional," *Iberoromania* 17 (1983): 71–73.

22. Dominant cultural assumptions with respect to femininity are explored in several of Valle-Inclán's previous texts, such as in the short story *Eulalia* in which they are contrasted with a mythical, prelapsarian world. See C. Nickel, "Recasting the Image of the Fallen Woman in Valle-Inclán's *Eulalia*," *Studies in Short Fiction* 24.3 (1987): 289–94. See also L. Ramos Kuethe, "El concepto de libertinismo en la narrativa temprana de don Ramón del Valle-Inclán," *Hispanic Journal* 4.2 (1983): 51–63.

enters the realm of melodramatic exaggeration as "a projection of 'irrational' fear."²³ In the words of one of the tenants, "[Rosa] Is a monster, and as such, evolves a bestial part. He who went hunting with that woman in the mountains and shot some game recently died" ["Es monstruo, y como tal desenvuelve una parte de bestia. Murió poco ha quien con esa mujer en el monte cazó y pieza cobró"] (63).

Rosa becomes less an individual than the projection or incarnation of evil itself, as the imagery of the play suggests. *Embrujado* opens with foreboding anaphoras about a rabid dog:²⁴

> *Juana de Juno* — Where did the dog bite her?
> *The Grandmother* — She was a shepardess in Lugar de Condes.
>   She was a shepardess!
> *Juana de Juno* — Where was it that the dog bit her?
> *The Grandmother* — Where was it that the dog bit her? In her own face!... In her own face!..."
>
> [Juana de Juno — ¿Dónde le mordió el can?
> La Abuela — Era pastora en Lugar de Condes.
>   ¡Era pastora!
> Juana de Juno — ¿Qué dónde le mordió el can?
> La Abuela — ¿Qué dónde le mordió el can? ¡En la misma cara!
>   ... ¡En la misma cara!...]   (15)

The play ends with the barks of "three white dogs" ["tres perros blancos"] (147), eloquent testimony to the bewitchment of Anxelo and Mauriña. Two more dogs—Anxelo and Mauriña under Rosa's spell—join the white dog that appears just before Rosa's final entrance. She is associated time and again with the dog, both by the author—"Rosa Galans appears [. . . .] A dog barks with fury" ["Aparece Rosa Galans [. . . .] Ladra con furia un perro"] (95)—and by the characters: Anxelo is speaking,

> Returning from mowing, the sun already set, a barking dog came upon me on the path with its eyes on fire. I hit it with my clog and it ran away with a howl that filled the darkness of the night like the voice of an imprisoned

---

23. E. Bentley, *The Life of the Drama* (London: Methuen & Co., 1965), 203.
24. Valle-Inclán accords the canine special importance. From *El miedo* to the *Los cuernos de don Friolera*, "[r]are is the work of Valle-Inclán where a dog does not appear" ["Rara es la obra de Valle-Inclán donde no aparezca un perro"] (M. A. Sanz Cuadrado, "*Flor de santidad* y *Aromas de leyenda*: estudio comparativo," *Cuadernos de literatura contemporánea* 18 [1946]: 522). In *Embrujado*, Valle-Inclán makes use of "[t]he traditional association between dogs and death," and a world of "ineffable realities" (Catherine A. Nickel, "Ramón del Valle-Inclán's *Retablo de la avaricia, la lujuria y la muerte*: The One-Act Plays," diss., U of Nebraska—Lincoln, [1985]: 26, 25). See, in this text, chapter three, footnote 22.

[wretched] woman. A little futher on, I find a small inn and her [Rosa] sitting at the door [. . . . Rosa] spat on her fingers, revived the wick of the lamp, and putting the light to my face she asked me, without moving her mouth: Who did you find on the path? And in that moment, I recognize in her voice, the howl of the dog when I hit its head with the clog. From then on, I was unable to leave her circle!

[Volviendo de la siega, ya puesto el sol, salióme al camino un can ladrando, los ojos en lumbre. Le di con el zueco y escapó dando un alarido que llenó la oscuridad de la noche como la voz de una mujer cautiva. A poco andar, descubro un ventorrillo y á ella sentada en la puerta [. . . .] Escupió en los dedos, espabiló el candil, y poniéndome la luz en la cara, me dijo sin mover la boca: ¿A quién topaste en el camino? Y en aquel momento, yo reconozco en su voz el alarido del perro al darle en la cabeza la zocada. ¡Ya no pude salir de su rueda!] (92–93)

Rosa can change form and appear in different guises. Specificity per se disembodies. As character, Rosa is subsumed under the desire to project satanic forces. Anxelo wants to redeem his soul (71) and confess his role in the murder of don Pedro's son ("my hands stained with blood" ["mis manos manchadas de sangre"] [74]). On the verge of confessing—"I will save my soul declaring the whole truth" ["Yo salvaré mi alma, declarando toda la verdad"] (74)—he is prevented from doing so by the "howling dog" ["can que aulla"] (140–41) that precedes Rosa's appearance on the scene. She forestalls his act of contrition in order to achieve salvation, leading both Anxelo and his wife "To Hell!" ["¡A los Infiernos!"] (146). Rosa prevents Christian sacraments—confession, absolution, and redemption—from taking place and instead casts her own binding spell.

The evil as well as the stable and commendable elements of *Embrujado* are welldefined. The importance lies in the characters' ability to ensure that these elements are manifested onstage. The tension in *Embrujado*, like that in all melodrama, derives from the simple enactment of a paradigm, not from the questioning of its parameters:

it is important that, in talking of [melodrama's] affective structure [. . . .] we not be deluded into thinking we are referring to the psychological structures of melodrama's characters. There is no "psychology" in melodrama in this sense; the characters have no interior depth, there is no psychological conflict. It is delusive to seek an interior conflict, the "psychology of melodrama," because melodrama exteriorizes conflict and psychic structure, producing instead what we might call the "melodrama of psychology."[25]

25. P. Brooks, *The Melodramatic Imagination* (New Haven: Yale University Press, 1976), 35.

Anxelo appears at first sight a complex, tortured character fraught with guilt due to his role in the murder. He projects his feelings onto his "soul" ["ánima"], and speaks with his conscience, repeatedly stressing his need to confess (see 68–71). Yet, the remorse he feels derives less from the guilt due to Miguel's murder than from his inability to warn Rosa's potential followers of the danger they confront:

> Every new young man the serpent [Rosa] takes into her company is a remorse for me on account of not being able to warn [dissuade] him of the deceit [. . . .] It is the remorse of letting a young man walk blindly straight to the gallows... The soul of the dead man, when it appears to me, accuses me mainly of this. It accuses me more for this than for his shed blood!

> [Cada nuevo mozo de quien se acompaña la serpiente es para mí un remordimiento, por no poder desengañarle [. . . .] Es remordimiento de dejar á un hombre mozo caminar ciego de cara á la horca... El alma del muerto, cuando se me aparece, nada me culpa tanto. ¡Más me culpa por ello que por su sangre derramada!] (83–84)

The psychological complexity of a moral quandary—the reflection that might enhance the character's autonomy—here cedes place to the melodramatic need to show the clash between good and evil. Anxelo has one principal role: to ensure without ambiguity the strength of Rosa's supernatural powers.

In a like manner, don Pedro forms part of this melodramatic world. The ambiguity as to the identity of those involved in the death of don Miguel surfaces time and again throughout the play. Innuendos about the role played by doña Isoldina's family (44–45) or about don Miguel's smuggling activities (48–49) abound. Someone continues to pay the Blind Man to recite verses with "more venom than a green scorpion" ["más veneno que un verde alacrán"] (25). The members of don Pedro's household incessantly mention possible culprits (28–29; 47–49). Malvín appears particularly intent on finding who is responsible for the Blind Man's verses: "Another fox plots them without leaving its lair. But be it from the head, be it from the tail, I will reveal it" ["Otro raposo las urde sin salir del tobo. Más sea de la cabeza, sea del rabo, yo lo he de sacar"] (26). Don Pedro remains aloof from these concerns and even rebukes Malvín: "Leave to God what pertains to God!" ["¡Deja sus incumbencias á Dios!"] (26). Don Pedro's subsequent (fruitless) questioning of the Blind Man reveals one sole preoccupation—that the poison of the verses might deter him from recognizing the child's legitimacy. "Your stories and those of others might frighten from my soul the love that I have placed in that child. If you achieve this, may your tongues be wrenched out! Cursed be you!" ["Acaso las historias tuyas y de otros espanten de mi alma el amor que tengo puesto en ese niño. ¡Si tal conseguís, arrancadas se vean vuestras lenguas! ¡Malditos seáis!"] (38). The questions do not lead to new evidence about don Miguel's murder, they simply vent the hatred don Pedro feels toward those elements blocking his adoption of Rosa's son. His life centers around the child: "Look at me, who cannot live without this grandchild outside of the church" ["Mírame á mí, que no puedo vivir sin ese nieto de tras la Iglesia"] (120). Doubts and vacillation are unknown. "The singleness of feeling that gives one the sense of wholeness,"[26] a feature instrinsic to melodrama, is that of *Embrujado*:

> The issue [. . . in melodrama] is not the reordering of the self, but the reordering of one's relations with others, with the world of people or things; not the knowledge of self but the maintenance of self, in its assumption of wholeness, until conflicts are won or lost. (Heilman, 86)

Interior strife stands waived and comes to be replaced by an emphasis on the sheer interplay, the visualization, of a struggle.

The dramatis persona in tragedy characterizes an individual and portrays a psyche. In melodrama, the dramatis persona projects "human laughableness, human loathsomeness, and human admirableness, as these are commonly identified in the author's day."[27] While tragedy needs to be understood, melodrama strives to be seen; the stress lies on how good and evil are intertwined—the diction, tone, gesture, and pathos of the embranglement. As a result, melodrama can be regarded as "drama in its elemental form; it is the quintessence of drama."[28] Melodrama "handles its feelings and ideas virtually as plastic entities, visual and tactile models held out for us all to see and to handle. Emotions are given a full acting-out, a full representation before our eyes."[29] Theatre comes to be displayed in immediately apprehensible terms. None other than Artaud, the promoter

---

26. R. B. Heilman, *Tragedy and Melodrama* (Seattle: University of Washington Press, 1968), 85. A. Lewis de Galanes notes the characters "singleness of feeling" (what Heilman denominates a "monopathic" nature) in the context of an issue of cosmic import: "*El Embrujado* is a tragedy to embody a situation of universal transcendence: evil in presence and reality that perseveres in its being without change" ["*El Embrujado* es una tragedia por corporeizar una situación de trascendencia universal: el mal en presencia y realidad que persevera en su ser sin modificarse"] ("El retablo de maese Valle-Inclán," *Revista de Estudios Hispánicos* 3.1 [1969]: 24–25).

27. R. B. Heilman, *Tragedy and Melodrama*, 78.
28. E. Bentley, *The Life of the Drama*, 216.
29. P. Brooks, *The Melodramatic Imagination*, 41.

of the "total spectacle [. . . .] a spectacle that addresses itself to the entire organism" ["spectacle total [. . . .] un spectacle qui s'adresse à l'organisme entier"], defends the validity of melodrama: "and I defy anyone to show me *here* a valid spectacle, and valid in the supreme sense of theatre, after the last great romantic melodramas" ["et je défie qu'on me montre *ici* un spectacle valable, et valable dans le sens suprême du théâtre, depuis les derniers grands mélodrames romantiques"].[30]

Don Pedro's expression of need for a grandchild, Anxelo's terror, Mauriña's fear reiterated time and again, the plasticity with which the subject Rosa/the demonic comes to be manifested—all exemplify the abandonment of psychological drama and the development of interior traits, in favor of an "exteriorization" of individuation as the characters stand, essentially helpless, in the grips of a "performance" that ensures complete and unambiguous apprehension. The melodramatic cast and tone explored in *Embrujado* foreshadow the stage characteristics of Valle-Inclán's subsequent works, as the 1927 inclusion of *Embrujado* with *Retablo de la avaricia, la lujuria y la muerte* suggests.[31]

---

30. A. Artaud, "En finir avec les chefs d'oeuvre," *Le Théâtre et son double* (Paris: Gallimard, 1964), 118. The preceding quotation in the body of the text comes from an essay in the same volume: "Le Théâtre de la cruauté," 134–35.

31. Both *La rosa de papel* and *La cabeza del bautista*, for example, are subtitled "Melodrama para marionetas." Nonetheless, this inclusion strikes many critics as forced. S. Greenfield states that *Embrujado*'s link with the other works of *Retablo* remains "basically thematic [. . . .] But in spite of the formal interrelation of *El Embrujado* with the four pieces written with the mature valleinclanesque technique of the other period 1920–1930, the tragedy is, after all, a naive work of another period of Valle-Inclán, already long gone in 1927" ["basicamente temática [. . . .] Pero a pesar de la interrelación formal de *El Embrujado* con las cuatro piezas escritas con la madura técnica valleinclanesca de la otra época 1920–1930, la tragedia es, a fin de cuentas, una obra ingenua de otra época de Valle-Inclán, ya bien desvanecida en 1927"] (*Valle-Inclán: Anatomía de un teatro problemático* [Madrid: Fundamentos, 1972], 134). The play's melodramatic characteristics receive little attention: "a forced melodrama is badly integrated with a profusion of stylized and not very original mannerisms" ["un melodrama forzado está mal integrado con una profusión de estilizaciones amaneradas y no muy originales"] (Greenfield, 134). E. González López remarks: "*El Embrujado*, united to the other four dramatic works of this *Retablo* by the role played in the work by the three powers that move Humanity (avarice, lust, and death), belongs to a dramatic art distinct from the other four works that accompany it in this volume" ["*El Embrujado*, unido a las otras cuatro obras dramáticas de este *Retablo* por el papel que juegan en él los tres poderes que mueven a la Humanidad (la avaricia, la lujuria y la muerte), pertenece a un arte dramático distinto a las otras cuatro obras que lo acompañan en este volumen"] (*El arte dramático de Valle-Inclán* [New York: Las Américas, 1967], 141). J. L. Brooks reduces *Embrujado*'s relation to the other plays to a minimum: "[*El Embrujado*] may justifiably be omitted from any general study of the book [*Retablo*] for, though thematically it may be related to the others, in technique and

Embrujado's transcendental evocations—evocations emanating from the melodramatic projection and revelation of supernatural forces—are also evident in *Cara de plata* (1923). Elements implicit in the presentation of the satanic in *Embrujado* are made explicit in *Cara de plata* (*Cara*). Rosa, to some extent, alludes to Christian sacraments insisting that Anxelo share a cup of brandy with her while Anxelo makes it clear that "From having drunk comes my chain!" ["¡De haber bebido viene mi cadena!"] (*Embrujado*, 104).[32] Don Juan Manuel (El Caballero), on the other hand, blatantly forces Sabelita to share his "supper" ["cena"] with him—"Sit [. . . .] Take my cup and drink" ["Siéntate [. . . .] Toma mi copa y bebe"] (*Cara*, 202–3). The scene ends when "[El Caballero] raises his cup and offers it to the kneeling shadow of his new concubine" ["levanta su copa y la ofrece a la sombra arrodillada de su nueva manceba"] (214). Within this framework reminiscent of the Last Supper and Communion, Sabelita condemns herself:

> *Sabelita* — I condemn my soul!
> *El Caballero* — Hand it over!
> *Sabelita* — Why do you want my soul?
> *El Caballero* — I want it for me. Hand it over!
> *Sabelita* — I give it to Satan.
> *El Caballero* — It is mine! [. . . .] I am Satan and I damn you!
>
> [*Sabelita* — ¡Mi alma condeno!
> *El Caballero* — ¡Entrégamela!
> *Sabelita* — ¿Para qué quiere mi alma?
> *El Caballero* — Para mí la quiero. ¡Entrégamela!
> *Sabelita* — A Satanás se la entrego.
> *El Caballero* — ¡Mía es! [. . . .] ¡Soy Satanás y te pierdo!]
> (205–6)

El Caballero has a "warlock's power" ["poder de brujo"] (214)— the force of evil itself is behind the outward appearance of the aris-

---

characterization it belongs to a very different period" ("Valle-Inclán's *Retablo de la avaricia, la lujuria y la muerte*," *Hispanic Studies in Honour of I. González Llubera*, ed. F. Pierce [Oxford: Dolphin Bks., 1959], 87). D. Ling also excludes *Embrujado* from his study of *Retablo*: "[*Embrujado*] by its very nature, its themes and its style, belongs to another period of Valle-Inclán's works" ("Human Dignity and Passions in Valle-Inclán's *Retablo de la avaricia, la lujuria y la muerte*," *Revista de Estudios Hispánicos* 8.2 [1974]: 271).

32. See also *Embrujado*, 135. Christian and mystic symbols are used throughout Valle-Inclán's oeuvre. See C. J. Paolini, *Valle-Inclán's Modernism: Use and Abuse of Religious and Mystical Symbolism* (Valencia: Albatros Hispanófila, 1986); A. Smith, "*Luces de bohemia* y la figura de Cristo; Valle-Inclán, Nietzsche y los románticos alemanes," *Hispanic Review* 57.1 (1989): 57–71.

tocrat. Yet, while the melodramatic mode is displayed onstage in all its glory (see especially the soliloquy so crucial to the genre in which don Juan Manuel expresses unrepentant evil, 272–73), the tone is different.

The Abbot's exaggerated melodramatic invocation of evil ("Satan, help me [. . . .] unchain your north winds! Set on fire your serpents!" ["¡Satanás, ayúdame [. . . .] desencadena tus aquilones! ¡Enciende tus serpientes!"] [223–24]) requires the Sacristan to feign death in a profanization of the Last Rites (see 230–46). Amidst the sobs of his small children—"Our dad! Our dad!" ["¡O noso paisiño! ¡O noso paisiño!"]—the disbelief of his daughter—"Don't act retarded, Father!" ["¡No alele mi Padre!"]—and that of his wife—"Did I make your life so miserable? Answer, you sot! [. . .] You have to be touched, damn it! ["¿Era tan mala la vida que te daba? ¡Responde, pellejo! [. . . .] ¡Hay que conmoverse, carajeta!"]—the Sacristán alternates imprecations—"Criminny, what a thrashing I gave you! [. . . .] I am going to prick your throats, villains!" ["¡Concho, qué tunda te daba! [. . . .] ¡Voy a picarvos el cuello, malvados!"]—with the language proper to his role—"Mother of the Word, come to the help of this devout [man] who is going to face the Supreme Tribunal" ["¡Madre del Verbo, ven en auxilio de este devoto, que va a comparecer ante el Supremo Tribunal!"]. All the stops of the melodramatic situation are pulled: the tearful deathbed benediction—"Beloved offspring, in this vale of tears we only find shelter in the bosom of the Holy Catholic Church. Do not let this go unheeded! Life is a passage!" ["Tiernos vástagos, en este valle de lágrimas solamente hallamos amparo en el seno de la Santa Iglesia Católica. ¡Qué no se os vaya de la cabeza! ¡La vida es un tránsito!"]—the use of the formulaic epithet—"Warm me a drop of wine with cinnamon, pious distraught wife" ["Témplame una gota de vino con canela, piadosa mujer desconsolada"]—and so forth. The Sacristan's words are those of melodrama, but they take place in the context of *teatralería* of the first water. The whole satanic tinge, the very seriousness of the Abbot's appeal to the devil, becomes more than questionable with the advent of, what for lack of better words might be best defined as, this ludicrous scene. Melodrama turns in on itself, effect separates from motive, and the outward gestures become the subject of theatrical presentation. The melodramatic gesture in this case stems not from any melodramatic cause, but from the machinations of an actor interested in playing a part well. Such use of form constitutes one of the prevalent features of the *esperpento*:[33] the audience is "establishing

33. Valle-Inclán emphasizes the presence of literature and literary codes in the theatre: "In the theatre [. . .] everything is literature" ["En el teatro [. . .] todo es literatu-

the difference between burlesque and stylization," and Valle-Inclán is "attempting to grasp the essential form of a literary convention and stylize it without touching the content."[34]

Two uses of melodrama coexist side by side: on the one hand, and very much in the mainstream of the melodramatic tradition, the revelation of a world of pure evil and malice; on the other hand, melodramatic language as the main component of a farcical situation, incongruous in a melodramatic framework. Januslike, *Cara de plata* looks back to the world of spiritual salvation depicted in *Romance de lobos*[35] while gazing directly at the world of the *esperpento*. The (implications of the) experiments with melodramatic form and gestures link Valle-Inclán's early and late oeuvre.

Further development of the visualization of cosmic forces as well as the characters' progressive subservience to these forces are characterstics marking the affirmation of Valle-Inclán's dramatic voice. Rosa Galana, as noted before, is crucial in this respect.[36] In *Divinas palabras* (*DP*), Mari-Gaila expands on *Embrujado*'s use of the *desasosegante*. Dissatisfied with her role as wife and mother, she becomes attracted to the encephalitic "freak" ["engendro"]: "If you only knew how outstanding his private parts are!" ["¡Y si supiéses qué completo es de sus partes!"] (*DP*, 70). Her attachment to this caged freak leads to the unsettling subculture of the maimed, the effeminate, and others ostracized from established society, in particu-

---

ra"] (D. Dougherty, *Un Valle-Inclán olvidado,* 264). The special esteem in which Valle-Inclán holds Muñoz-Seca (see Dougherty, *Un Valle-Inclán olvidado,* 271), the creator of "a magnificent theatre" ["un teatro magnífico"], stems, in part, from the fact that (in Valle-Inclán's words) "Perhaps Muñoz-Seca's theatre is the one that has the most literature" ["Tal vez el teatro de Muñoz-Seca es el que tiene mayor cantidad de literatura"] (Dougherty, *Un Valle-Inclán olvidado,* 264). Valle-Inclán, of course, manipulates literary presence for his own iconoclastic purposes. Other revolutionary dramaturges also recognize and avail themselves of this presence. The prevalence of rhetorical conventions in theatre underlies and permits Brecht's *Gest*: "All discourse is gestic or rhetorical, but some—dramatic discourse—is more rhetorical than the rest. It *needs* to be, since its task is to reveal the repressed rhetoricity of nontheatrical utterances [. . . .] The function of theater is to show that all the world's a stage." (T. Eagleton, "Brecht and Rhetoric," *New Literary History* 16.3 [1985]: 634).

34. P. Ilie, "The Grotesque in Valle-Inclán. A Monograph," *Ramón del Valle-Inclán. An Appraisal of His Life and Works*, ed. A Zahareas (New York: Las Américas, 1968), 504.

35. See, in this chapter, footnote 19.

36. The victimization of the character in the grip of forces beyond his control comes to be further developed, in both theme and form, in the four remaining one-act plays of *Retablo*. The one-act play, as Peter Szondi indicates, is the "drama of the unfree human being" (cited in G. Finney, "Theater of Impotence: The One-Act Tragedy at the Turn of the Century," *Modern Drama* 28.3 [1985]: 460).

lar, Séptimo Miau, whose vision is that of a warlock (256) and whose tricks are Devil's art (354).[37] The toponyms which fix the play's setting in Galicia[38] are slowly defamiliarized in the course of Mari-Gaila's steady descent into the unknown. An inchoate amalgamation of yearnings, her search for fulfillment unveils another world:

> The place changes [. . . .] Witches dance around [. . . .] The Billy-Goat bursts in guffaws [. . . .] Mari-Gaila feels herself being carried in a gust, she hardly touches the ground. The impulse grows, she dangles in the air, she soars and sighs in carnal delight. She feels beneath her skirts the thrust of a wooly haunch, stretches her hand so as not to fall, and her hands find the twisted horn [antler] of the Billy-Goat [. . . .] Mari-Gaila faints, and in a swoon, she feels herself carried through the clouds.
>
> [El paraje se trasmuda [. . . .] Las brujas danzan en torno [. . . .] El Cabrío revienta en una risada [. . . .] Mari-Gaila se siente llevada en una ráfaga, casi no toca la tierra. El impulso acrece, va suspendida en el aire, se remonta y suspira con deleite carnal. Siente bajo las faldas la sacudida de una grupa lanuda, tiende los brazos para no caer, y sus manos encuentran la retorcida cuerna del Cabrío [. . . .] Mari-Gaila se desvanece, y desvanecida se siente llevada por las nubes.] (184–91)

The magical scene foregrounds the inner world of sensual longing and concretizes the plunge into the demonic. Moreover, the interlude takes place between two episodes in which Mari-Gaila learns about the "freak's" death at the tavern and confronts her family with this information. The scene alternates quite freely with these depictions of Galician life. The boundaries between the fantastic and the normal are in flux. Valle-Inclán's stage defines the interplay of its elements and operates within a framework of its own.

Valle-Inclán exteriorizes psychic reality amid characters more ostensibly mimetic with complete mastery in figures like Fuso Negro in *Cara de plata* (*Cara*). In the comparison, "the madman [Fuso] twists and turns under the hoofs, disheveled and frightful, like the moors of Saint James" ["el loco se revuelve bajo las herraduras, greñudo y espantable, como los moros del Señor Santiago"] (*Cara*, 150), Fuso garners an epic, larger-than-life dimension through the similarity of this description with the imagery of *Romance de lobos* (*Romance*). While ravaging the presbytery, one of don Juan Manuel's sons finds a lamp in

---

37. The pagination should be 254. The number 354 is an evident misprint.
38. J. Caamaño Bournacell describes a tour of Galicia, based on the towns and places named or evoked in Valle-Inclán's works. See *Por las rutas turísticas de Valle-Inclán* (Madrid: Privately printed, 1971). Although by no means a scholarly work, it indicates the extent to which an audience would associate Valle-Inclán's plays with Galicia.

which ";[t]he eyes of the scabby Satan laugh, bloodshot, under the Archangel's feet [. . . . don Juan Manuel's son] places his hand familiarly over that black moor's head that sticks out its snake's tongue as it is trampled by the angelic soles" ["Los ojos del tiñoso Satanás ríen encarnizados bajo las plantas del Arcangel [. . . .] posa familiarmente una mano sobre aquella cabeza de moro negro, que saca la lengua de sierpe al ser aplastada por las angélicas plantas"] (*Romance*, 96–97). Fuso, the "moor" ["moro"] in *Cara*, recreates the statue in *Romance*, in which the "black moor/Satan" struggles under the angel's feet.[39] Fuso's demonic nature comes to be even more explicitly declared. The Abbot clamors "Help me, Satan!" ["¡Acúdeme Satanás!"] to which Fuso Negro immediately responds, "Here, my Captain! // On the white path, the madman dances his frenetic dance" ["¡Presente, mi Capitán! // Sobre el albo camino baila el loco su baile frenético"] (*Cara*, 224). Fuso will indeed answer the Abbot's entreaty and play a satanic role, rankling Cara de Plata until he leaves Pichona's side and, like Benito el Penitente, wields the parricidal axe.

However, more than a visible manifestation of evil onstage, Fuso incarnates the interior *dark* forces of the play. Father and son are pitted against one another in a struggle for Sabelita's affection. Cara de Plata has told Sabelita he will break down her door and share her bed (33), while don Juan Manuel has warned Sabelita to stay clear of his son while bemoaning the fact that he is not ten years younger (43). Seething envy, lust, and violence finally break into the open. Cara de Plata threatens to carry off Sabelita but desists—"Because of the asylum of the church, I do not grasp you now by the waist and carry you stolen over my horse!" ["¡Por el asilo de la iglesia no te prendo ahora por la cintura y te llevo robada sobre mi caballo!"] (144)—while don Juan Manuel carries through where his son falters. The prize of the abduction is ostensibly Sabelita, but more specifically, the conquest of Sabelita, the taking of her virginity; and this is left for Fuso to act out. Just after Cara's abortive abduction and before don Juan Manuel's successful one, Fuso finds Sabelita:

> *Fuso Negro* — Beautiful face, show me your legs!
> *Sabelita* — Go away!

39. The visual arts are constantly present in Valle-Inclán's theatre at all levels of textual structure and organization. J. Lyon's groundbreaking essay stresses the importance of "graphically immediate images" ("Valle-Inclán and the Art of the Theatre," *Bulletin of Hispanic Studies* 46.2 [1969]: 148). "The *Comedia bárbara*, more than written, is painted like a fresco" ["*La Comedia bárbara* está, diríamos, más que escrita, pintada al fresco"] (C. Rivas Cherif, "*La Comedia Bárbara* de Valle-Inclán," *España*, 16 February 1924: 9). See Eva Llorens for a study of plastic interpresence in Valle-Inclán's aesthetic proceedings (*Valle-Inclán y la plástica* [Madrid: Insula, 1975]).

Dissemination

> *Fuso Negro* — I don't want to.
> *Sabelita* — Go away, or I'll yell!
> *Fuso Negro* — Show me your legs, damn it!
> *Sabelita* — Don't frighten me, Fuso Negro!
> *Fuso Negro* — Toporroutóu! How white you are! Give me a piece, damn it! Holy Mother, what a hymen you have!
> In the romantic portico, under the stone saints, the triumphant phallus, laughter in waves, eyes on fire, the frantic shock of hair.
>
> [*Fuso Negro* — ¡Cara bonita, amuéstrame las piernas!
> *Sabelita* — ¡Vete!
> *Fuso Negro* — No quiero.
> *Sabelita* — ¡Vete, o doy voces!
> *Fuso Negro* — ¡Amuéstrame las piernas, puñela!
> *Sabelita* — ¡No me asustes, Fuso Negro!
> *Fuso Negro* — ¡Toporroutóu! ¡Qué blanca eres! ¡Dame una vicada, concho! ¡Madre Santísima, qué virgo tienes!
> En el romántico pórtico, bajo los santos de piedra, el fálico triunfo, la risa en balandros, los ojos en lumbre, la greña frenética.] (149–50)

Although the triumphant phallus and the allusion to the toughness of Sabelita's hymen certainly connote the consummation of Fuso's attack, her virginity appears to remain intact (260; 265–66). Ambiguity shrouds the facts and envelopes the event in uncertainty, for a reason—the event is less an act per se than an enactment. Gesture takes over. Fuso becomes the onstage visual embodiment of the force motivating the father/son rivalry and, more particularly, Sabelita's abduction. The characters are stage entities in the full sense of the word—entities understood only within the context of the stage world and its functions.

In a period where reigning theatrical conventions are guided by the identification of the outside "real" of the spectators with the "real" presented within the artistic space of the play—or by a reduction to a minimum of the discrepancies between them—Valle-Inclán stands aloof. In his works, the world of the stage and that of the audience are no longer perforce mutually translatable, nor are they on an equal footing. The dialogue, free of any (necessary) connection to the audience, simply functions within stage parameters:

> *Juana de Juno* — [Rosa] Galana had dealings with many [men].
> *La Navora* — [This is] Well-known!
> *Juana de Juno* — A year ago, on the day of St. James's fair, I saw her sitting in La Braña laughing with a young man and tying her kerchief.
> *La Navora* — A kerchief is just as likely to be untied by a hand

as it is by the wind.
Juana de Juno — I had an evil thought and I frightened it away so as not to condemn my soul. Dissembling, I passed behind, and see I did see... Her back and her shoulders full of dirt! What are you doing, girls? Don't you cry or laugh?
La Navora — What desire to gad about and to stir up gossip some young women have! With pastures and corn fields that are gorgeous, to go and pick one's fare in La Braña! The young women of today do not look out for their honor nor for the jewel they wear clothed.
The Older Daughter of Everyone's Rosa — What are you saying? Heavens! Those [women] that don't have a hard time attaining it do not look out, but the rest of us certainly do.
La Navora — If they find a beau that will give them a doubloon, it won't help them.
The Older Daughter of Everyone's Rosa — Beaus with a doubloon, earrings, and a necklace! They are not around these days, Mrs. Andrea La Navora! [. . . .]
Juana de Juno — [Rosa] Galana has two enemies that are eating her: The wine jug and the court.
La Navora — Say three enemies, because [. . . .]

[*Juana de Juno* — La Galana tuvo conversa con muchos.
La Navora — ¡Notorio!
Juana de Juno — Cumple un año para la feria del Santiago, que la vi sentada en La Braña, riendo con un mozo, y atándose el pañuelo.
La Navora — Un pañuelo, por igual lo desata una mano que lo desata el viento.
Juana de Juno — Tuve un mal pensamiento y lo espanté para no condenar mi alma. Al disimulo pasé por detrás, y vi que le vi... ¡La espalda y los hombros llenos de tierra! ¿Qué hacéis, rapazas? ¿No lloráis ni reís?
La Navora — ¡Afanes de loquear y de dar que decir tienen algunas mozas! ¡Con prados y maizales que es una gloria, ir á recoger esquilmo en La Braña! Las mozas de hoy no miran por su honra ni por la buena prenda que llevan vestida.
La Hija Mayor De Rosa De Todos — ¿Qué está diciendo? ¡Santa del Cielo! No miran aquellas que les cuesta poco trabajo ganarlo, que las demás bien reparamos.
La Navora — Si encuentran un cortejo que les deje una onza de oro, de nada les aprovecha.
La Hija Mayor De Rosa De Todos — ¡Cortejos de onza de oro, pendientes y gargantilla! ¡No son de este tiempo, señora Andrea la Navora! [. . . .]
Juana de Juno — La Galana tiene dos enemigos que la comen: El jarro de vino y la curia.
La Navora — Di tres enemigos, porque [. . . .]]

(*Embrujado*, 29–31)

Here the dialogue moves from the tight strictures of a language that has to communicate information—more an audience directed rather than a character preocuppied language—to the more general function of language establishing phatic contact. La Navora's insinuations as to Juana de Juno's complicity in the dubious characteristics of "some young women" who go to pick their "fare in La Braña" signals a change. With the phrase beginning "The young women of today [. . .]" the dialogue loses contact with the content of Juana's message or any element bearing information about Rosa's characteristics and continues in this vein until Juana again brings up the subject of interest, "[Rosa] Galana has two enemies [. . .]" From a level of high tension and constant pressure with respect to what is spoken—the information about the dramatis personae and their actions that impel the play—language relaxes to a point where what comes to be conveyed is of little substantive import. The impetus behind a very specific and purposeful revelation seemingly disappears. Language is loosed from its labors and simply indulges in a dispute between generations. The restful interlude, though, serves as a literary lightning rod grounding the preceding tension—the consciousness of language in its role as disseminator of information. Audience-directed theatrical language is subsumed into an underlying language category—the *private* exchange of the characters making general references to the world they inhabit.[40]

Valle-Inclán's stage simply posits itself. Audience expectations are exploited to highlight the stage as such: the *private* stage, for Valle-Inclán returns theatre to the artist. Spanish theatrical discourse becomes a vehicle for personal expression—an expression that, in Valle-Inclán's case, shatters prevalent dramatic format. The stage bears the stamp of Valle-Inclán's own unique vision.[41] Two

40. See A. Ubersfeld, *Lire le théâtre* (Paris: Editions Sociales, 1978), 251, for theatrical dialogue as "enclosed within the interior of an enclosure" ("*englobé à l'intérieure d'un englobant*"). For the "deictic-performative articulation" of the written/stage text, see A. Serpieri, et al., "Towards a Segmentation of the Dramatic Text," *Poetics Today* 2.3 (1981): 171.

41. As a result, Valle-Incláns plays are largely not staged, and indeed, their very status as plays is called into question. S. de Madariaga considers the *Comedias bárbaras* "dramatic novels" ["novelas dramáticas"] (*Semblanzas literarias contemporáneas* [Barcelona: Cervantes, 1924], 204), as does E. Gómez de Baquero, along with other works ("Valle-Inclán, novelista," *La Pluma* 4.32 [1923]: 7–14). The close link between the dramatic and the novelistic is thereby underlined. See, for example, C. Barja, *Libros y autores contemporáneos* (Madrid: Librería General de Victoriano Suárez, 1935), 389. Azorín affirms that Valle-Inclán is not a "professional dramaturge" ["dramaturgo profesional"] (*Insula* 176–77 [1961]: 4), a doubt that lingers on well into the second half of the century. See, *ABC* 15 April 1966: 103, responded to by R. Domenech in "Para una visión actual de los esperpentos," *Cuadernos Hispanoamericanos* 199–200 (1966): 455–57. Indeed, the whole issue soon becomes embrangled in

aspects of this vision are particularly significant: obscurity and linguistic tradition ("Wise words that come from old people" ["Las palabras sabias, que vienen de los viejos"] [43]).[42] When El Ciego de Gondar utters the phrase, "The white dove began to pull the leaves off her olive branch in the air, between the clear sun and the wretched earth" ["¡La paloma blanca se puso á deshojar su ramo de oliva en los aires, entre el claro sol y la tierra cativa!"] (41), a multitude of interpretations are proffered:

> *Juana de Juno* — Such words—that are from the old people—come to mean that the sun is like a splendor of the Sky and a black coal from Hell the wretched earth.
> *La Navora* — Such words come to signify that the sun is the power that don Pedro Bolaño wields and that the wretched earth is the status of the poor, who only have a sheet of earth, and a quilt of earth, and a mattress of earth... And this when they die!
> *Juana de Juno* — Perhaps such a statement could also mean that the sun is don Pedro Bolaño's charity and the wretched earth, the black soul who wants to prevent it.
> *La Navora* — You are deluding yourself, woman! Whosoever you ask will explain it in a different fashion.
> *Juana de Juno* — And no one will explain it to the satisfaction of the grandmother.
> *La Navora* — Nor do I pretend to maintain anything different. Wise words, that come from the old people, say a different thing to each person, as happens with music.
> *One of the Five Young Women* — An ear [of wheat] has many grains to give, and much flour to knead, and much bread to offer. And good words—our grandmother used to say—are ears in God's threshing ground.

---

a series of controversies over genres: the dramatic versus the novelistic, the status of the dialogue novel and its precedents in Spanish literary history, the role of stage directions in the dramatic text, and so forth. Regardless of the view taken—D. Pérez Minik, for example, holds that Valle-Inclán's works are "[a]ll stageable. Lucidly prepared for the stage" ["Todas representables. Lúcidamente preparadas para la escena"], and claims that if they were in their majority not staged, this is only because "there were no theatrical groups capable of doing them justice" ["no existían compañias dramáticas capaces de llevarlas a cabo"] ("Valle-Inclán o la restauración del bululú," *Debates sobre el teatro español contemporáneo* [Santa Cruz de Tenerife: Goya Ediciones, 1953], 131–32)—there is no doubt that Valle-Inclán broke reigning theatrical horizons of expectations. See also M. Fernández Almagro, "Teatro al margen," *Insula* 100–101 (1954): 3; "Encuesta sobre el teatro de Ramón del Valle-Inclán," *Insula* 236–37 (1966): 6; R. Domenech, *El teatro, hoy* (Madrid: Cuadernos para el diálogo, 1966), 124–26; B. Losado, "Valle-Inclán entre Galicia y Brecht," *Estudios Escénicos* 13 (1969): 61–80.

42. See, in this text, chapter 1, section 2, for Valle-Inclán's use of literary tradition.

[*Juana de Juno* — Tales palabras—que son de los
  viejos—vienen á representar que el sol es como un res-
  plandor del Cielo, y un carbón negro del Infierno la
  tierra cativa.
La Navora — Vienen á decir tales palabras, que el sol es
  el poderío que tiene Don Pedro Bolaño, y la tierra cativa la condición del pobre, que sólo tiene una sábana de
  tierra, y un cobertor de tierra, y un jergón de tierra...
  ¡Y eso al morir!
Juana de Juno — Si acaso, tal sentencia puede contener
  que el sol es la caridad que hace Don Pedro Bolaño, y
  la tierra cativa el alma negra que la quiere estorbar.
La Navora — ¡Te engañas, moza! Cualquiera á quien
  interrogues te lo explicará de distinta conformidad.
Juana de Juno — Y ninguno lo explicará al conforme de
  la abuela.
La Navora — Ni otra cosa aventuro. Las palabras sabias,
  que vienen de los viejos, á cada uno le dicen una cosa
  distinta, como acontece con las músicas.
Una De Las Cinco Mocinas — Una espiga tiene muchos
  granos que desgranar, y mucha harina que amasar, y
  mucho pan que dar. Y las buenas palabras—nuestra
  abuela decía—son espigas de la era de Dios.]

(42–43)

Like the audience outside the stage world proper, the characters within this world confront a dizzying multivalency of signification—delphic words. Dramatic speech taps mystic sources.

Perspectival Stance

As previously noted, *El Embrujado* (*Embrujado*), dating from 1913, along with *La rosa de papel* and *La cabeza del bautista* (both from 1924, the year of the revised edition of *Luces de bohemia*), *Ligazón* (1926), and *Sacrilegio* (1927) form part of *Retablo de la avaricia, la lujuria y la muerte* (1927). The title aptly reflects the concerns dominating the collection—lust and avarice in the presence, and from the perspective, of death. The prophetic mode adopted by The Blind Man of Gondar (see above) bears witness to the transcendent interests surfacing time and again throughout Valle-Inclán's theatrical career.

As a spokesman for, and integrant of, those marginated throngs—lepers, thieves, puppeteers, and fools—populating Valle-Inclán's works, The Blind Man of Gondar waxes eloquent:[43]

---

43. El Pobre de San Lázaro in *Romance de lobos*, is an important precursor in Valle-Inclán's development of the beggar figure.

> The sins of an almsman are not like those of a rich gentleman. The almsman can do many bad things without condemning his soul. The almsman says that there are no robbers in the world because no one robs him. The almsman says that there are no assassins in the world because no one wishes him harm. The almsman says that there is no hate between families because he is like a rolling stone. The almsman says that there are no lawsuits over inheritances because he has nothing to bequeath. The true almsman needs alms in order to be buried, and since he undergoes so many plights, even when he does a bad thing, he does not condemn himself as do the rich.
>
> [Los pecados de un pobre de pedir no son como los de un rico caballero. El pobre de pedir puede hacer muchas cosas malas sin condenar su alma. El pobre de pedir dice que no hay ladrones en el mundo, porque á él nadie le roba. El pobre de pedir dice que no hay asesinos en el mundo, porque á él nadie le quiere mal. El pobre de pedir dice que no hay odio entre las familias, porque él es como una piedra que rueda. El pobre de pedir dice que no hay pleitos por las herencias, porque él no tiene nada que dejar. Al verdadero pobre de pedir hay que enterrarlo de limosna, y como pasa tantos trabajos, aun cuando haga alguna cosa mala, no se condena como los ricos.] (*Embrujado*, 50–51)

The "almsman" stands untouched by the afflictions troubling those who surround him. Don Pedro's fear of losing his possessions, motivated by the avarice and greed shown by Rosa, Mauriña, and others does not affect him, "no one robs him." The deep-seated hatred extant between doña Isoldina's family and don Pedro's will never be experienced by the beggar, "he is like a rolling stone." The lawsuits with which now Rosa Galana, now don Pedro, are threatened, the accompanying bitterness and grudges, don Pedro's anguish as to the bequeathment of his possessions, will never be felt by the "almsman," "he has nothing to bequeath." The position that The Blind Man of Gondar represents stands in sharp contrast to the machinations revolving around the self, and to the other characters who are preoccupied with increasing or maintaining the authority, wealth, and power of the individual.[44] The beggar stands isolated, an island of passivity unaffected by the swirl of activity centered on personal profit that surrounds him.

The Blind Man of Gondar's pronouncements satisfy Valle-Inclán's penchant for a literary work replete with contrasts—the prevalent

---

44. The Blind Man of Gondar himself stands far from incarnating the attributes of the "almsman"—witness his litigation with The Blind Man of Flavia over María Virula, the girl who guides him (*Embrujado*, 104–7)—and is by no means an Adega-like figure of innocence (*Flor de santidad*), a role perhaps best suited to doña Isoldina. Nevertheless, the text utilizes the description of the beggar's status, not the characteristics of the particular beggar, The Blind Man of Gondar.

atmosphere of *Embrujado* comes to be viewed from a totally different vantage point.⁴⁵ This result resembles the literary effect produced by another blind figure, the Godmother ["Madrina"] in *La Lámpara maravillosa* (*Lámpara*).⁴⁶ Valle-Inclán recollects his first "literary intuition" ["intuición literaria"]: "I had been able to incarnate in the substance of life and in its most beautiful shadows the pious stories and the stories of princesses that my grandmother [Valle-Inclán's Madrina] told me" ["Yo había llegado á encarnar en la substancia de la vida y en sus sombras más bellas las historias piadosas y los cuentos de princesas que mi abuela me contaba"] (*Lámpara*, 194–95).⁴⁷ "Life" ["vida"] and "stories" ["historias"]

45. From the vantage point of the "almsman," the disinterested perspective (essential to mystic comprehension) is unveiled. The ego, the "satanic serpent of the I" ["sierpe satánica del yo"] (*La lámpara maravillosa* [*Lámpara*], 152) prevents one from going beyond the confines of time and limits one to the realm of the particular: "Before reaching this aesthetic quietism, divine delight, I went through an enormous aridness, always distressed by the sensation of movement and of sterile living [. . . .] I have spent many years looking at how everything changed and perished, blind to their eternity. The foundation of my egoism was so strong that I only managed to know that which in some fashion was related to the strivings of each hour, and my senses learned coordinated with them, without ever disengaging themselves, without being able to rend the veils that hide the mystic enigma of the world" ["Antes de llegar á este quietismo estético, divino deleite, pasé por una aridez muy grande, siempre acongojado por la sensación del movimiento y del vivir estéril [. . . .] He consumido muchos años mirando como todas las cosas se mudaban y perecían, ciego para ver su eternidad. Era tan firme el cimiento de mi egoísmo, que sólo alcanzaba á conocer aquello que en algún modo guardaba relación con los afanes de cada hora, y los sentidos aprendían coordinados con ellos, sin desvincularse jamás, sin poder rasgar los velos que ocultan el enigma místico del Mundo"] (*Lámpara*, 38). The wandering of the alms seeker, devoid of patrimony and family, a veritable "rolling stone" (*Embrujado*, 51) reduced to the most elemental of belongings, typifies the detachment from preoccupations, the "anxieties of each hour," that Valle-Inclán seeks. See chapter 1, footnotes 14 and 26.

46. Blindness exercises a particular fascination on Valle-Inclán. See E. Segura Covarsi, "Los ciegos de Valle-Inclán," *Clavileño* 3.17 (1952): 49–52. V. Garlitz compares being blind to the "physical world" ["al mundo físico"] and to "what lies beyond" ("lo más allá"), which explains "the great importance that the blind and that the use of the play between vision and blindness and their complements, light and shadow, have in Valle-Inclán's entire work" ["la gran importancia que tienen los ciegos y el empleo del juego entre la visión y la ceguera y sus complementos la luz y la sombra, por toda la obra de don Ramón"] ("El centro del círculo: *La lámpara maravillosa* de Valle-Incán," diss., University of Chicago, 1978, 215–16). "Happy are the eyes that go blind after having seen because they purify their knowledge of geometry and chronology!" ["¡Felices los ojos que ciegan después de haber visto, porque purifican su conocimiento de geometría y de cronología!"] (*La lámpara mararillosa*, 206)—blindness leads to the comprehension in which "the bonds of place and of the hour" ["los lazos del lugar y de la hora"] stand "broken" ["rotos"] (206).

47. This childhood "sacred emotion" ("emoción sagrada") that the adult Valle-Inclán confesses, "I still evoke and relive" ["Aun evoco y revivo en mí"] (*Lámpara*, 194) results from listening to, not reading, literature. The "statements of the folios"

combine, and the resulting experience, in Valle-Inclán's words, "shook my child's soul like a nocturnal wind" ["estremeció mi alma de niño como un viento nocturno"] (202). What grips Valle-Inclán so is the manner in which the blind Godmother narrates: "That village blind woman, when she told her stories, seemed to be looking at them in the bottom of her soul" ["Aquella ciega de aldea cuando contaba sus historias parecía estar mirándolas en el fondo de su alma"] (205). In particular: "All things were infused with a static mysticism: Souls in penance [. . .] thefts, and deaths mixed in profound and silent actions that appeared to be seen more from the stars of the sky than from human eyes" ["Todas las cosas estaban imbuídas de un misticismo estático: Las almas en pena [. . .] los robos y las muertes se mezclaban en acciones profundas y silenciosas que más parecían vistas por las estrellas del cielo que por ojos humanos"] (204–5). The subject matter of the stories is narrated from afar. The blind Godmother's stories partake of the essential characteristics Valle-Inclán ascribes to one of his *Comedias—Cara de plata*, published in 1923—where "the funambulism of the action [. . . .] has something of the [stage] machinations of sleep, by which spectres can talk with the living" ["el funambulismo de la acción [. . . .] tiene algo de tramoya de sueño, por donde las larvas pueden dialogar con los vivos"].[48] The aesthetic object is made different: "Her stories [the blind Godmother's] never took place in the world of our senses. They had a translucent landscape. They were country narrations that the millenary soul of that blind village woman converted into

---

["sentencias de los infolios"] (30) recede before the importance of the auditory in the literary context: "It is important that throughout *La lámpara maravillosa* the poet's magic does not occur because of a written text but because of his ability to use language orally (the spoken word) or musically (the sound and evocative power of words)" Carol S. Maier, "Symbolist Aesthetics in Spanish: The Concept of Language in Valle-Inclán's *La lámpara maravillosa*," *Wating for Pegasus*, ed. R. Grass and W. R. Risley [Illinois: Western Illinois University Press, 1979], 79). For the theatrical implications of this emphasis on aural (Spanish), see, in this text, chapter 4, section 1, in particular, 96–99. Valle-Inclán uses drama (the audible form of literature) as a vehicle to express his return to the infantile, to the fairy-tale "story" ["cuento"] form (e.g., *La cabeza del dragón*)—a return that has a specifically mystic (nontemporal) cause/effect. The "evocative character" ["caractère d'évocation"] and the "return backwards in time [. . . .only have] as their objective situating action a little outside of time" ["retour en arrière dans le temps [. . . . n'ont] pour objet que de situer l'action un peu en dehors du temps"] (Francisco Nieva, *Le Théâtre moderne: Hommes et tendances*, ed. Jean Jacquot [Paris: Editions du Centre National de la Recherche Scientifique, 1958], 227).

48. Ramón del Valle-Inclán, "Autocrítica," *España* 8 March 1924: 6. Reproduced in *Ramón del Valle-Inclán, Artículos completos y otras páginas olvidadas*, ed. J. Serrano Alonso [Madrid: Istmo, 1987], 269–71.

myths" ["Sus cuentos nunca sucedían en el mundo de nuestros sentidos. Tenían un paisaje translúcido. Eran relatos campesinos que convertía en mitos el alma milenaria de aquella aldeana ciega"] (203). A simple story, purposefully differentiated, but not entirely separated from the quotidian perception at its root, reveals (hidden) mythic dimensions. The blind Godmother's narrative technique allows for the transcendence of the specific. She is party to the comprehension of those realizing that:

> The unity of the world is broken in the eyes as the unity of light in the triangular prism of crystal. It is necessary to have emotively contemplated the same image from different places, so that it ignites in the memory the ideal gaze outside of a geometrical position and outside of a position in Time. The blind pupils of the gods in the Grecian marbles symbolize this supreme vision that imprisons in a circle all that it regards. It is the matutinal and plural grace [....] communion with the eternal substance
>
> [La unidad del mundo se quiebra en los ojos, como la unidad de la luz en el prisma triangular de cristal. Es preciso haber contemplado emotivamente la misma imagen desde parajes diversos, para que alumbre en la memoria la ideal mirada fuera de posición geométrica y fuera de posición en el Tiempo. Las pupilas ciegas de los dioses en los mármoles griegos, simbolizan esta suprema visión que aprisiona en un círculo todo cuanto mira. Es la gracia plural y matinal [....] comunión con la eterna substancia]. (187–88)

The lesson Valle-Inclán draws from his blind Godmother's stories—the perspectival variance or distancing that breaks temporal and spatial confines—lies at the heart of his aesthetic. The pilgrim seeking eternal understanding must realize that "there is no more refined fortune than weeping one's own tribulations as if they were someone else's" ["no hay más acendrada ventura que llorar las propias tribulaciones, como si fuesen ajenas"] (233). The self must be contemplated from the other side of death, under the light of eternity:

> My life is repeated in the incorporeal world of spirits, and when death arrives, with my soul free of its clay prison, I will see all the past in the eternal circle of my shadows. At every moment, the carnal form sheds an impalpable part of itself, and it leaves its track along the way. Where we once passed, there we remain. And everything remains unchanged!
>
> [Mi vida se repite en el mundo incorpóreo de los fantasmas, y cuando llegue la muerte, con el alma libre de la cárcel de barro, veré todo el pasado en el círculo eterno de las sombras mías. La forma carnal se despoja en todos los instantes de una parte impalpable de sí misma, y deja su rastro á lo largo del camino. Por donde una vez más pasamos, allí perduramos. ¡Y todo perdura

igual!] (213)

Death breaks through temporal and spatial strictures to reveal a new world of myriad, latent possibilities, an infinitely renewable re-creation of the past:

> my heart went in pilgrimage to my infancy and it returned garbed in a new grace. As I walked under the sacred shade of [my] memories, I did not experience the sensation of living once again in those distant years, but something more ineffable, for I understood that nothing in my psyche was abolished. Up until then, I had never discovered that intuition of eternity shown at once by evoking childhood and making it immediately applicable [real] in another circle of Time.
>
> [peregrinó mi corazón hacia la infancia y tornó revestido de una gracia nueva. Al caminar bajo la sombra sagrada de los recuerdos, no experimenté la sensación de volver á vivir en los años lejanos, sino algo más inefable, pues comprendía que nada de mi psiquis era abolido. Hasta entonces nunca había descubierto aquella intuición de eternidad que se mostraba de pronto al evocar la infancia y darle actualidad en otro círculo del Tiempo.] (53)

The pilgrim does not relive the past in identification with the event and its context. The eternal view implies situating the incident or memory in a different context, where it becomes the center of new evocations radiating possibilities for new linkage. The self becomes the vortex, the center of an eternal re-creation and placement in "another circle."

The distance traversed in order to attain the perspective offered by death leads to mystic comprehension—the final goal of an enterprise both personal and aesthetic. Don Estrafalario, in the quite evident fictive confines of *Los cuernos de don Friolera*, immortalizes the *sub specie aeternitatis* personal dictum: "I would like to see this world from the perspective of the other shore. I am like that relative of mine that you met, and who once, when the local boss asked him what he wanted to be, he answered: I, dead" ["Yo quisiera ver este mundo, con la perspectiva de la otra ribera. Soy como aquel mi pariente que usted conoció, y que una vez, al preguntarle el cacique qué deseaba ser, contestó: Yo difunto"] (22). Valle-Inclán, in the biographical, exhortative, religious compendium that constitutes *Lámpara*, simply universalizes his need for an aesthetic imperative: "Pilgrim of the world [. . . .] Infuse in your soul the joy of what is beautiful, create beauty, live in beauty, and when contemplating your past from the remote shore, you will contemplate love. Do not forget that the ultimate and supreme reason that all things treasure to be loved is to be beautiful" ["Peregrino del mundo [. . . .] Infunde en tu alma el goce de lo bello, crea belleza, vive en belleza, y al contemplar tu pasado desde la ribera remota, contemplarás amor. No olvides que la última y suprema razón que todas las cosas atesoran para ser amadas, es ser bellas"] (243).

Valle-Inclán's own biography, with the constant presence of *historias*, eloquently confirms the convergence of personal and aesthetic pursuits in the search for Unity.[49] The confusion between Valle-Inclán and his literary characters,[50] or the confusion of the characters with Valle-Inclán—ontological priority is difficult to ascertain—poses the fundamental inability to fix and delimit the Valle-Inclanesque oeuvre. *La Marquesa Rosalinda* offers, especially in the figure of Arlequín, the confusion between a play and the moments pointing out the play, between fiction and a seeming nonfictional, thereby presenting in microcosm the entire Valle-Inclanesque macrocosmic confusion of life and art. Like *Luces de bohemia*, *La Marquesa Rosalinda* depicts the creation of an artwork, and true to Valle-Inclán's principles, the aesthetic implicates the personal. Arlequín's life becomes the revelation of the birth of a theatrical performance in which the seeming autonomy of the troupe's actions is progressively subsumed under the

---

49. The affirmations are numerous: Valle-Inclán's "life is a manifestation at one with and inseparable from his work [. . . .] In Valle, the mask is one with the face [. . . .] without doubt a personality in unitary orientation towards aesthetic values" ["vida es manifestación solidaria e inseparable de su obra [. . . .] En Valle, la máscara es una con el rostro [. . . .] sin duda alguna, una personalidad unitariamente orientada en dirección a los valores estéticos"] (Franciso Ayala, "Nota al centenario de Valle-Inclán," *Insula* 236-37 [1966]: 5). "Valle-Inclán was a magnificent literary character. Everything in him was literature." ["Valle-Inclán era un magnífico personaje literario. Todo en él era literatura"] (J. Benavente, *La Voz* 8 January 1936: 3). Valle-Inclán himself is notorious for his contributions to this literary/biographical confusion. The incidents are myriad and one will serve as an example. Valle-Inclán calls the Marquis of Bradomín his uncle only to subsequently identify himself with this protagonist of the *Sonatas*: "On board the *La Dalila*—I remember with pride—I assassinated Sir Robert Yones" ["A bordo de *La Dalila*—lo recuerdo con orgullo—asesiné a Sir Roberto Yones"] ("Juventud militante," *Alma Española*, 27 December 1903: 7).

50. The Marquis of Bradomín comes immediately to mind, although there are many incidents of such possible Valle-Inclanian projections. The intervention of the soldier who has an amputated arm in *Divinas palabras* (*DP*), for example, is particularly suggestive given Valle-Inclán's own physique. In addition, Valle-Inclán frequently acknowledges his own inclination for the military (see *Lámpara*, 13-15; or A. Reyes, "La parodia trágica," *Simpatías y diferencias: Segunda serie* [Madrid: E. Teodoro, 1921], 21, where Valle-Inclán confesses that "I am not a writer. I am a military [man]" ["Yo no soy escritor. Soy militar"]), and admits to the militaristic view of his literature. The soldier's role in *DP* is brief, yet authoritative, announcing beyond a doubt and against the affirmations of the other characters that the encephalitic freak has died (*DP*, 176).

ever-enveloping folds of a theatrical depiction. Similarly in *Luces de bohemia*, the birth of the *esperpento* claims the life of Max Estrella. An explicit "devouring aestheticality" becomes a—indeed, the—principal characteristic of things Valle-Inclanesque. Valle-Inclán forever perpetuates a created Valle-Inclán.[51] The Galician writer blurs the interstice lying between the model and its image, so that determining the degree of possible iconization becomes a blurred and blurring impossibility. The ever-present oscillation between an act and its simulation or recreation is constitutive of *La Marquesa Rosalinda*. The constant image making/theatre making-as-activity proclaimed at any given moment indicates that the aesthetic imperative, with its mystic import, does not remain confined to exposition in *Lámpara*. A "devouring aestheticality" stitches together the very fabric of Valle-Inclán's life and artistic manifestations.

Like Midas, but with an aesthetic touch, Valle-Inclán endows all activity with an aesthetic onus that transcends temporal limitations. The "remote shore" ["ribera remota"] (*Lámpara*, 243) perspective becomes the hallmark of aesthetic expression in search of mystic truth. *La cabeza del dragón* inscribes the "made different" perspective in its very texture. At the same time that the *didascalies* insert a distanced view of the action onstage—deflationary comments, incongruous comparisons, and so forth—the stage doubles the distancing action of the *didascalies*, mirroring/mimicking the nonintegration of the authorial perspective vis-à-vis the constructed world. The piece ceaselessly interiorizes and displays a distanced/distancing view.

Valle-Inclán's spatial concern, his desire for perspective in literature, becomes apparent with the title of the 1927 work under which he subsequently included *El Embrujado (Embrujado)*—"retablo" in which "two factors generally intervene: the joy itself of representing scenes very much in relief as well as a moral intention" ["intervienen, generalmente, dos factores: la alegría misma de representar escenas muy en relieve, a la par que una intención moral"].[52] The vantage point from which the characters are so frequently glimpsed—"they come from far away" ["vienen de muy lejos"]; "They evanesce along the shore between the weightless folds of the drizzle: They fade away

---

51. Manuel Azaña exclaims: "At times, going to meet Valle-Inclán, I asked myself which one I would find of the various that exist" ["Alguna vez, yendo a encontrarme con Valle-Inclán, me he preguntado a cuál hallaría, de los varios que existen"] ("El secreto de Valle-Inclán," *La Pluma* 4.32 [1923]: 84). Even in his own lifetime, attempts are made to pare away the fabricated versions and arrive at the *real* Valle-Inclán: see, Alberto Ghiraldo, "Como perdió su brazo D. Ramón María del Valle-Inclán," *Diario de la Plata* 9 September 1923: N.p.

52. Jean Paul Borel, "Reflexiones sobre un retablo," *Insula* 176–77 (1961): 14.

Dissemination 129

and disappear under the branches that drip flaccid, sad" ["Se esfuman á lo largo de la ribera, entre los pliegues ingrávidos de la llovizna: Se desvanecen y desaparecen bajo los ramajes, que gotean lacios, tristes"] (*Embrujado*, 76; 87)—a use of theatrical resources often portrayed by critics as cinematic,[53] derives, in part, from the desire to inscribe the perspective inherent in the mystic view. Anxelo and Mauriña are often encased in a setting that provides the distancing effect redolent of the stories told by Valle-Inclán's childhood blind Godmother:

> An autumn afternoon. A tranquil river spread in still waters under the green shade of the poplars and willows. On both shores, twin fields of hay and flax that, like the river, ripple with the breeze. It rains softly, softly, in great peace. A man and a woman are seated on the course sand of the shore that crunches [as if] threshed. To their rear, open and empty, the house built out of rough rocks, covered with corn straw, and surrounded by smoke. The figures appear to be very far away in the sifting light rain. Two spirits on the shore of the river. They speak in a secretive and fearful manner, as if they did not wish to disturb the calm of the landscape, the silence of the leaves, and of the crystal of the water, the peace of all things that speak of the perfection of ecstasy and the hermetic and eternal meaning of happiness.
>
> [Tarde de otoño. Un río tranquilo, espaciado en remansos bajo la verde sombra de chopos y mimbrales. A las dos riberas, agros mellizos de heno y de linar que, á par del río, se rizan con la brisa. Llueve menudo, menudo, en una gran paz. Sobre la arena fuerte de la ribera, que cruje desgranada, están sentados un hombre y una mujer. A su espalda, abierta y vacía, la casa alzada con pedruscos, cubierta con paja de maíz y envuelta en humo. Las figuras parecen muy lejanas en el cernir de la lluvia menuda. Dos larvas en la orilla del río. Hablan de una manera fugitiva y medrosa, como si quisiesen no alterar el reposo del paisaje, la quietud de las hojas y del cristal del agua, la paz de todas las cosas que dice la perfección del éxtasis y el sentido hermético y eterno de la felicidad.] (67–68)[54]

All that Anxelo and Mauriña represent, their greed and lust—which for Valle-Inclán implies remaining within the confines of the particular—comes to be viewed from afar. Even contemporary critics com-

---

53. See, for example, Carlos Jerez Farrán, *El expresionismo en Valle-Inclán: Una reinterpretación de su visión esperpéntica* (Coruña: Ediciós do Castro, 1989), 209–64; R. Osuna, "Un 'guión cinematográfico' de Valle-Inclán: *Luces de bohemia*," *Bulletin of Hispanic Studies* 59.2 (1982): 120–28; J. Urrutia, "Sobre el carácter cinematográfico del teatro de Valle-Inclán: A propósito de *Divinas palabras*," *Insula* 491 (1987): 18.

54. For comments on this and other citations from *Embrujado*, see L. González del Valle, "La unidad conceptual de *El Embrujado*," R. Johnson, ed., *Studies in Honor of José Rubia Barcia* (Lincoln, Neb.: Society of Spanish and Spanish-American Studies, 1982), 71–82.

ment on this aspect of the work: "The staging willingly distances the crudeness [primitiveness] of this tragic intrigue, as if slowing it and evanescing it" ["La representación aleja voluntariamente la crudeza de esta intriga trágica, como deteniéndola y esfumándola"], and from this vantage point the play has "many similarities [. . .] with static drama even in the moments of heightened violence" ["mucho [. . .] de drama estático, aun en los momentos de mayor violencia"].[55] The moral aspects associated with the "retable" are brought out by these differences in perspective—"the perfection of ecstasy" provides the base from which the figures are seen as "spirits on the shore of the river," their passions and troubles so distinct, so far from (a morally incumbent) eternal happiness. The ambiance that surrounds the characters, and the characters themselves, partake, as in the blind Godmother's stories, of an "static mysticism" ["misticismo estático"] (*Lámpara*, 204). In don Pedro's house, "They speak quietly. They have a mysterious air. The figures, the shadows, the voices ready to fade away, as unsubstantial as the undulations of the flame under the black stones of the chimney where the wind whistles" ["Hablan en voz baja. Tienen un aire de misterio. Las figuras, las sombras, las voces próximas á desvanecerse, inconsistentes como el ondular de la llama bajo las negras piedras de la chiminea donde silba el viento"]; "there is a row of faded figures, diluted, monotonous. Gesture and speech in the gray register" ["hay una hilera de figuras desvanecidas, diluidas, monótonas. Gesto y voz en la gama del gris"] (*Embrujado*, 114; 122). The figures are testimony to one moment of Valle-Inclán's ongoing desire to mold characters in the light of "the stars of the sky" ["las estrellas del cielo"] rather than from the perspective of "human eyes" ["ojos humanos"] (*Lámpara*, 205).

55. E. Díez Canedo, *Artículos de crítica teatral*, v. 4, 30, 29.

Select Bibliography

The select bibliography consisits of three sections: I. the editions of Valle-Inclán's works cited in this text; II. articles by Valle-Inclán and literature on Valle-Inclán; and III. general bibliography.

I. Editions of Valle-Inclán's Works Cited in This Text

Valle-Inclán, Ramón del. *Aguila de blasón: Comedia bárbara dividida en cinco jornadas*. Madrid: Sociedad general española de librería, 1915. Opera Omnia, vol. 14. (Abbreviated *Aguila* in the text.)

———. *La cabeza del dragón: Farsa*. Madrid: Perlado, Paez y Cía, 1914. Opera Omnia, vol. 10. (Abbreviated *CdD* in the text.)

———. *Cara de plata: Comedia bárbara* Madrid: Imprenta Cervantina, 1923. Opera Omnia, vol. 13. (Abbreviated *Cara* in the text.)

———. *Los cuernos de don Friolera. Esperpento*. Madrid: Renacimiento, Imp. Cervantina, 1925. Opera Omnia, vol. 17. (Abbreviated *Cuernos* in the text.)

———. *Divinas palabras: Tragicomedia de aldea*. Madrid: Yagües, 1920. Opera Omnia, vol. 17. (Abbreviated *DP* in the text.)

———. *El Embrujado: Tragedia de Tierras de Salnés*. Madrid: Imprenta José Izquierdo, 1913. Opera Omnia, vol. 4. (Abbreviated *Embrujado* in the text.)

———. "Farsa italiana de la enamorada del rey." *Tablado de marionetas para educación de príncipes*. Madrid: Rivadneyra, 1926. Opera Omnia, vol. 10.

———. "Farsa y licencia de la reina castiza." *Tablado de marionetas para educación de príncipes*. Madrid: Rivadneyra, 1926. Opera Omnia, vol. 10

———. *La lámpara maravillosa: Ejercicios espirituales*. Madrid: Imp. Helénica, 1916. Opera Omnia, vol. 1. (Abbreviated *Lámpara* in the text.)

———. *Luces de bohemia*. Ed., A. Zamora Vicente. Madrid: Espasa-Calpe, 1973. (Abbreviated *Luces* in the text.)

———. *El Marqués de Bradomín: Coloquios románticos*. Madrid: Pueyo, 1907.

———. *La Marquesa Rosalinda: Farsa sentimental y grotesca*. Madrid: Imprenta Alemana, 1913. Opera Omnia, vol. 3. (Abbreviated *MR* in the text.)

———. *Romance de lobos*: *Comedia bárbara dividida en tres jornadas*. Madrid: Perlado, Paez y Cía. 1914. Opera Omnia, vol. 15. (Abbreviated *Romance* in the text.)

———. *Sonata de estío: Memorias del Marqués de Bradomín*. Madrid: Imprenta Helénica, 1913. Opera Omnia, vol. 6.

———. *Sonata de invierno: Memorias del Marqués de Bradomín*. Madrid: Imprenta Helénica, 1913. Opera Omnia, vol. 8.

———. *Voces de gesta: Tragedia pastoril*. Madrid: Imprenta Alemana, 1911[2]. (Abbreviated *VdG* in the text.)

II. Articles by Valle-Inclán and Literature on Valle-Inclán

Abrams, Fred. "The Onomastic Link Between Valle-Inclán and the Marqués de Bradomín." *Romance Notes* 14 (1972): 242–43.

Adamov, Arthur. "Une pièce progressiste quand même." *Cahiers Renaud-Barrault* 43 (1963): 56–58.

Allegra, Giovanni. "Sobre unas claves 'históricas' y teóricas de la gnosis modernista." In *La Chispa '85,* edited by Gilbert Paolini, 27–38. New Orleans: Tulane University Press, 1985.

Alonso, Amado. "La musicalidad de la prosa en Valle-Inclán." In *Materia y forma en poesía*, 313–69. Madrid: Gredos, 1955.

Alonso, F. "Estreno de *La Marquesa Rosalinda*." *Nuevo Mundo,* 7 March 1912. n.p.

Alonso, José Luis. "Mi cuaderno de dirección de tres obras de Valle." *Primer Acto* 82 (1967): 28–31.

Alvarez, Carlos Luis. "En el Martín Guerrero se presentó *Aguila de blasón* de Valle-Inclán." *ABC* 15 April 1966: 103.

Ambía, Isabel de. "Magia en la vida y en la obra de don Ramón del Valle-Inclán." *Cuadernos de literatura contemporánea* 18 (1946): 479–84.

Amor y Vázquez, José. "Valle-Inclán y las musas: Terpsicore." In *Homenaje al profesor William L. Fichter*, edited by D. Kossof and J. Amor y Vázquez, 11–31. Madrid: Castalia, 1971.

Aub, Max. "Prólogo acerca del teatro español en los años veinte de este siglo." *Papeles de Son Armadans* 15, nos. 69–96 (1966): 66–96.

Ayala, Francisco. "Nota al centenario de Valle-Inclán." *Insula* 236–37 (1966): 5.

———. "Valle-Inclán and the Invention of Character." In *Valle-Inclán Centennial Studies*, edited by Ricardo Gullón, 27–39. Austin: University of Texas Press, 1968.

Azaña, Manuel. "El secreto de Valle-Inclán." *La Pluma* 6.32 (1923): 82–89.

Barja, César. *Libros y autores contemporáneos*. Madrid: Librería General de Victoriano Suárez, 1935. 360–421.

Baroja, Pío. *El escritor según él y según los críticos*. In *Obras completas,* vol. 7, 387–494. Madrid: Biblioteca Nueva, 1949.

Bary, David. "La 'inaccesible categoría estética' de Valle-Inclán." *Papeles de Son Armadans* 52 (1969): 221–38.

Batal Batal, Carlos. "Las primeras narraciones de Valle-Inclán." Diss., University Complutense Madrid, 1978.

Benavente, J. *La Voz* (Madrid) 8 January 1936: 3.

Select Bibliography 133

Benítez Claros, Rafael. "Metricismos en las *Comedias bárbaras*." *Revista de literatura* 3, no. 5 (1953): 247–91.

Bermejo Marcos, M. *Valle-Inclán. Introducción a su obra*. Spain: Anaya, 1971.

Blanquat, Josette. "Symbolisme et 'esperpento' dans *Divinas palabras*." In *Mélanges à la mémoire de Jean Sarrailh*, vol. 1, 145–65. Paris: Centre de Recherches de l'Institut d'Etudes Hispaniques, 1966.

Borel, Jean-Paul. "Reflexiones sobre un *Retablo*." *Insula* 176–77 (1961): 14.

———. *El teatro de lo imposible*. Madrid: Ediciones Guadarrama, 1966. 171–223.

Boudreau, Harold. "The Creation of Valle-Inclán's *Sacrilegio*. *Symposium* 22, no. 1 (1968): 16–24.

———. "The Circular Structure of Valle-Inclán's *Ruedo ibérico*." *PMLA* 82, no. 1 (1967): 128–35.

Brooks, J. L. "Los dramas de Valle-Inclán." *Estudios dedicados a D. Ramón Menéndez Pidal*. 7, no. 1 (1957): 177–98.

———. "Valle-Inclán's *Retablo de la avaricia, la lujuria y la muerte*." In *Hispanic Studies in Honour of I. González Llubera*, edited by Frank Pierce, 87–104. Oxford: Dolphin, 1959.

Buero Vallejo, A. "De rodillas, en pie, en el aire." *Revista de Occidente* 15, nos. 44–45 (1966): 132–45.

Caamaño Bournacell, J. "Valle-Inclán y el concepto del teatro." In *Mélanges à la mémoire d'André Joucla-Ruau*, vol. 1, 501–15. Aix-en-Provence: Editions de l'Université de Provence, 1978.

———. *Por las rutas turísticas de Valle-Inclán*. Madrid: Privately published, 1971.

Cano, José Luis. "Valle-Inclán y la crítica." *Insula* 2, no. 22 (1947): 3.

Canoa Galiana, J. *Semiología de las 'Comedias bárbaras'*. Madrid: Cupsa, 1977.

Cardona, Rodolfo, and A. Zahareas. *Visión del esperpento*. Madrid: Castalia, 1970.

Caro Baroja, Julio. "Recuerdos valleinclanesco-barojianos." *Revista de Occidente* 15, nos. 44–45 (1966): 302–13.

Cervera, Juan. *Historia crítica del teatro infantil*. Madrid: Editora Nacional, 1982. 349–67.

Cuenca, Luis A. de. "El teatro de Valle-Inclán." *Cuadernos Hispanoamericanos* 309 (1976): 441–44.

Díaz Ortiz, Pedro. "Valle-Inclán y el teatro contemporáneo." *Cuadernos Hispanoamericanos* 199–200 (1966): 445–50.

Díaz Plaja, Guillermo. *Las estéticas de Valle-Inclán*. Madrid: Gredos, 1965.

Díez Canedo, E. *Artículos de crítica teatral. El teatro español de 1914–1936*. México: Joaquín Mortiz, 1968.

Domenech, R. *El teatro, hoy*. Madrid: Cuadernos para el diálogo, 1966.

———. "Para una visión actual del teatro de los esperpentos." *Cuadernos Hispanoamericanos* 199–200 (1966): 455–66.

Dougherty, Dru. *Un Valle-Inclán olvidado: entrevistas y conferencias*. Madrid: Fundamentos, 1983.

———. "Theater and Eroticism: Valle-Inclán's *Farsa y licencia de la reina castiza*." *Hispanic Review* 55, no. 1 (1987): 13–25.

Drake, William A. "Ramón del Valle-Inclán." In *Contemporary European Writers*, 130–37. New York: John Day Co., 1928.

Select Bibliography

Durán, Manuel. "Del Marqués de Sade a Valle-Inclán." *Asomante* 2 (1954): 40–47.

Edwards, Gwynne. "The *Comedias bárbaras*: Valle-Inclán and the Symbolist Theatre." *Bulletin of Hispanic Studies* 60, no. 4 (1983): 293–303.

———. "Valle-Inclán and the New Art of the Theatre." *Neophilolgous* 68, no. 1 (1984): 48–62.

———. Encuesta sobre el teatro de Ramón del Valle-Inclán." *Insula* 176–77 (1961): 4–5.

———. Encuesta sobre el teatro de Ramón del Valle-Inclán." *Insula* 236–37 (1966): 6.

Entrambasaguas, J. de "Leyendo a Valle-Inclán (Notas al margen)." *Cuadernos de literatura contemporánea* 18 (1946): 539–91.

Esteban, José. *Valle-Inclán visto por.* . . . Madrid: Editorial Gráficas Espejo, 1973.

Fernández Almagro, Melchor. "Teatro al margen." *Insula* 100–101 (1954): 3.

———. *Vida y literatura de Valle-Inclán.* Madrid: Editora Nacional, 1943.

Fernández Santos, A. "La dificultad de representar a Valle-Inclán." *Indice* 219–20 (1967): 47.

Franco, Jean. "The Concept of Time in *El ruedo ibérico*." *Bulletin of Hispanic Studies* 39, no. 3 (1962): 177–87.

La gaceta literaria, 1 February 1928: 5.

Garcia Pavón, F. "*Cenizas* (primer drama de Valle-Inclán)." *Insula* 236–37 (1966): 10.

García Sabell, Domingo. "Españoles mal entendidos: Don Ramón María del Valle-Inclán." *Insula* 176–77 (1961): 1, 19.

———. "El verdadero don Ramón." In *Ramón María del Valle-Inclán. 1866–1966. (Estudios reunidos en conmemoración del centenario),* 62–68. La Plata: Universidad Nacional de La Plata, 1967.

Garlitz, Virginia Milner. "El centro del círculo: *La lámpara maravillosa* de Valle-Inclán." Diss., University of Chicago, 1978.

George, D. "Harlequin Comes to Court: Valle-Inclán's *La Marquesa Rosalinda*." *Forum for Modern Language Studies* 19, no. 4 (1983): 364–74.

Ghiraldo, A. "Como perdió su brazo don Ramón María del Valle-Inclán." *Diario de la plata* (Buenos Aires), 9 September 1923. N.P.

Gómez de Baquero, E. "Las marionetas de Valle-Inclán." *El Sol* 24 April 1926: 1.

———. "Valle-Inclán novelista." *La Pluma* 4, no. 32 (1923): 7–14.

Gómez de la Serna, G. "Ideas e ideales permanentes de don Ramón María." *La estafeta literaria* 320–21 (1965): 36–37.

González del Valle, Luis. "La unidad conceptual de El Embrujado." In *Studies In Honor of José Rubia Barcia,* edited by Roberta Johnson, 71–82. Lincoln, NE: Society of Spanish and Spanish-American Studies, 1982.

González López, E. *El arte dramático de Valle-Inclán* New York: Las Americas, 1967.

———. "El *Cuento de abril* de Valle-Inclán: Sus fuentes y su arte." *Revista Hispánica Moderna* 32, nos. 3–4 (1966): 186–90.

———. "El melodrama expresionista de Valle-Inclán y el extrañamiento dramático." *Estudios escénicos* 21 (1976): 95–110.

Greenfield, Sumner M. *Valle-Inclán: Anatomía de un teatro problemático.* Madrid: Fundamentos, 1972.

———. "Valle-Inclán en transición: una brujería dialogada." *La Torre* 13, no. 51 (1965): 175–92.

Select Bibliography

Guerrero, Obdulia. *Valle-Inclán y el novecientos: apuntes para un estudio biográfico-literario.* Madrid: Editorial Magisterio Español, 1977.

Hardison, Felicia. "Valle-Inclán and Artaud: Brothers Under the Skin." *Educational Theatre Journal* 19, no. 4 (1967): 455–66.

Hormigón, Juan Antonio. *Ramón del Valle-Inclán: la política, la cultura, el realismo y el pueblo.* Madrid: A. Corazón, 1972.

———. *Valle-Inclán, cronología y documentos.* Madrid: Ministerio de Cultura, 1978.

———. "Valle-Inclán y el teatro de la Escuela Nueva." *Estudios Escénicos* 16 (1972): 10–21.

Ilie, Paul. "The Grotesque in Valle-Inclán." In *Ramón del Valle-Inclán. An Appraisal of His Life and Works*, edited by A. Zahareas, 493–539. New York: Las Américas, 1968.

Jérez Ferran, Carlos. *El expresionismo en Valle-Inclán: Una reinterpretación de su visión esperpéntica.* Coruña: Ediciones do Castro: 1989.

Jiménez, Juan Ramón. "Ramón del Valle-Inclán" *University of Miami Hispanic-American Studies* 2 (1941): 108–18.

Kirkpatrick, Susan. "From *Octavio Santino* to *El yermo de las almas:* Three Phases of Valle-Inclán." *Revista Hispánica Moderna* 37 (1972-3): 56–72.

Lavaud, Etienne. *Valle-Inclán: Du journal au roman (1888–1915).* Dijon: L'Université de Dijon, 1979.

Lavaud, Jean-Marie. "Realidad y esperpento en *La cabeza del dragón.*" In *Ramón del Valle-Inclán (1866–1936)*, edited by H. Wentzlaff-Eggebert, 115–24. Tübingen: Max Niemeyer, 1988.

———. "Une collaboration de Valle-Inclán au journal 'Nuevo Mundo' et l'Exposition de 1912." *Bulletin Hispanique* 71, nos. 1–2 (1969): 286–311.

LeMay, A. H. "The Verse Plays of Ramón del Valle-Inclán: A Poetic Vision." Diss., Indiana University—Bloomington, 1971.

Lewis de Galanes, A. "El retablo de maese Valle-Inclán." *Revista de Estudios Hispánicos* 3, no. 1 (1969): 3–31.

Lima, R. *An Annotated Bibliography of Ramón del Valle-Inclán.* University Park: Pennsylvania State University Libraries, 1972.

———. "The Commedia dell'Arte and *La Marquesa Rosalinda.*" In *Ramón del Valle-Inclán. An Appraisal of His Life and Works*, edited by A. Zahareas, 386–415. New York: Las Américas, 1968.

———. *Valle-Inclán: The Theatre of His Life.* Columbia: University of Missouri Press, 1988.

Ling, D. "Valle-Inclán's Compromise with the Spanish Stage. A Comparative study of *El Marqués de Bradomín* and Its Source, the *Sonatas.*" *Revue des Langues Vivantes* 39, no. 1 (1973): 46–58.

Llorens, Eva. *Valle-Inclán y la plástica.* Madrid: Insula, 1975.

Losada, B. "Valle-Inclán entre Galicia y Brecht." *Estudios Escénicos* 13 (1969): 61–80.

Lyon, J. E. *The Theatre of Valle-Inclán.* Cambridge: Cambridge University Press, 1983.

———. "Valle-Inclán and the Art of the Theatre." *Bulletin of Hispanic Studies* 46, no. 2 (1969): 132–52.

McGrady, D. "Elementos folclóricos en tres obras de Valle-Inclán." *Thesauras. Boletín del Instituto Caro y Cuervo* 25, no. 1 (1970): 49-58.

Machado, A. "Ramón del Valle-Inclán visto por Juan de Mairena." *Insula* 236–37 (1966): 26.

Madariaga, Salvador de. *Semblanzas literarias contemporáneas*. Barcelona: Cervantes, 1924. 185–211.

Madrid, F. *La vida altiva de Valle-Inclán*. Buenos Aires: Poseidón, 1943.

Maier, Carol S. "Notas hacia una definicion del concepto de historia en *La lámpara maravillosa*." *Explicación de textos literarios* 9, no. 2 (1981): 153–58.

———. "Symbolist Aesthetics in Spanish: The Concept of Language in Valle-Inclán's *La lámpara maravillosa*." In *Waiting for Pegasus*, edited by R. Grass and W. R. Risley, 77-87. Macomb: Western Illinois University Press, 1979.

———. "Untwisting the Castillian Tongue: Some Suggestions from Valle-Inclán's *La lámpara maravillosa*." *Hispanic Journal* 6, no. 2. (1985): 59–67.

———. "Valle-Inclán y *La lámpara maravillosa*: Una poética iluminada." Diss., Rutgers University, 1975.

Maldonado Macías, H. A. *Valle-Inclán gnóstico y vanguardista*. México: University Nacional Autónoma de México, 1980.

March, M. E. *Forma e idea de los esperpentos de Valle-Inclán*. No. 10 of *Estudios de Hispanófila*. Chapel Hill: Department of Romance Languages, University of North Carolina, 1969.

Marrast, R. "Quelques clés pour *Divines paroles*." *Cahiers de Renaud-Barrault* 43 (1963): 18–35.

Marías Aguilera, Julián. *La imagen de la vida humana y dos ejemplos literarios: Cervantes, Valle-Inclán*. Madrid: Ediciones de la Revista de Occidente, 1971.

Marsillach, A. "*Aguila de blasón*." *Primer Acto* 82 (1967): 22–28.

Mas y Pi, J. "*El Embrujado*." *Nosotros* 7, no. 53 (1913): 296–97.

Maza, Ana María S. "'Tablado de Marionetas': un proceso de desmitificación." *Estudios filológicos* 8 (1972): 69–87.

Monleón, José. "Crítica sobre *Aguila de blasón*." *Primer Acto* 75 (1966): 60–62.

———. *El teatro del '98 frente a la sociedad española*. Madrid: Castalia, 1975.

Montesinos, J. F. "Modernismo, esperpentismo o las dos evasiones." *Revista de Occidente* 15, nos. 44–45 (1966): 146–65.

Morón Arroyo, C. "*La lámpara maravillosa* y la ecuación estética." In *Ramón del Valle-Inclán. An Appraisal of His Life and Works*, edited by A. Zahareas, 443–59. New York: Las Américas, 1968.

Moya del Pino, J. "Valle-Inclán y los artistas." *La Pluma* 32 (1923): 63–65.

Navas, Federico. *Las esfinges de Talía*. El Escorial: Imprenta del Real Monasterio de El Escorial, 1928.

Nicholson, D. "Valle-Inclán's *The Dragon's Head*: Symbolist Fairy Tale and Satyr Play." *Modern Drama* 29, no. 3 (1986): 460–71.

Nickel, C. A. "Ramón del Valle-Inclán's *Retablo de la avaricia, la lujuria y la muerte*: The One-Act Plays." Diss., University of Nebraska—Lincoln, 1985.

———. "Recasting the Image of the Fallen Woman in Valle-Inclán's *Eulalia*." *Studies in Short Fiction* 24, no. 3 (1987): 289–94.

———. "The Secret of *La Marquesa Rosalinda*: From the Physical to the Metaphysical." *Hispanic Journal* 5, no. 2 (1984): 75–87.

Nieva, F. "Vertus plastiques du théâtre de Valle-Inclán." In *Le théâtre moderne:*

Hommes et tendances, edited by Jean Jacquot, 223–40. Paris: Editions du Centre National de la Recherche Scientifique, 1958.

Paolini, Claire J. "Mystical Symbolism in the *Sonatas* of Valle-Inclán." *Discurso Literario* 3, no. 1 (1985): 133–44.

———. *Valle-Inclán's Modernism: Use and Abuse of Religious and Mystical Symbolism*. Valencia: Albatros Hispanófila, 1986.

Pérez de Ayala, R. "Valle-Inclán dramaturgo." *La Pluma* 32 (1923): 19–27.

Pérez Minik, D. "Valle-Inclán o la restauración del bululú." *Debates sobre el teatro español contemporáneo*, 121–40. Santa Cruz de Tenerife: Goya Ediciones, 1953.

Phillips, Allen. "Rubén Darío y Valle-Inclán: historia de una amistad literaria." *Temas del modernismo hispánico y otros estudios*, 159–207. Madrid: Gredos, 1974.

Posse, R. "Notas sobre el folclore gallego en Valle-Inclán." *Cuadernos Hispanoamericanos* 199–200 (1966): 493–520.

Quentin-Mauroy, Dominique. "Ramón del Valle-Inclán. L'amour créateur et le temps." In *Le temps et la mort dans la philosophie espagnole contemporaine*, edited by Georges Hahn, 162–66. Toulouse: Edouard Privat, 1968.

Quinto, J. M. de. "Obras de una noche y gracias." *Primer Acto* 28 (1961): 18–19.

Ramos-Kuethe, L. "El concepto de libertinismo en la narrativa temprana de don Ramón del Valle-Inclán." *Hispanic Journal* 4, no. 2 (1983): 51–63.

Reyes, A. "La parodia trágica." In *Simpatías y diferencias (segunda serie)*, 17–33. Madrid: E. Teodoro, 1921.

———. "Valle-Inclán, teólogo." In *Cartones de Madrid*, 59-62. Madrid: Hiperión, 1988.

Risco, A. *El demiurgo y su mundo: Hacia un nuevo enfoque de la obra de Valle-Inclán*. Madrid: Gredos, 1977.

———. *La estética de Valle-Inclán en los 'esperpentos' y en el 'Ruedo ibérico.'* Madrid: Gredos, 1966.

———. "El juglar en la obra de Valle-Inclán: Proyecto de estudio." In *La juglaresca*, edited by M. Criado de Val, 469–72. Madrid: Edi-6, 1986.

Rivas Cherif, Cipriano. "Los 'Amigos de Valle-Inclán.' Segunda carta abierta sobre un teatro nuevo." *España* 6, no. 278 (1920): 12–13.

———. "La *Comedia barbara* de Valle-Inclán." *España* 16 February 1924: 8–9.

———. "El viaje de Valle-Inclán." *España* 11 May 1916: 10–11.

Rogerio Sánchez, J. *El teatro poético: Valle-Inclán, Marquina. Estudio crítico*. Madrid: Sucesores de Hernando, 1914.

Rojas, R. "Valle-Inclán, el hombre imaginario." In *Retablo español*, 278–81. Buenos Aires: Losada, 1938.

Romens, Thomas L. "A Sociolinguistic Approach to Dramatic Literature: The Case of Valle-Inclán's *Aguila de blasón*." Diss., University of Minnesota, 1980.

Rubia Barcía, J. *Mascarón de proa*. La Coruna: Ediciós Do Castro, 1983.

———. "Secuela, realidad y profecía del teatro de Valle-Inclán." *Cuadernos Americanos* 199 (1975): 200–222.

Ruiz de Gallarreta, J. "El humorismo de Valle-Inclán." *Cuadernos Hispanoamericanos* 199–200 (1966): 65–99.

Ruiz Fernández, Ciriaco. *El léxico del teatro de Valle-Inclán*. Salamanca: University de Salamanca, 1981.

Saillard, S. "De D'Annunzio à Valle-Inclán ou la naissance d'un auteur dramatique." *Cahiers Renaud-Barrault* 43 (1963): 36–44.

Salinas, P. "Significacion del esperpento o Valle-Inclán, hijo pródigo del '98." In *Literatura española siglo XX,* 86–114. Madrid: Alianza, 1972.

Salper, Roberta L. *Valle-Inclán y su mundo: ideología y forma narrativa.* Amsterdam: Rodopi, 1988.

Salvat, R. "Els camins de la creació poètica. Teatre de fira, guinyol i *esperpento*: Valle-Inclán." In *Teatre contemporani I,* 259–66. Barcelona: Ediciones 62, 1966.

Sánchez, Roberto. "Gordon Craig y Valle-Inclán." *Revista de Occidente* 4 (1976): 27–37.

Sanz Cuadrado, M. A. "*Flor de santidad* y *Aromas de leyenda*: estudio comparativo." *Cuadernos de literatura contemporánea* 18 (1946): 503–38.

Saz Sánchez, Agustín. del. *El teatro de Valle-Inclán.* Barcelona: Gráfica, 1950.

Schiavo, Leda. "Tradición literaria y nuevo sentido en *La Marquesa Rosalinda*." *Filología* 15 (1971): 291–97.

Seelman, R. "Folkloric Elements in Valle-Inclán." *Hispanic Review* 3, no. 2 (1935): 103–19.

Segura Covarsi, E. "Las acotaciones dramáticas de Valle-Inclán." *Clavileño* 7, no. 38 (1956): 44–52.

———. "Los ciegos de Valle-Inclán." *Clavileño* 3, no. 17 (1952): 49–52.

Sender, R. *Valle-Inclán y la dificultad de la tragedia.* Madrid: Gredos, 1965.

Serrano Alonso, J. *Ramón del Valle-Inclán, Artículos completos y otras páginas olvidadas.* Madrid: Istmo, 1987.

Sinclair, Alison. "Nineteenth Century Popular Literature as a Source of Linguistic Enrichment in Valle-Inclán's *Ruedo ibérico.*" *Modern Language Review* 70, no. 1 (1975): 84–96.

Smith, Alan E. "*Luces de Bohemia* y la figura de Cristo: Valle-Inclán, Nietzsche y los románticos alemanes." *Hispanic Review* 57, no. 1 (1989): 57–71.

Soriano, Ignacio. "*La lámpara maravillosa* clave de los esperpentos." *La Torre* 62 (1968): 144–50.

Speratti-Piñero, E. S. *El ocultismo en Valle-Inclán.* London: Támesis, 1974.

———. "Los brujos de Valle-Inclán." *Nueva Revista de Filología Hispánica* 21, no. 1 (1972): 40–70.

———. "La farsa de *La cabeza del dragón*, pre-esperpento." In *De 'Sonata de otoño' al esperpento.* 35–45. London: Támesis, 1968.

Torre, Guillermo de. "La evolución de Valle-Inclán." *Insula* 176–77 (1961): 1, 19.

Umpierre, Gustavo. *'Divinas palabras': Alusión y alegoría.* Estudios de Hispanófila 18. Chapel Hill: University of North Carolina Press, 1971.

———. "Occultism and Allegory in Valle-Inclán's *La Marquesa Rosalinda.*" *Symposium* 28, no. 3 (1974): 259–73.

Unamuno, Miguel de. "De algunos juicios acerca de Valle-Inclán." *Ahora* 7 January 1936: 9.

Urrutia, J. "Sobre el carácter cinematográfico del teatro de Valle-Inclán: A propósito de *Divinas palabras.*" *Insula* 491 (1987): 18.

Valle-Inclán, Ramón del. "Autocrítica." *España* 8 March 1924: 6

———."Juventud Militante." *Alma Española* 27 December 1903, 7.

Williamson, W. "Las *Comedias bárbaras* de Valle-Inclán: estudio temático, estructural y estilístico." Diss., Indiana University, 1972.
Young, G. J. "Sade, los decadentistas y Bradomín." *Cuadernos Hispanoamericanos* 298 (1975): 112–31.
Zabalbeascoa Bilbao, J. A. "Los constantes del teatro de Valle-Inclán en *El yermo de las almas*." Tesis de licenciatura, University Barcelona, 1956.
Zahareas, Anthony, ed. *Ramón del Valle-Inclán. An Appraisal of His Life and Works*. New York: Las Américas, 1968.
Zamora Vicente, Alonso. *La realidad esperpéntica (aproximación a 'Luces de bohemia')*. Madrid: Gredos, 1969.

III. General Bibliography

Abirached, Robert. *La Crise du personnage dans le théâtre moderne*. Paris: Grasset, 1978.
Alter, Jean. "From Text to Performance: Semiotics of Theatricality." *Poetics Today* 2, no. 3 (1981): 113–39.
———. "Performance and performance: On the Margin of Theatre Semiotics." *Degrés* 30 (1982): d1–d14.
Artaud, Antonin. *Le Théâtre et son double*. Paris: Gallimard, 1964.
Avigal, Shoshana, and S. Rimmon-Kenan. "What Do Brook's Bricks Mean? Toward a Theory of the 'Mobility' of Objects in Theatrical Discourse." *Poetics Today* 2, no. 3 (1981): 11–34.
Badiou, Maryse. "L'Objet et le sacré dans le processus de dramatisation." *Degrés* 32 (1982): I1–I7.
Bal, Mieke. "Mise en abyme et iconicité." *Littérature* 29 (1978): 116–28.
Barrault, Jean Louis. "Du théâtre total et de 'Cristophe Colomb.'" *Cahiers Renaud-Barrault* 88 (1975): 24–42.
———. "Le Corps magnétique." *Cahiers Renaud-Barrault* 99 (1979): 71–135.
———. "Le Roman adapté au théâtre." *Cahiers Renaud-Barrault* 91 (1976): 27–58.
———. "On Stanislavski and Brecht." *Theatre Quarterly* 3, no. 10 (1973): 2–3.
———. "The Rehearsal, The Performance." "*Yale French Studies* 5 (1950): 3–4.
Barthes, R. "Baudelaire's Theater." In *Critical Essays*, 25–31. Evanston, IL: Northwestern University Press, 1972.
———. "L'Effet de réel." *Communications* 11 (1968): 84–89.
———. "Theatre and Signification." *Theatre Quarterly* 9, no. 33 (1979): 29–30.
Bascompte, Ramiro. "El juego de la farsa y su puesta en escena." *Yorick* 5–6 (1965): 11–12.
Beaumont, C. W. *History of Harlequin*. New York: B. Blom, 1967.
Behar, Henri. "Le Théâtre expérimental, de la synthèse à l'improvisation." *Littérature* 30 (1978): 111–23.
Bentley, Eric. *The Life of the Drama*. London: Methuen, 1965.
———. *The Theory of the Modern Stage*. Harmondsworth: Penguin, 1968.
Bergson, Henri. *Le Rire*. Paris: Félix Alcan, 1911.

Bermel, Albert. *Farce.* New York: Simon & Schuster, 1982.

Bersani, Leo. *A Future for Astyanax.* Boston: Little, Brown and Co., 1976. 259–315.

Bloch, Ernst. "'Entfremdung,' 'Verfremdung': Alienation, Estrangement." *Tulane Drama Review* 15, no. 1 (1970): 120–25.

Body, Jacques. "Du genre théâtral défini par la réception différentielle synchrone." *Rivista di letterature moderne e comparate* 34, no. 3 (1981): 169–74.

Bogatyrev, Petr. "Costume as Sign." In *Semiotics of Art: Prague School Contributions,* edited by Ladislav Matejka and Irwin Titunik, 13–19. Cambridge: M.I.T. Press, 1976.

―――. "Forms and Functions of Folk Theatre." In *Semiotics of Art: Prague School Contributions,* edited by Ladislav Matejka and Irwin Titunik, 51–56. Cambridge: M.I.T. Press, 1976.

―――. "Les Signes du théâtre." *Poétique* 8 (1971): 517–30.

―――. "Semiotics in the Folk Theatre." In *Semiotics of Art: Prague School Contributions,* edited by Ladislav Matejka and Irwin Titunik, 33–50. Cambridge: M.I.T. Press, 1976.

Booth, Michael. "Theatre History and the Literary Critic." *The Yearbook of English Studies* 9 (1979): 15–27.

Bradbury, Gail. "Irregular Sexuality in the Spanish 'Comedia.'" *The Modern Language Review* 76, no. 3 (1981): 566–80.

Brater, E. "Brecht's Alienated Actor in Beckett's Theatre." *Comparative Drama* 9, no. 3 (1975): 195–205.

Breton, A. *Anthologie de l'humour noir.* Paris: Sagittaire, 1950.

Brook, P. *Empty Space.* New York: Atheneum, 1968.

―――. "The Influence of Gordon Craig in Theory and Practice." *Drama* 37 (1955): 33–36.

Brooks, Peter. *The Melodramatic Imagination.* New Haven: Yale University Press, 1976.

Brustein, R. *The Theatre of Revolt: An Approach to Modern Drama.* Boston: Little, Brown, 1964.

Bueno, Manuel. *Teatro español contemporáneo.* Madrid: Biblioteca Renacimiento, 1909.

Bunjevac, Milan. "La Marque de la théâtralité." *Degrés* 32 (1982): e1–e-6.

Calandra, Denis. "Jessner's 'Hintertreppe': A Semiotic Approach to Expressionist Performance." *Theatre Quarterly* 9, no. 35 (1977): 31–42.

Carlson, Marvin. "The Golden Age of the Boulevard." *The Drama Review* 18, no. 1 (1974): 25–33.

Caro Baroja, Julio. *Teatro popular y magia.* Madrid: Ediciones de la Revista de Occidente, 1974.

Chambers, Ross. "La Marque et le miroir: Vers une théorie relationelle du théâtre." *Etudes Littéraires* 13, no. 3 (1980): 397–412.

Champigny, Robert. "Theatre in a Mirror: Anouilh." *Yale French Studies* 14 (1954): 57–64.

―――. "Trois définitions du symbolisme." *Comparative Literature Studies* 4, no. 1 (1967): 127–34.

Chateau, Dominique. "Note sur la fonction de l'acteur de théâtre." *Degrés* 30 (1982): c1–c5.

Conrad, Randall. "Mystery and Melodrama: A Conversation with Georges Franju." *Film Quarterly* 35, no. 2 (1981–82): 31–41.
Copeau, Jacques. "A Theatre of National Renewal." *Theatre Quarterly* 6, no. 23 (1976): 30–42.
Copeland, Roger. "Brecht, Artaud and the Hole in the Paper Sky." *Theater* 9, no. 3 (1978): 42–49.
Corvin, Michel. "La Redondance du signe dans le fonctionnement théâtral." *Degrés* 13 (1978): c1–c23.
Craig, E. G. "The Actor and the Uber=Marionette." *The Mask* I, no. 2 (1908): 3–15.
Cravetto Letizia, María. "Paradoxe théâtral: jeu de miroir/jeu d'échec." *Littérature* 43 (1981): 75–88.
Deák, Frantisek. "The Grand Guignol." *The Drama Review* 18, no. 1 (1974): 34–43.
———. "Structuralism in Theatre: The Prague School Contribution." *The Drama Review* 20, no. 4 (1976): 83–94.
Deleito y Piñuelo, José. *Origen y apogeo del 'género chico.'* Madrid: Revista de Occidente, 1949.
De Man, Paul. "The Double Aspect of Symbolism." *Yale French Studies* 74 (1988): 3–16.
Derrida, J. "Le Théâtre de la cruauté et la clôture de la représentation." In *L'Écriture et la différence*, 341–68. Paris: Editions du Seuil, 1967.
Díaz Plaja, Guillermo. *Modernismo frente a noventa y ocho*. Madrid: Espasa-Calpe, 1951.
Dichy, Albert. "Objets, acteurs, personnages dans le discours scénique." *Littérature* 43 (1981): 89–99.
Dick, Kay. *Pierrot*. London: Hutchinson, 1960.
Dodd, William N. "Metalanguage and Character in Drama." *Lingua e Stile* 14, no. I (1979): 135–50.
Dort, Bernard. "Epic Form in Brecht's Theatre." *Yale/Theatre* 2 (1968): 24–33.
Dougherty, Dru. "Talía convulsa: La crisis teatral de los años 20." In *2 ensayos sobre teatro español de los 20*, 85–157. Murcia: Cuadernos de la cátedra de teatro de la universidad de Murcia: 1984.
Dubois, Jacques. "Code, texte, métatexte." *Littérature* 12 (1973): 3–11.
Durand, Régis. "La Voix et le dispositif théâtral." *Etudes Littéraires* 13, no. 3 (1980): 387–96.
———. "Problèmes de l'analyse structurale et sémiotique de la forme théâtrale." In *Sémiologie de la représentation*, edited by André Helbo, 112–20. Brussels: Editions Complexe, 1975.
Eagleton, Terry. "Brecht and Rhetoric." *New Literary History* 16, no. 3 (1985): 633–38.
Eco, Umberto. "Semiotics of Theatrical Performance." *The Drama Review* 21, no. 1 (1977): 107–17.
Elam, Keir. *The Semiotics of Theatre and Drama*. London: Methuen, 1980.
Erenstein, Robert L. "Satire and the Commedia dell'Arte." In *Western Popular Theater*, edited by D. Mayer and K. Richards, 29–47. London: Methuen, 1977.
Esslin, Martin. *The Theatre of the Absurd*. New York: Overlook Press, 1969.
Eynot, Von Irene. "Adolphe Appia: De la Communication au Jeu." *Maske und Kothurn* 22 (1976): 238–52.

Fanto, James A. "Speech Act Theory and its Applications to the Study of Literature." In *The Sign: Semiotics Around the World*, edited by R. W. Bailey, et al., 280–304. Ann Arbor: University of Michigan Press, 1978.

Feibleman, James. *In Praise of Comedy*. New York: Russel & Russel, 1962.

Feral, Josette. "Performance and Theatricality: The Subject Demystified." *Modern Drama* 25, no. 1 (1982): 170–81.

Fergusson, Francis. *The Idea of Theatre*. Princeton: Princeton University Press, 1949.

Fernández Cifuentes, Luis. "García Lorca y el teatro convencional." *Iberoromania* 17 (1983): 66–99.

Finney, Gail. "Theatre of Impotence: The One-Act Tragedy at the Turn of the Century." *Modern Drama* 28, no. 3 (1985): 451–61.

Fischer-Lichte, Erika. "Theatrical Communication." *Degrés* 29 (1982): f1–f9.

Fowlie, Wallace. "Mystery of the Actor." *Yale French Studies* 5 (1950): 5–11.

Frye, Northrop. "Three Meanings of Symbolism." *Yale French Studies* 9 (1952): 11–19.

George, David. "The Commedia dell'Arte and the Circus in the Works of Jacinto Benavente." *Theatre Research International* 6, no. 2 (1981): 92–109.

Germain, Edward B. "Automatism and the Birth of Language." *Forum for Modern Language Studies* 18, no. 2 (1982): 172–82.

Gerould, Daniel. "Henry Monnier and the Erotikon Theatron: The Pornography of Realism." *The Drama Review* 25, no. 1 (1981): 17–19.

Goffman, Erving. "Performances." In *Ritual Play and Performance*, edited by Richard Schechner and Mady Schuman, 89–96. New York: Seabury Press, 1976.

———. "The Theatrical Frame." In *Frame Analysis*, 123–55. New York: Harper & Row, 1974.

Green, André. "La Déliaison." *Littérature* 3 (1971): 33–52.

Gruber, D. E. "The Imperfect Action of Comedy." *Genre* 10, no. 1 (1977): 115–30.

Guimbretière, André. "Approche du référent." *Degrés* 3 (1973): f1–f7.

Gullón, R. "Ideologías del modernismo." *Insula* 291 (1971): 1, 11.

Gumpel, L. "The Essence of 'Reality' as a Construct of Language." *Foundations of Language* 2, no. 2 (1974): 167–85.

Halpern, Joséph. "Describing the Surreal." *Yale French Studies* 61 (1981): 89–106.

Handke, Peter. "Nauseated by Language." Interview by A. Joseph. *Tulane Drama Review* 15, no. 1 (1970): 56–61.

Hamon, Philippe. "Rhetorical Status of the Descriptive." *Yale French Studies* 61 (1981): 1–26.

———. "Texte littéraire et métalanguage." *Poétique* 31 (1977): 261–84.

Heilman, Robert B. *Tragedy and Melodrama*. Seattle: University of Washington Press, 1968.

Helbo, André. "Le Discours théâtral: une sémantique de la relation." In *La relation théâtrale*, edited by Régis Durand, 97–104. Lille: Presses Universitaires de Lille, 1980.

———. "Le Théâtre: une communication en déni?" *Etudes Littéraires* 13, no. 3 (1980): 461–70.

Heller, Erich. "The Dismantling of a Marionette Theater; or, Psychology and the Misinterpretation of Literature." *Critical Inquiry* 4, no. 3 (1978): 417–32.

Hinchliffe, Arnold P. "Literature in the Theatre?" *The Yearbook of English Studies* 9 (1979): 1–14.

Hogendoorn, Wiebe. "Notes on Deixis and Simultaneity in Theatre Performance." *Degrés* 30 (1982): e1–e6.

Homan, Sidney. "When the Theatre Turns to Itself." *New Literary History* 2, no. 3 (1971): 407–18.

Honzl, Jindrich. "Dynamics of the Sign in the Theatre." In *Semiotics of Art: Prague School Contributions*, edited by Ladislav Matejka and Irwin Titunik, 74–93. Cambridge: M.I.T. Press, 1976.

Howarth, W. D. "Word and Image in Pixérécourt's Melodramas: The Dramaturgy of the Strip Cartoon." In *Performance and Politics in Popular Drama*, edited by David Bradby, Louis James, and Bernard Sharratt, 17–32. Cambridge: Cambridge University Press, 1980.

Hristic, Jovan. "The Problem of Realism in Modern Drama." *New Literary History* 8 (1977): 311–18.

Hubert, Judd D. "Symbolism, Correspondence and Memory." *Yale French Studies* 9 (1952): 46–55.

Huston, Hollis. "Dimensions of Mime Space." *Educational Theatre Journal* 30, no. 1 (1978): 63–72.

Ingarden, Roman. "Les Fonctions du langage au théâtre." *Poétique* 8 (1971): 531–38.

Innes, C. *Holy Theatre: Ritual and the Avant Garde*. New York: Cambridge University Press, 1981.

Ionesco, Eugène. *Notes and Counternotes*. New York: Grove Press, 1964.

Issacharoff, Michael. "Space and Reference in Drama." *Poetics Today* 2, no. 3 (1981): 211–24.

Jacob, André. "Langage et vérité." *Degrés* 3 (1973): d1–d12.

Jameson, Fred. "The Laughter of Nausea." *Yale French Studies* 23: 26–32.

Jiménez, J. R. *El modernismo*. México: Aguilar, 1962.

Jrade, C. L. *Rubén Darío and the Romantic Search for Unity: The Modernist Recourse to Esoteric Tradition*. Austin: University of Texas Press, 1983.

Kellman, Steven G. "The Function of Self-Begetting." *Modern Language Notes* 91, no. 6 (1976): 1243–56.

Kennedy, Andrew. "Mimesis and the Language of Drama: A Reply to Michael Anderson." In *Drama, Dance and Music*, edited by J. Redmond, 225–33. Cambridge: Cambridge University Press, 1981.

———. "Natural, Mannered, and Parodic Dialogue." *The Yearbook of English Studies* 9 (1979): 28–54.

———. "The Theatre Breeds Comedy." *Modern Drama* 31, no. 4 (1988): 473–8.

Kern, E. "Beckett and the Spirit of the Commedia dell'Arte." *Modern Drama* 9, no. 3 (1966): 260–67.

Kierkegaard, Sören. "Farce Is Far More Serious." *Yale French Studies* 14 (1954): 3–9.

Kirby, E. T. "The Mask: Abstract Theatre, Primitive and Modern." *The Drama Review* 16, no. 3 (1972): 5–21.

Kirby, Michael. "Structural Analysis/Structural Theory." *The Drama Review* 20, no. 4 (1976): 52–68.

Kleist, Heinrich von. "On The Marionette Theatre." *The Drama Review* 16, no. 3 (1972): 22–26.

Koelb, Clayton. "The Problem of 'Tragedy' as a Genre." *Genre* 8, no. 3 (1975): 248–66.

Koritz, Amy. "Woman Dancing: The Structure of Gender in Yeats's Early Plays for Dancers." *Modern Drama* 32, no. 3 (1989): 387–400.

Kowzan, Tadeusz. "The Sign in the Theatre." *Diogenes* 61 (1968): 52–80.

Krysinski, Wladimir. "Changed Textual Signs in Modern Theatricality: Gombrowicz and Handke." *Modern Drama* 25, no. 1 (1982): 3–16.

Lambert, Bernard. "Les Grandes théories: Nietzsche et le théâtre." *Littérature* 9 (1973): 3–30.

Larthomas, P. "Le Langage dramatique." *L'Information Littéraire* 24, no. 4 (1972): 164–66.

Leclaire, Serge. "Le Réel dans le texte." *Littérature* 3 (1971): 30–32.

Levaillant, Jean. "Histoire/Sujet." *Littérature* 13 (1974): 125–27.

Lewis, Thomas E. "Notes Toward a Theory of the Referent." *PMLA* 94, no. 3 (1979): 459–75.

McCollom, William G. "Verse Drama: A Reconsideration." *Comparative Drama* 14, no. 2 (1980): 99–116.

McLuhan, M. "Roles, Masks and Performances." *New Literary History* 2, no. 3 (1971): 517–31.

Martin, Graham Dunstan. "A Measure of Distance: The Rhetoric of the Surrealist Adjective." *Forum for Modern Language Studies* 18, no. 2 (1982): 108–25.

Martin Jarret-Kerr, C. R. "The Conditions of Tragedy." *Comparative Literature Studies* 2, no. 4 (1965): 363–74.

Mayer, David. "The Sexuality of Pantomime." *Theatre Quarterly* 4, no. 13 (1974): 55–64.

Mazzone-Clementi, Carlo. "Commedia and the Actor." *The Drama Review* 18, no. 1 (1974): 59–64.

Melançon, Joseph. "Theatre as Semiotic Practice." *Modern Drama* 25, no. 1 (1982): 17–24.

Merrell, Floyd. "Metaphor and Metonomy: A Key to Narrative Structure." *Language and Style* 11, no. 3 (1978): 146–63.

Monk, Philip. "Common Carrier: Performance by Artists." *Modern Drama* 25, no. 1 (1982): 163–69.

Monleón, José. *El teatro del 98 frente a la sociedad española*. Madrid: Cátedra, 1975.

Mukarovsky, Jan. "An Attempt at a Structural Analysis of a Dramatic Figure." In *Structure, Sign and Function*, edited by John Burbank and P. Steiner, 171–77. New Haven: Yale University Press, 1978.

———. "On the Current State of the Theory of Theater." In *Structure, Sign and Function*, edited by John Burbank and P. Steiner, 201–19. New Haven: Yale University Press, 1978.

———. "Standard Language and Poetic Language." In *A Prague School Reader on Esthetics, Literary Structure and Style*, edited by P. L. Garvin, 17–30. Washington, D.C.: Georgetown University Press, 1964.

———. "Two Studies of Dialogue." In *The Word and Verbal Art*, edited by John Burbank and Peter Steiner, 81–115. New Haven: Yale University Press, 1977.

Nicoll, Allardyce. *Masks Mime and Miracles: Studies in the Popular Theatre.* New York: Cooper Square Publishers, 1963.

———. *World of Harlequin: A Critical Study of the Commedia dell'Arte.* Cambridge: Cambridge University Press, 1963.

Ohmann, Richard. "Literature as Act." In *Approaches to Poetics,* edited by Seymour Chatman, 81–107. New York: Columbia University Press, 1973.

———. "Speech, Action and Style." In *Literary Style: A Symposium,* edited by Seymour Chatman, 241–54. London and New York: Oxford University Press, 1971.

Olson, Elder. *The Theory of Comedy.* Bloomington: Indiana University Press, 1968.

Oreglia, Giacomo. *The Commedia dell'Arte.* London: Methuen, 1968.

Orgel, Stephan "The Poetics of Spectacle." *New Literary History* 2 (1971): 367–89.

Pasquier, Marie-Claire. "L'Image de ce qui n'est pas l'image de ce qui est." *Cahiers Renaud-Barrault* 96 (1977): 36–46.

Pavis, Patrice. "On Brecht's Notion of 'Gestus.'" In *Languages of the Stage,* 37–49. New York: Performing Arts Journal, 1982.

———. "Remarques sur le discours théâtral." *Degrés* 13 (1978): h1–h10.

———. "The Interplay between Avant-Garde Theatre and Semiology." *Performing Arts Journal* 5, no. 3 (1980): 75–86.

Paz, Octavio. *Los hijos del limo.* Barcelona: Seix Barral, 1974.

Pérez Minik, Domingo. "Se trata de la farsa, una forma incordia del teatro europeo." *Yorick* 5–6 (1965): 4–5.

Piemme, J. M. "L'Organisation de l'espace scénique et les problèmes du lieu théâtral." *Revue des Langues Vivantes* 34, no. 3 (1968): 245–60.

Pirandello, Luigi. "On Humor." *Tulane Drama Review* 10, no. 3 (1966): 46–59.

Pohl, Jaques. "Rire et parole." *Revue des Langues Vivantes* 32, no. 3 (1966): 318–23.

Pugliatti, Paola Guilli. "The Distribution of Implicit Information in the Opening Scenes of Dramatic Texts." *Lingua e Stile* 16, no. 3 (1981): 481–94.

Rahill, Frank. *The World of Melodrama.* University Park: The Pennsylvania State University Press, 1967.

Rey, Alain. "Référence et littérature." *Degrés* 3 (1973): h1–h8.

Roda, Federico. "Aquí se habla del mimo y de la pantomima como elementos predilectos de la farsa." *Yorick* 5–6 (1965): 13–15.

Ruff, Loren, and W. R. Stump. *Imitation: The Art of the Theatre.* North Carolina: Hunter, 1979.

Salinas, P. *La poesía de Rubén Darío.* Buenos Aires: Losada, 1948.

Sartre, J. P. *L'Imaginaire.* Paris: Gallimard, 1948.

Savona, Jeannette Laillou. "'Didascalies' as Speech Acts." *Modern Drama* 25, no. 1 (1982): 22–35.

———. "Narration et actes de parole dans le texte dramatique." *Etudes Littéraires* 13, no. 3 (1980): 471–93.

Schade, G. D. "La mitología clásica en la poesía hispanoamericana." In *La cultura y la literatura iberoamericanas,* edited by Luís Monguió, 123–29. México: Audrea, 1957.

Schechner, Richard. "Actuals: Primitive Ritual and Performance Theory." *Theatre Quarterly* 1, no. 2 (1971): 49–66.

———. "Drama, Script, Theatre, and Performance." *The Drama Review* 17, no. 3 (1973): 5–36.

Scherillo, Michele. "The Commedia dell'Arte." *The Mask* 3 (1910–11): 108–27.

———. "The Geneology of Pulcinella." *The Mask* 3 (1910–11): 22–29.

Scott, Virginia P. "The *Jeu* and the *Rôle*: Analysis of the Appeals of the Italian Comedy in France in the Time of Arlequin-Dominique." In *Western Popular Theatre*, edited by David Mayer and Kenneth Richards, 1–27. London: Methuen, 1977.

Schwarz, Heinrich "The Mirror in Art." *The Art Quarterly* 15, no. 2 (1952): 96–118.

Searle, John. "The Logical Status of Fictional Discourse." *New Literary History* 6, no. 2 (1975): 319–32.

Segal, Charles. "Tragédie, oralité, écriture." *Poétique* 50 (1982): 131–54.

Serpieri, Alessandro, et al. "Toward a Segmentation of the Dramatic Text." *Poetics Today* 2, no. 3 (1981): 163–200.

Sheringham, Michael. "Breton and the Language of Automatism: Alterity, Allegory, Desire." *Forum for Modern Language Studies* 18, no. 2 (1982): 142–58.

Siniscalchi, Marina Maymon. "E. G. Craig: The Drama for Marionettes." *Theatre Research International* 5, no. 2 (1980): 122–37.

Smith, Willard. *The Nature of Comedy*. Norwood, PA: Norwood Editions, 1978.

Sontag, Susan. "The Death of Tragedy." In *Against Interpretation*, 132–39. New York: Octagon Books, 1978.

———. "Marat/Sade/Artaud." In *Against Interpretation*, 163–74. New York: Octagon Books, 1978.

States, B. O. "The Actor's Presence: Three Phenomenal Modes." *Theatre Journal* 35, no. 3 (1983): 359–75.

Storey, Robert. *Pierrots on the Stage of Desire*. Princeton: Princeton University Press, 1985.

Styan, J. L. *Dark Comedy: The Development of Modern Comic Tragedy*. London: Cambridge University Press, 1968.

———. "Pirandellian Theatre Games: Spectator as Victim." *Modern Drama* 23, no. 2 (1980): 95–101.

Tindemans, C. "Coherence. Putting 'Pieces' Together." *Degrés* 31 (1982): i1–i6.

Tonelli, Franco, and Judd Hubert. "Theatricality: The Burden of the Text." *Substance* 21 (1978): 79–102.

Tort, Patrick. "Masque, écriture, doublure." *Poétique* 15 (1973): 313–19.

Trussler, Simon. "A Chronology of Early Melodrama." *Theatre Quarterly* 1, no. 4 (1971): 19–21.

Ubersfeld, Anne. "Le Discours du comédien." *Degrés* 30 (1982): a1–a11.

———. *Lire le théâtre*. Paris: Editions Sociales, 1977.

———. "Notes sur la dénégation théâtrale." In *La relation théâtrale*, edited by Regis Durand, 11–25. Lille: Presses Universitaires de Lille, 1980.

———. "The Pleasure of the Spectator." *Modern Drama* 25, no. 1 (1982): 127–39.

Urmson, J. O. "Dramatic Representation." *The Philosophical Quarterly* 22, no. 89 (1972): 333–43.

Varey, J. E. *Títeres, marionetas y otras diversiones populares de 1758–1859*. Madrid: Instituto de Estudios Madrileños, 1959.

Veinstein, André. *La Mise en scène théâtrale et sa condition esthétique* Paris: Flammarion, 1955.

Veltrusky, Jiří. "Basic Features of Dramatic Dialogue." In *Semiotics of Art: Prague School Contributions,* edited by Ladislav Matejka and Irwin Titunik, 128–33. Cambridge: M.I.T. Press, 1976.

———. "Contribution to the Semiotics of Acting." In *Sound, Sign and Meaning: Quinquagenary of the Prague Linguistic Circle,* edited by Ladislav Matejka, 553–606. Ann Arbor: Department of Slavic Languages & Literatures, University of Michigan, 1976.

———. "Dramatic Text as a Component of Theatre." In *Semiotics of Art: Prague School Contributions,* edited by Ladislav Matejka and Irwin Titunik, 94–117. Cambridge: M.I.T. Press, 1976.

———. "Man and Object in the Theatre." In *A Prague School Reader on Esthetics, Literary Structure and Style,* edited by Paul L. Garvin, 83–91. Washington, D.C.: Georgetown University Press, 1964.

Vilar, Jean. "The Director and the Play." *Yale French Studies* 5 (1950): 12–26.

Weiss, Aurélia. "Truth and Theatre." *Comparative Drama* 4, no. 1 (1970): 63–74.

Wilcox, Leonard. "Modernism vs. Postmodernism: Shepard's *The Tooth of Crime* and the Discourses of Popular Culture." *Modern Drama* 30, no. 4 (1987): 560–73.

Wilshire, Bruce W. *Role Playing and Identity: The Limits of Theatre as Metaphor.* Bloomington: Indiana University Press, 1982.

Zurita, Marciano. *Historia del género chico.* Madrid: Prensa Popular, 1920.

Index

Actor, role of the, 37–38, 48, 58–59, 62–63
Aguila de blasón, 4–5, 102, 103, 104
Alonso, F., 100n.13
Alter, J., 91n.42
Amor y Vázquez, J., 73n.28
Aromas de leyenda, 107n.24
Art: mystic dimensions of, 9–10, 24–25, 27–28, 123–30; sensuous aspects of, 12, 14–15; Valle-Inclán's view of, 7 n.15, 10n.1
Artaud, Antonin, 51n, 110, 111n.30
Ayala, F., 127n.49
Azaña, M., 128n.51

Ballet, 70–71
Barja, C., 119n.41
Baroja, Pío, 10n
Barrault, Jean-Louis, 53, 53n.32, 55n.1, 61n.13, 74n.29
Barthes, R., 21n.20
Benavente, Jacinto, 5, 33n.4, 127n.49
Bentley, E., 107n.23, 110n.28
Bergson, Henri, 69–70, 69n.25
Bermejo Marcos, M., 99n.11
Bermel, A., 68n
Booth, M. R., 55n.2
Borel, J. P., 100n.14, 128n.52
Brater, E., 69n.24
Brecht, B., 91n.43, 114n.33, 120n.41
Breton, A., 69n.23
Brooks, J. L., 111n.31
Buero Vallejo, A., 74, 74n.30
Bunjevac, M., 61n.14

Caamaño Bournacell, J., 99n.10, 115n.38
Cabeza del bautista, 111n.31, 121
Cabeza del dragón, La:
—audience, role of the, 59–61
—authorial presence, affirmation of, 65–69
—character/actor versus author, 58–59, 61–63
—director versus author, 63–64
—discourse, 81–87, 89–91
—distancing and the mechanical, 69–71, 128
—farce, relation to, 55–56
—literary interplay, 64–65, 74–81
—*mise en scène* and the author, 55–81
Calderón, Pedro, 21, 30n.28, 56n.4, 75, 92
Cara de Plata, 104–5, 112–14, 115–17, 124
Cardona, R., 57n.7
Celestina, La, 98
Cenizas, 3n.2, 4
Champigny, R., 57n.9
Comedias bárbaras, 4–5, 18n.15, 19n.17, 96n, 101–2, 104, 104n.19, 105–6, 116n, 119n.41, 124. See also *Aguila de blasón; Cara de Plata; Romance de lobos*
Commedia dell'arte, 20n.18, 32–54; Spanish/non-Spanish differences, in the context of, 18–22, 26–28, 30n.28; temporal dimensions, 29–31
Copeau, J., 70
Criado de Val, M., 64n.19
Cuento de abril, 19n.17, 96n

150 Index

Cuernos de don Friolera, Los, 7, 31 n.30, 56, 65, 69, 70, 74, 75, 107 n.24, 126

Dance, 72n
Darío, Rubén, 12, 12 n.6, 13, 13 n.7, 15 n.12, 29
Death, 7, 30–31, 34, 89, 121, 126–27
De Man, P., 14n
Demonic, the, 103–5
Derrida, J., 52 n.30
Díaz de Mendoza, Fernando, 100 n.13
Díaz Plaja, G., 12 n.4, 29n, 105, 105n
Dicenta, Joaquín, 5
Dichy, A., 63 n.17
Didascalies: defined, 64 n.18
Díez Canedo, E., 101n, 130n
Disinterestedness, 4–5, 17 n.14, 28 n.26, 30 n.29, 122, 123 n.45
Distancing, 7, 56–58, 65, 69–70, 74–75, 81, 124–30
Divinas palabras, 18 n.15, 28 n.26, 56, 77, 114–15, 127 n.50, 129 n.53
Dodd, W.n., 57 n.8
Domenech, R., 119 n.41, 120 n.41
Dougherty, D., 10n, 33 n.4, 73 n.28, 95 nn. 2 and 3, 96n, 98n, 99 nn. 9 and 11, 100 nn. 12 and 13, 114 n.33
Duchartre, P. L., 38 n.11
Durand, R., 54n

Eagleton, T., 114 n.33
Embrujado, El:
 —melodrama, use and development of, 107–17
 —perspective: disinterestedness, 121–22, 123 n.45; distancing, 122–30; *La lámpara maravillosa,* relation to 123–30
 —social order, role of, 100–102
 —*sosegante* versus *desasosegante,* 103–5; feminine functions, 105–8
 —stage independence, 117–21
 —tradition versus innovation, aspects of, 99–100, 111 n.31
Entrambasaguas, J. de, 4 n.4
Erotic, significance of, 15, 16n. See also *La Marquesa Rosalinda*—pagan aspects
Esperpento, 3, 4 n.3, 6, 6 n.9, 7, 8, 10n, 56 n.3, 57 n.7, 74, 75, 82n, 86, 86n, 96n, 100, 113, 114, 128, 129 n.53

Espronceda, José de, 44, 105n
Eulalia, 106 n.22

Farsa italiana de la enamorada del rey, 56
Farsa y licencia de la reina castiza, 43 n.22, 73 n.28
Feral, J., 43 n.21, 48n
Fernández Almagro, M., 6 n.8, 120 n.41
Fernández Cifuentes, Luis, 106 n.21
Finney, G., 114 n.36
Fischer-Lichte, E., 55 n.2
Flor de santidad, 107 n.24, 122n
Fowlie, W., 70n

Garlitz, V., 4 n.4, 123 n.46
Ghiraldo, A., 128 n.51
Goffman, I., 76 n.33
Gómez de Baquero, E., 119 n.41
González del Valle, L., 129 n.54
González López, E., 96n, 111 n.31
Greenfield, S., 111 n.31
Gruber, D. E., 67n
Guerrero, María, 100 n.13
Gullón, R., 15 n.12
Guimbretière, A., 73 n.29

Heilman, R. B., 110, 110 nn. 26 and 27
Helbo, A., 54n
Hinchliffe, A., 61 n.15
Homan, S., 57 n.8
Honzl, J. 43 n.20
Hormigón, J. A., 6 n.10, 60n
Huston, H., 43 n.20

Ilie, P., 24n, 114 n.34
Improvisation, 31, 37–38, 56 n.5
Intereses creados, Los, 33 n.4

Jameson, F., 87 n.38
Jerez Farrán, C., 129 n.53
Jiménez, J. R., 12 n.4
Joseph, A., 32 n.3
Jrade, C. L., 15 n.12

Kearn, E., 32 n.2
Kennedy, A., 35n, 38 n.12, 76 n.32
Kirby, M., 40 n.15
Koritz, A., 72n
Krysinski, W., 32 n.3

Lámpara maravillosa, La:
— aesthetic/mystic pilgrimage, 9–10
— analogic vision, 13–15
— biography/literature, 123–24, 127–28
— *Comedias bárbaras,* in the context of, 4–5
— dance and music, 72n, 73n.29
— disinterestedness, 17n.14, 123n.45, 129–30
— *El Embrujado,* in the context of, 122–30
— intellect, the role of the, 18n.15
— language and cultural renovation, 93–99; theatrical language, 95–99
— *La Marquesa Rosalinda,* in the context of, 9–31
— nontemporal view, 4–5, 14–15, 25, 27–28, 29–31, 123nn.46 and 47, 124–30
— opposition and contrast, the interplay of, 27–28
— perspective, the distancing, 124–30
— sensuous/mystic unity, 14–15
Langer, S., 43n.20
Larthomas, P., 57n.9
Lavaud, J. M., 3n.1, 7n.15
Lewis, T. A., 65n
Ligazón, 30n.29, 121
Lima, R., 4n.4, 33n.4
Ling, D., 112n.31
Llorens, E., 116n
López Heredia, I., 100n.12
Losado, B., 120n.41
Luces de bohemia, 10n, 12n.2, 22n, 47, 74, 112n.32, 121, 127, 128, 129n.53
Lundeberg, O. K., 56n.4
Luz Uribe, M. de la, 44n.23
Lyon, J., 4n.5, 7n.14, 44n.24, 99n.7, 116n

Madariaga, S. de, 119n.4
Maier, C. S., 6n.13, 124n.47
Marqués de Bradomín, El, 3n.2, 104
Marquesa Rosalinda, La:
— aesthetic/mystic search, the manifestation of, 10–15, 27–28, 29–31, 127–28
— author to *mise en scène,* relation of, 58–59
— characters, 43–48

— citation, role of the, 22–25
— frame, 32–38
— *La lámpara maravillosa,* relation to, 9–31
— language, 38–41, 87–89
— objects, status of the, 41–43
— pagan aspects: aesthetic significance of pagan versus nonpagan (Spanish) differences, 16–22; aesthetic/mystic significance of pagan versus nonpagan (Spanish) differences, 26–28; *modernista* sources, 12–14; sensuous/mystic implications, 11–15, 16n
— perspective shifts, 26–28
— rhythm, 71–74
— textual characteristics, 50–54
— time, passage of, 28–31
Marrast, R., 28n.26
McGrady, D., 104n.18
Mechanical, inscription of the, 69–74
Melodrama, 99n.11, 107–17
Miedo, El, 107n.24
Mitry, J., 31n.32
Modernista, 9, 10n, 12–14, 15n.12, 29n, 64n.19, 112n.32
Monguió, L., 12n.5
Monk, P., 40n.16
Moya del Pino, J., 6n.10
Mukarovsky, J., 39n
Muñoz-Seca, P., 114n.33
Music, 71–74
Mythology. See *La Marquesa Rosalinda*—pagan aspects

Navas, F., 5n.7, 6n.11
Nicholson, D., 65n
Nickel, C., 106n.22, 107n.24
Nicoll, A., 38n.11
Nieva, F., 124n.47
Nontemporal view. See *La lámpara maravillosa*—nontemporal view

Octavia Santino, 3n.2
Ohman, R., 23n
Oreglia, G., 20n.18
Osuna, R., 129n.53

Paolini, C. J., 112n.32
Pavis, P., 91n.43
Paz, Octavio, 13nn. 9 and 10
Pérez de Ayala, R., 6n.11

Pérez Galdós, Benito, 99n.11
Pérez Minik, D., 120n.41
Performance, popular culture and, 55–56
Perspective, statement of Valle-Inclán's aesthetic, 56n.7. See also *El Embrujado*—perpective; *La Marquesa Rosalinda*—perspective shifts
Phillips, A. W., 13n.6
Pugliatti, P. G., 59n.11

Ramos Kuethe, L., 106n.22
Retablo de la avaricia la lujuria y la muerte, 3, 28n.26, 99, 107n.24, 111n.31, 114n.36, 121. See also *El Embrujado, La cabeza del bautista; Ligazón; Rosa de papel; Sacrilegio*
Reyes, A., 127n.50
Risco, A., 82n.35, 86n
Rivas Cherif, Cipriano, 6n.10, 92, 96n, 99n.10, 116n
Romance de lobos, 4–5, 102, 104, 105, 114, 115–16, 121n
Romero Cuesta, J., 100n.12
Rosa de papel, 111n.31, 121
Ruiz Fernández, C., 6n.9

Sacrilegio, 18n.15, 121
Sainete, 86
Salinas, P., 4n.3, 13n.7, 56n.3
Salper, R. L., 4n.3
Sanz Cuadrado, M. A., 107n.24
Sartre, J. P., 53, 53n.33
Savona, J. L., 64n.18
Schade, G. D., 12n.5
Schechner, R., 38n.10, 50–51, 50n.28
Scherillo, M., 20n.18, 37n
Script, 50–51
Seeleman, R., 104n.18
Segal, C., 56n.5
Segura Covarsi, E., 123n.46
Serpieri, A., 119n.40
Serrano Alonso, J., 124n.48
Shakespeare, William, 60n
Smith, A., 112n.32
Sonata de estío, 7, 10n, 30n.29, 96n
Sonata de invierno, 7
Sonata de otoño, 3n.2
Sonatas, 5, 7, 96n, 127n.49. See also

Sonata de estío; Sonata de invierno; Sonata de otoño
Spain, Valle-Inclán's vision of, 7, 19n.17, 94–95, 96n. See also *La Marquesa Rosalinda*—pagan aspects: aesthetic significance of pagan versus nonpagan (Spanish) differences; aesthetic/mystic significance of pagan versus nonpagan (Spanish) differences
Spanish. *See* Theatre: Spanish, Valle-Inclán's view of the Spanish language and theatre
Speratti-Piñero, E. S., 104n.18
Spinoza, B., 7n.16
States, B., 89n.41
Storey, R., 53n.34
Styan, J. L., 41n
Szondi, P., 114n.36

Tablado de marionetas para educación de príncipes, 3. See also *La cabeza del dragón; Farsa italiana de la enamorada del rey; Farsa y licencia de la reina castiza*
Theatre: renovation of, Valle-Inclán's, 5–6, 32n.4, 55–56, 96–99, 119n.41; Spanish, Valle-Inclán's views of the Spanish language and theatre, 6, 27n, 56n.4, 92–99
Tindemans, C., 76n.33

Ubersfeld, A., 34n.6, 63n.16, 89n.41, 119n.40
Unamuno, M. de, 95n.3
Urmson, O., 76n.33
Urrutia, J., 129n.53

Veltrusky, J., 42n.18
Vilar, J., 56n.6
Voces de gesta, 19n.17, 56, 64n.19, 96n

Wagner, R., 66
Weiss, A., 81n
Wilcox, L., 87n.39
Williamson, W., 104n.19

Yermo de las almas, El, 3n.2, 19n.17

Zahareas, A., 24n, 57n.7, 114n.341